P9-BYB-061

Days in the Lives of
Gerontological Social Workers

44 Professionals Tell Stories From "Real-Life" Social Work Practice With Older Adults

Edited by

Linda May Grobman and
Dara Bergel Bourassa

White Hat Communications
Harrisburg, Pennsylvania

Days in the Lives of Gerontological Social Workers
44 Professionals Tell Stories From "Real-Life" Social Work Practice With Older Adults

Edited by Linda May Grobman and Dara Bergel Bourassa

Published by:

White Hat Communications

Post Office Box 5390
Harrisburg, PA 17110-0390 U.S.A.
717-238-3787 (voice)
717-238-2090 (fax)
http://www.socialworker.com

All rights reserved. No part of this book may be reproduced or transmitted in any form or by any means, electronic or mechanical, including photocopying, recording or by any information and retrieval system without written permission from the publisher, except for the inclusion of brief quotations in a review.

Copyright © 2007 by Linda May Grobman and Dara Bergel Bourassa

The publisher can be contacted by e-mail at *lindagrobman@socialworker.com*. For more information related to this book and other *Days in the Lives of Social Workers* books, please see *http://www.daysinthelivesofsocialworkers.com*.

Note: The names and identities of social work clients mentioned in this book have been carefully disguised in accordance with professional standards of confidentiality.

Photo credit: cover and interior photos by Marianne Gontarz York

Library of Congress Cataloging-in-Publication Data

Days in the lives of gerontological social workers : 44 professionals tell stories from real-life social work practice with older adults / edited by Linda May Grobman and Dara Bergel Bourassa.
p. cm.
Includes bibliographical references.
ISBN-13: 978-1-929109-21-0
1. Social work with older people–Case studies. 2. Social workers–Biography. 3. Gerontology. I. Grobman, Linda May. II. Bourassa, Dara Bergel.
HV1451.D39 2007
362.6–dc22
2007015562

Days in the Lives of Gerontological Social Workers

Table of Contents

About the Editors

Linda May Grobman, MSW, ACSW, LSW, is the founder, publisher, and editor of THE NEW SOCIAL WORKER®, the magazine for social work students and recent graduates, and the editor of Days in the Lives of Social Workers and More Days in the Lives of Social Workers. She is co-author of The Social Worker's Internet Handbook. She has practiced social work in mental health and medical settings, and is a former interim executive director of the Pennsylvania and Georgia state chapters of the National Association of Social Workers. She received her MSW and BM (Music Therapy) degrees from the University of Georgia.

Dara Bergel Bourassa, Ph.D., MSW, LSW, is an assistant professor of social work and director of the gerontology program at Shippensburg University in Pennsylvania. She received her BSW and MSW from the University of Pittsburgh. She received her Ph.D. in social work from the University of Maryland at Baltimore in 2007. Her practice experience is primarily in hospital settings, working with stroke, nephrology, orthopedics, intensive care, and cardiology patients. She also worked in a Level 1 Trauma unit as an emergency department social worker in Pittsburgh, PA, and was a senior services volunteer through Jewish Family Services in Baltimore, MD.

About the Contributors

Renee R. Adams, MSW, LCSW, has worked at Hospice of the Valley in Scottsdale, Arizona for seven years. Previously, she was Social Service Director at Phoenix Mountain Nursing Center. She has also taught a graduate course at Arizona State University West in Social Work Practice With Elders and enjoys training second-year graduate student interns in the field.

Gary E. Bachman, MSSW, LSCSW, is an associate professor at Park University Department of Social Work in Parkville, Missouri, and clinical instructor at the University of Kansas School of Medicine, Department of Family Medicine. The event described in his chapter occurred in the emergency department of Brackenridge Hospital in Austin, Texas. The lessons learned and insights gained that evening have been put to use on a regular basis in his work as a social worker and medical educator for the past 25 years.

Mary Jo Garcia Biggs, Ph.D., LCSW, is an assistant professor at Texas State University–San Marcos. She is currently involved in "gerontologizing" the curriculum as part of a curriculum development institute Gero-Ed project, a John A. Hartford grant. Her research interests include gerontology, crsis intervention, secondary trauma, and social justice issues. She is the faculty advisor for Latinas Unidas, a university support group for Latina women.

Kimberly McClure Cassie, MSSW, MA, is a doctoral candidate at the University of Tennessee and a Hartford Doctoral Fellow. She holds master's degrees in social work and gerontology. The setting described in her chapter is a state survey agency responsible for the licensing and certification of skilled nursing facilities in a southeastern state.

Jennifer Clements, Ph.D., MSW, LCSW, is an assistant professor in the Department of Social Work at Shippensburg University. Her chapter is based on work she performed as a contractual social worker at a nursing home facility. She received her BA in social work/psychology, MSW, and Ph.D. from the University of Maryland.

Andrea Shankman Eisenstein, MSW, LCSW, is a geriatric care manager in Houston, Texas. She is a member of NAPGCM, the Houston Gerontological Society, and NASW. She would like to thank all her senior teachers for preparing her for her own aging process. "They all have personal experience to share with me and have trained me to be the best geriatric care manager I can be," she says.

Christina L. Erickson, Ph.D., MSW, LISW, is an assistant professor at Augsburg College in Minneapolis, Minnesota. She was formerly the program coordinator for the National Parkinson Foundation–Center of Excellence at the University of Illinois at Chicago. She received her Ph.D. in 2005 from the Jane Addams College of Social Work at the University of Illinois at Chicago.

Cynthia Garthwait, MSW, LCSW, ACSW, is professor and chair, School of Social Work, the University of Montana. She is director of the Geriatric Social Work Initiative at the School of Social Work and is a member of the Institute for Gerontology Education, the Montana Gerontology Society, and the Association for Gerontology Education in Social Work. She also serves as a social services consultant to nursing homes and retirement centers.

Trevor Gates, MSW, ACSW, LMSW, is a therapist at a community mental health agency in Arlington, Texas. He is a social work generalist with experience including work in community mental health and managed care organizations. His field placement in geriatric case management provided him the generic skills to work with other populations across the lifespan. His professional interests include social work with lesbian, gay, bisexual, and transgender persons, as well as work with persons overcoming chemical dependency.

Karen V. Graziano, MSW, LCSW, is a geriatric care manager in private practice in New York City and is affiliated with New York Presbyterian Hospital in Manhattan as the Lifeline Marketing and Development Director. Her chapter is based on her work at a naturally occurring retirement community (NORC) located in the New York City Housing Authority, Ravenswood public housing complex, Long Island City, New York. She wishes to express a heartfelt thanks to all the Ravenswood residents who helped to orchestrate the program, especially Felipe Rosado, Hector Muniz, Mannie Wilson, and the late Marion Fernandes, who is deeply missed.

Susan J. Harper, MSW, LSW, ACSW, was a care manager at Ursuline Senior Services in Pittsburgh, Pennsylvania. With more than 15 years of experience as a social worker, Harper has spent more than half of her professional career working in gerontology.

Debra Hartley, BSW, MSW, is a community social worker for the Seniors Services, the City of Calgary, Alberta, Canada. She has been a gerontological social worker since graduating with her BSW in 1977. Her focus changed to gerontological community development in 2000, when she graduated with her MSW.

Erica Holman, LLMSW, LNHA, is a licensed nursing home administrator in Michigan. She is a participant in a grant project at Michigan State University to train gerontological social workers and currently supervises several MSW interns. Ms. Holman's long-term care experience includes holding positions as director of social services, opening and supervising an Alzheimer's unit, public speaking, and presenting seminars on various topics related to psychosocial wellness and best standards of practice.

Thomas Horn, BA (Hons.), MSW, is a Registered Social Worker in Ontario, Canada. He currently works on an acute mental health inpatient ward, which is the setting of his chapter in this book. He received his MSW and BA from Wilfrid Laurier University.

Heidi Hovis, BSW, is a licensed social worker and assistant director of social services at Golden Living Center in St. Louis Park, Minnesota. She received her BSW from Winona State University.

JoAnn T. Jarolmen, Ph.D., MSW, ACSW, LCSW (New York and New Jersey), is an assistant professor of social work at Dominican College of Blauvelt, located in Orangeburg, New York. She was a school social worker in Hillsdale, New Jersey for 27 years. Her chapter describes a project that took place during her tenure there.

Sally Hill Jones, Ph.D., LCSW, is an assistant professor and MSW Coordinator at Texas State University School of Social Work in San Marcos, Texas. She worked as a social worker and consultant in hospice settings, was a caregiver for her mother, who had Alzheimer's, and is currently involved in "gerontologizing" the curriculum and field placements with John Hartford Foundation grants. She has published on the topics of assessment of self-care in caregivers and self-care for hospice workers.

Lisa Krinsky, MSW, LICSW, is director of the LGBT Aging Project in Boston, Massachusetts. She earned an AB at Vassar College and an MSW in clinical social work at Simmons College School of Social Work. She has nearly 20 years of experience in community-based elder services. She joined the LGBT Aging Project in 2001 and frequently consults with mainstream aging service providers about cultural competency with LGBT elders.

Dale K. Laninga, MSW, ACSW, is a consultant in Harrisburg, Pennsylvania. He was Co-Director of the Long Term Care Reform Project in the Governor's Office of Health Care Reform and Executive Director of the Intra-Governmental Council on Long Term Care. His background includes 25 years in planning, policy, and program development for the elderly in the Pennsylvania Department of Aging, organizing a community mental health center for teenagers in Detroit, Michigan, and working in community mental health in Sydney, Australia. He taught at the University of New South Wales in Sydney, Australia.

Patricia Levy, Ph.D., LMSW, ACSW, is an assistant professor in the Department of Sociology and Social Work at Fort Hays State University. She worked as a social worker in Israel for 18 years, including two years at the Day Center for the Chronically Ill Elderly. She comes from an extensive background in multicultural practice with children, families, and the aged both in the U.S. and in Israel. Her skilled expertise with culturally diverse groups has culminated in a richness of professional experience while working with Native Americans, African Americans, and a wide range of Middle Eastern and European populations. She has published articles on topics including social work practice and terrorism, and the dilemmas of American rural medical social work. Dr. Levy has continued research in gerontology, disability, and spirituality in health.

Denice Goodrich Liley, Ph.D., ACSW, BCD, is Associate Professor at the Boise State University School of Social Work. Dr. Liley has more than 20 years of clinical social work practice experience, primarily in aging and health care.

Kay A. Long, BSW, RSW, is a 20-year retiree of the government of Alberta, master log builder, writer, and women's group facilitator. She is employed by Meals on Wheels in Lethbridge, Alberta, Canada. She previously worked for the government of Alberta as a program officer for the Department of Housing, which involved traveling to remote aboriginal communities via unpaved roads and small aircraft. In 2003, at age 65, she returned to school and received her BSW.

Man Wai Alice Lun, Ph.D., is an assistant professor at the Borough of Manhattan Community College, CUNY, in New York City. She worked in a NORC as Interim Director, providing overall administration of programs, including re-strategizing program direction and compiling reports. She also monitored provision of services including case assistance, case management, counseling, and health services. She received her Ph.D. from Columbia University School of Social Work in 2003.

Nicole Sarette MacFarland, LCSW-R, DCSW, CASAC, is Clinical Director of Senior Hope Counseling, Inc., an outpatient clinic for people age 50 and over who struggle with alcohol and/or drug addiction. She is also a Ph.D. student at SUNY Albany School of Social Welfare. She holds a CASAC in the state of New York and has devoted her career to helping clients with mental illness and chemical addictions. She has lectured on the topic of older adults and addictions and plans to complete her dissertation on the topic of geriatric addictions. She resides in Glenmont, New York with her husband, Gary, and son, Jared.

Kathryn C. Maclean, BA, completed her Hartford Practicum Partnership Program experience at the three sites described in her chapter—assisted living, AAA, and the Alzheimer's Association. She will graduate in 2007 with her MSW from St. Louis University. She is also an MSW graduate admissions assistant at St. Louis University and after graduation will work as Outreach Coordinator for the Alzheimer's Association.

Kelly Mills-Dick, BSW, MSW, LMSW, is a lecturer in social work at Skidmore College and a Ph.D. student at Boston University. Her research and practice experience have been in the area of gerontological social work, including geriatric mental health and substance abuse, as well as housing for older adults. Her research interests include geriatric mental health, retirement, lifelong learning, care giving, and long-term care. The setting described in her chapter is the Over 60 Health Center in Berkeley, California, which began in 1976 as an outgrowth of the Gray Panthers, a senior citizens' advocacy organization.

Murali D. Nair, MS, MSW, DSW, is Professor in the School of Social Work, Cleveland State University, Cleveland, Ohio. He is also Co-Director of the Center for Healing Across Cultures, Director of the India Experience Program at Cleveland State, and a Fulbright scholar. He has an MS in computer science from New York Institute of Technology and a DSW from Columbia University. For the past 10 years, he has conducted field studies on centenarians in Kerala, India, mainly to identify their secrets to long life, beyond modern medicine, especially their lifestyles. Every summer, he offers a study abroad program in India for university students. His Web site is at http://www.csuohio.edu/india_experience.

C. Michelle Niedens, BSW, MSW, LSCSW (Kansas), LCSW (Missouri), is the education/program director for the Alzheimer's Association, Heart of America Chapter.

Laura N. Norman, MSSA, received her graduate degree and certificate in gerontology in 2004 from Case Western Reserve University. She is currently Quality Assurance Specialist for the Maryland Department of Aging. Her chapter is based on employment as a Long Term Care Ombudsman in a large metropolitan area covering five counties, where she monitored 65 nursing homes and assisted living facilities.

Emma Giordano Quartaro, DSW, ACSW, LCSW, established and chaired the nationally accredited Department of Social Work at Seton Hall University in South Orange, New Jersey, where she introduced and directs the Multidisciplinary Certificate Program in Gerontology (MCPG). The mission of the MCPG is to infuse content about aging into academic offerings across the disciplines and to give leadership to service delivery innovations in the community in both traditional and emerging settings. Dr. Quartaro was named the Gerontologist of the Year by the Society on Aging, received the Mirror of Justice Award of the Women's Faculty Association, and received the Advocate Award of the Community Health Law Project.

Jinsheng (Jane) Qiu, Ph.D., LMSW, is the director and social worker at a senior center in Flushing, New York. She earned her MSW in 1999 and Ph.D. in social welfare in 2005 at the Wurzweiler School of Social Work at Yeshiva University.

Karen Horwitz Rubin, MSW, ACSW, LCSW-C, is the Rehabilitation Continuum Coordinator at Good Samaritan Hospital in Baltimore, Maryland. She has worked in medical settings, primarily in physical rehabilitation, since her field placement at Magee Memorial Hospital in 1968. Much of her work has been with older adults.

Della Govea Sanchez, MSW, is Ombudsman for the South Alabama Regional Planning Commission, Area Agency on Aging, in Mobile, Alabama. She received her MSW in 2006 from the University of Alabama and received her Ombudsman State Certification in 2005. She also holds a Thanatology Certificate from the University of Alabama.

Grantlin Schafer received his BSW from James Madison University and will receive his MSW in May 2007 from the University of Houston. He would like to thank Professor Cindy Hunter at James Madison University for her knowledge, guidance, and support.

Gary B. Schwartz, MSW, is a medical social worker in private home health in Fort Myers, Florida. He works with elders in a tri-county area in southwest Florida, where there are more Medicare-age persons per capita than almost anywhere else. Being able to help this population is the most rewarding work he has ever done.

Karen L. Sheriff will graduate with her BSW from Shippensburg University in May 2007.

Laurie Silvia, BSW, MSW, LCSW, is currently employed at Seven Hills Behavioral Health in New Bedford, Massachusetts. She is a clinical social worker and works with a diverse client population that includes children, adolescents, adults, and the elderly. Her time is divided between two programs, the outpatient clinic, where she works with individuals, and the day treatment center, where she is a group therapist. Her chapter is based on her work at a private nonprofit nursing care center in Rhode Island.

Dorothy C. Stratton, MSW, ACSW, LISW, is a professor of social work at Ashland University. She conducts qualitative research on older widowed men with Dr. Alinde J. Moore, professor of psychology. Their book, *Resilient Widowers: Older Men Speak for Themselves,* was published in 2002. They have also published a book chapter and several scholarly articles based on their study, and have presented at many conferences. In a new study that will begin in 2008, they plan to interview "Baby Boom" era widowers.

Mary Pat Sullivan, Ph.D., BSW, MSW, is a lecturer and MA social work course director at the School of Health Sciences and Social Care, Brunel University, Uxbridge, Middlesex, United Kingdom. Her chapter is based on her 11 years working for a large acute care hospital in northeastern Ontario, Canada, where she was a medical social worker and then Clinical and Administrative Coordinator of an interdisciplinary outreach geriatric mental health service.

Marian Swindell, Ph.D., MSW, is an assistant professor of social work at Mississippi State University–Meridian. Her home health care practice took place in Orlando, Kissimmee, St. Cloud, and Windemere, Florida. She received both her Ph.D. and her MSW from the University of Alabama.

Roseanne Tzitzouris, LMSW, is a forensic social worker at the Legal Aid Society, Brooklyn Office for the Aging, in Brooklyn, New York. She received her MSSW from Columbia University School of Social Work and her BSW from Anna Maria College.

Gerald W. Vest, MSW, BSW, ACSW, LISW, is Professor Emeritus at New Mexico State University School of Social Work and Team Leader for Las Cruces Health Promotion Team With Elders. In addition to teaching and practicing social work, he administers and supports an international community of certified partners of the *15-Minute StressOut Program* for individuals, couples, groups, families, and communities. He facilitates stress management classes for U.S. Army Community Services in Ft. Bliss, Texas.

Karen Zgoda, MSW, LCSW, is a social worker at the Veronica B. Smith Multi-Service Senior Center in Brighton, Massachusetts. Her research interests include the role of technology in social work, social informatics, and the aging population. She is currently working on her Ph.D. in social work at Boston College. See Karen's Web site at http://www.karenzgoda.org.

About the Photographer

Marianne Gontarz York, MSW, LCSW, is a baby boomer who has been a gerontological social worker and photographer for the past 35 years. Originally from Boston and now living in northern California, Marianne has directed a number of community-based programs providing direct services to elders. These days, she is the Director of Social Services at Villa Marin, a life care retirement community. Feel free to check out her Web page at *http://www.mariannegontarzyork.com* to learn more about her and her photography.

Introduction
• • • • • • • • • •

There is a growing need for social workers who specialize in the field of gerontology. And there are social workers who are doing some amazingly exciting work in this area. This book highlights a cross-section of these social workers.

We all have probably known someone in a nursing home. And maybe we have had contact with a senior center or, perhaps, a hospice as a loved one became older. It was exciting to me to read about the variety of roles professional social workers play in the field of gerontology. Some of the chapters inspired me to think, "Hmm...I would really like to do something like that." I think they might inspire you in the same way.

This book is divided into seven parts, each focusing on a specific population, type of setting, or method. You will read about social work in communities, large and small agencies, private practice, international settings, and more. Social workers from throughout the United States and around the globe are doing this important work. Social workers at the BSW, MSW, and PhD levels have contributed stories, illustrating the fact that social workers at all levels play valuable roles in serving the older population.

Each chapter in this book tells a compelling story and teaches a valuable lesson (or two) on its own. In addition, once you have read the entire book, you will see several themes begin to emerge. Among them are the interdisciplinary nature of gerontological social work, the use of creativity, and the issue of self determination.

You may also notice that the field of gerontology has a language of its own. ADL, MDS, MMSE—what does it all mean? The glossary in the back of the book is designed to help you decipher these new and, perhaps, unfamiliar terms.

The language of our culture and our profession is ever-changing. You may notice, as you read this book, that social workers refer to people as clients, patients, consumers, customers, members, or participants. What is the most respectful manner in which you can address people? Does it change depending on the setting or situation? Does it change across time or geographic lines? Does it change on an individual basis?

You will also notice that some social workers use the term *gerontology,* and others use the term *geriatrics.* There is a subtle difference between the two. Gerontology is the study of aging, and geriatrics is the study of the diseases of the aging.

My hope is that by reading this book, you will gain an appreciation for the important work gerontological social workers do every day, that you will learn new ideas and skills, and that maybe you will discover that you want to do this work yourself.

You will find some questions at the end of each chapter. The questions are designed to serve as a starting point for further thought about the material that has been presented in each chapter. Certainly, many other questions will come to mind as you read about each social worker's day. Use the questions provided and your own additional questions to "think about it" further with classmates, co-workers, or on your own as you explore the variety of roles gerontological social workers play.

You may find that you want to do some more reading on a particular area of social work practice. Use the appendices in the back of the book to find readings, organizations, and Web sites on the areas that interest you the most.

So, through the "days" presented in the pages that follow, you can "follow" the writers for a day and feel the challenges, excitement, and rewards they experience. What are you waiting for? Let's get started!

Linda May Grobman, ACSW, LSW

I am extremely pleased that this book has come to fruition. The idea for this book was derived from my personal experiences in teaching a social work course on aging. My teaching experience was cultivated in the urban environment of Baltimore, Maryland, where there were many different opportunities available for social workers who are interested in working with older adults.

The university where I currently teach, Shippensburg University, is located in a rural part of Pennsylvania. I discovered that it was difficult to find gerontological social workers who worked in unique aging settings. My goal was to offer the students in the class a broader perspective of all the various opportunities available to social workers who want to work with older adults.

A chance meeting with the co-editor of this book and the owner of White Hat Communications, Linda Grobman, provided me with this vehicle, which I hope will encourage social work students to want to work with older adults. I also hope that this book may influence current social workers to pursue the gerontological field, because working with older adults is not limited.

By reading the 44 vignettes in this book, I hope that you will gain a broadened perspective on working with the elderly. I also hope that this book will inspire an increase in the number of social workers who are currently working with older adults. In the near future, this specific line of work will become increasingly important, as baby boomers move into retirement age and medical advancements and technology continue to develop.

It is important to note that these vignettes do not represent all of the roles and responsibilities that gerontological social workers perform. There are many other interesting and important aspects of social work with older adults. I believe that our roles as social workers will continue to expand as our society's demographics continue to change.

I also want to add that Linda and I are delighted to feature the photography of Marianne Gontarz York on the cover and throughout this book. Marianne is a social worker, gerontologist, and photographer whose work portrays older adults positively and realistically, whether they are active, frail, receiving care, or giving care. We encourage you to think about the stories that these visual images tell, as well as to think about the images you have of working with this population.

Will your images change after reading this book? Read on and see for yourself!

Dara Bergel Bourassa, Ph.D., MSW, LSW

Acknowledgments

● ● ● ● ● ● ● ● ● ● ● ● ● ● ● ● ●

DAYS IN THE LIVES OF GERONTOLOGICAL SOCIAL WORK-ERS has become a reality as a result of a joint effort by many people. We would like to thank the social workers who contributed chapters to the book. They are committed professionals who took time out of their busy days to share their experiences, in the hope that their experiences will inspire and educate you. We thank social worker and photographer Marianne Gontarz York for her ground-breaking work in portraying older adults through photography, and for making these images a part of this project.

Thanks also go to the BPD, MSW-EDUCATION, AGE-SW, and IASWR e-mail lists, the Geriatric Social Work Initiative, and other newsletters for providing a means for getting the word out about this project, and to the readers of *The New Social Worker's Social Work E-News* for their response to the call for manuscripts.

Thank you to the many social work educators and students who have read and used the first and second volumes in this series, and who have taken the time to give us their input by mail, telephone, e-mail, and at conferences throughout the country.

Linda would like to thank Dara Bergel Bourassa for suggesting the idea for this book, and for co-editing it while at the same time finishing and defending her doctoral dissertation. She is also grateful to her husband Gary for his support and input on all aspects of this book, and to their son Adam, who finds great pleasure in hearing stories of the older generation in his family.

Dara Bergel Bourassa would like to thank Linda Grobman for providing her with the wonderful opportunity to impart her love for gerontological social work to future and current social work professionals. She would also like to thank her husband, Eric Bourassa, for encouraging her to take on this endeavor, when he knew that she had many other tasks to accomplish in the same time period. Her parents, Vivian R. Bergel and Norman Bergel, deserve a special acknowledgment for loving her and supporting her through whatever she desires to achieve. Last, she would like to thank the faculty and staff at Shippensburg University, especially in the Department of Social Work and Gerontology. Without their encouragement, she would not have been able to pursue and undertake this project.

PART 1:
Community

Chapter 1

The Blessings of Meals on Wheels

• •

by Kay A. Long, BSW, RSW

G ood morning, Meals on Wheels, Kay speaking." Thus starts my day, five days a week, every other week, in Lethbridge, Alberta, Canada. I am part of an army of people throughout North America (maybe even the world) who feed people who can no longer prepare their own meals as a result of illness, disability, or age (in some cases all three). And, as we all know, a steady diet of canned soup, potato chips, and cookies is not conducive to healing and/or good health. Our bodies require a balanced, varied diet to promote physical, mental, and emotional well being. That's where Meals on Wheels comes in. We provide a nutritious, hot meal, five days per week, for those who need our help, either on a short- or long-term basis. Meals on Wheels is a wonderful example of people helping people, and I believe passionately in our mission. In fact, I am such a strong supporter of this service that I came out of retirement for the third time to become a job-share coordinator for this nonprofit organization. At my age, a half-time position is perfect. It provides exercise for both mind and body, and I am able to help others—an important objective for all social workers.

You have to be inspired or crazy to go back to work at 68. Perhaps I'm a little of both, but as a board member and a volunteer driver for Meals on Wheels, I saw firsthand the need for the service. So, when the newest job-share coordinator quit suddenly after only six months, I said I'd take the job. Most of the clients fit the category of the frail elderly, and many are living alone in their own homes. The majority of our volunteers are also senior citizens. Several have said that they support the service so it will be there when they need it. Our office is located in a seniors' lodge, so I have daily interaction with seniors who have made the choice to be where lodging and meals are provided. There is always a variety of cheerful "good mornings" from people who are still mobile, often with various types of walkers. At my age, I am honored to be surrounded by those who are older and less active than I am; it also makes me feel like a "kid."

My "on duty" days start at 8:00 a.m., when I unlock the door to our small office and switch on the lights. The first task of the day is to retrieve any messages from our voice mail. If clients have been hospitalized or invited out for lunch the night before, they call and leave a message that they will not need a meal for the next day. Most Mondays there will be at least one message from a client who has lost track of the days of the week and has called on Saturday, wondering why his or her meal is late. (We deliver meals Monday through Friday only.)

After all changes are made, I am ready to make the final count of clients to be served that day, process the billing on the computer, and ensure that the client cards in the route books match the roster for the day. The route books contain client cards with names, addresses, special dietary needs and delivery instructions (i.e., front door, back door, leave meal with neighbor, and so forth) for the volunteers who deliver the meals. Three days per week (Monday, Wednesday, Friday), there are seven color-coded routes. On Tuesday and Thursday, there are five routes. On a weekly basis, five days a week (even during holidays), we process, coordinate, and deliver approximately 350 meals. To further complicate the process of route preparation, not all clients receive meals five days a week. Meal delivery days are scheduled according to the client's individual lifestyle and budget. Some of our clients get meals only three days a week, and their weekly scheduling varies in all possible combinations.

At 9:30 a.m., it is time to go to the kitchen and prepare the work area. Two young women who are employed through Lethbridge Family Services' DaCapo Program carry out the actual process of placing the hot meal with accompanying soup, bun, crackers, and dessert in the styrofoam meal boxes. DaCapo is a program that trains the mentally and physically challenged people in our community, with the help of their job coach, to learn the basics of employment skills. Working with this team is one of the best parts of the job.

By 10:00 a.m., we are ready to roll. As the kitchen staff dishes up the meals, the DaCapo staff places the packaged food items into the styrofoam containers and I begin bundling the containers into the route groups. The first meals to be handled and sorted are the specials: diabetics, no gravy, no sauces, ground meat, or ground meat and vegetables. The meal boxes are strapped together in bundles of three to five boxes and color-coded with clip-on ribbons. As a bundle is completed, I load it onto a flat-bed dolly. On days when we serve large numbers of meals, we also use a large kitchen cart. If all goes well, we complete the job by 10:45 a.m. and take the meals down in the elevator to the volunteers who are waiting to deliver the meals to each individual client.

On a good day, everything goes according to plan. We have the correct number of meals, all the volunteer drivers and couriers show up, and all the clients are at home, waiting to get their meals. My best guess is that a good day happens about 50% of the time. If one of the above doesn't happen according to plan, it is my responsibility to make it right. This means that there are days when we have to go back to the kitchen to get an extra meal, or I have to deliver a route, or act as a courier, or I have to get on the phone and call until I find out if a client is in the hospital, at home in distress, or just forgot it was a meal day and left home. Part of our service is a safety check for our clients and we, at times, have been the first alert that a client is in trouble.

Once the meals are gone, I begin to prepare for the next day. Before I go home at 4:00 p.m., I have completed the meal count, the client list, and the volunteers' route assignments for tomorrow (all subject to change, of course).

This job is never dull, and we often operate in crisis mode. It is the personification of old Murphy's Law: "If anything can go wrong, it will." Along with the primary duty of getting the meals out each day, there is the daily bookkeeping, monthly collections, computer work, client applications and terminations, and phone and receptionist duties. Most important, we handle all exceptions to the rule as they arise and, trust me, they do. During any given month, there is interaction with approximately 100 clients who use the service, and at least that many volunteers.

For a social worker who has always described herself as a people person, it doesn't get much better. I am blessed to have my December days of employment be the best I have experienced in more than 40 years of a working career.

Think About It

1. What are some ways that the Meals on Wheels program helps people, besides simply providing food?

2. Think about your own career development process as you age. How do you envision yourself at age 60, 68, or beyond?

Chapter 2
Adult Protective Services

● ● ● ● ● ● ● ● ● ● ● ● ● ● ● ●

by Mary Jo Garcia Biggs, Ph.D., LCSW

When you read the newspaper headlines, some of the stories are traumatic, shocking, and unimaginable. While much of the focus is on children, older adults are making an impression, and the headlines have now become inclusive of that population. Too often, stories include family perpetrators, tales of abuse, neglect, and exploitation that occur within the family unit. Adult Protective Services (APS) is the agency charged with investigation of those types of allegations, and it is at this agency that I will share a day in my life as a social worker.

I was a BSW student ready to start my internship when my faculty liaison suggested I interview at Adult Protective Services. It wasn't what I wanted to do. I enjoyed working with children, and the thought of working with older adults didn't appeal to me. "Try something outside your comfort zone," he insisted, so, within days of our conversation, I applied, interviewed, and unbeknownst to me began my long career with the Department of Family and Protective Services (formerly the Department of Protective and Regulatory Services).

It's not always easy working for a large bureaucracy—deadlines, management, cynicism, red tape, and public scrutiny, being constantly on the run, and having little "down time." Adult Protective Services came with its share of burdens and stressors. Reflecting on my decade of employment at the agency brings back positive emotions as I think of the life lessons, the wonder, and the joy I experienced as an Adult Protective Services caseworker.

The charge of the Adult Protective Services program is to protect older adults and persons with disabilities from abuse, neglect, and exploitation by investigating and arranging for services to alleviate or prevent further maltreatment. The basic job duties of a caseworker range from conducting basic assessments to developing service plans while juggling various social work roles. At times, you are a broker, linking up your client with community resources and services. In the enabler role, you might help the client cope with life stressors such as eviction issues or transitional living by assisting in problem solving and identifying or supporting personal strengths. The advocacy role may involve speaking on behalf of the client system, possibly with a government agency, regarding benefits for disability issues. Many times the client does not understand options, choices, and processes, or may have other concerns. The APS caseworker may act as an educator to effectively communicate information to the client in a way that is clear and understandable. APS workers must have a bachelor's degree—not necessarily one in social work, although it is the preferred choice. The salary for an APS worker in my area (as of early 2007) ranges between $29,281 and $39,450 annually. It is part of a state agency with a variety of benefits, including medical and retirement plans.

Each day at the agency is unlike any other day. There is no predictability of what the days' events will bring—often a crisis, but sometimes basic follow-up on existing cases. There are easy cases and tough cases and even cases that are invalid or untrue, but for this "day in the life," I will share a story of one of my most difficult cases. The case was not difficult in terms of investigation or collection of evidence, but difficult in terms of images and smells of neglect that are etched in my mind.

The report came in as a low priority, verbal abuse of an older adult, allegedly by the daughter. The case was on my workload for about two weeks and I had been unable to make contact with the alleged victim or alleged perpetrator. I had visited the home and knocked on the door and it seemed as if people were inside, watching through the peep hole, but no one would open the door, and no one would answer when I called out. Telephone calls to the home had been met with resistance. I was told that I could not speak with the alleged victim as she was sleeping, not living at the home, or did not want to talk with me.

This day was different. I knocked on the door and someone cursed at me to go away. I explained that I had to visit with Mrs. L. She screamed that the only way I was going to see her mother was if I showed up with a police officer. I went to my car and called the police department, requesting a courtesy visit from the community officer. It seemed as if only minutes had passed before the officer arrived and we were knocking on the door. This time the woman, still agitated, was less resistant when I asked if we could come in and visit with her mother.

I knew immediately that something was wrong at the home. The stench was horrible. The officer and I were escorted to the back of the home. I thought this was a verbal abuse case, so I hadn't used my Vicks Mentholated (you rub a small amount under your nose to mask odors). The police officer was getting uncomfortable with the smell—I could tell by his body language and the look of disgust on his face.

There in the middle of the room was a cot; Mrs. L lay there, unresponsive, almost comatose. The daughter stood at the door, just as unresponsive as her mother. I introduced myself to the client, and she just blinked her eyes. I asked if I could move the sheet, and she didn't respond. I moved the sheet and could see that she was an amputee. The bed mattress was heavily soaked in urine and covered with feces; the sheets were stuck to Mrs. L's body. My heart broke as I saw movement on the sheets. It wasn't rice; they were maggots. The officer began to gag and quickly left the room. I asked the daughter: *What happened? Why is your mother like this? Where did these maggots come from?* The closer I looked, the more I could see maggots were everywhere, including the leg crevice and vaginal area. I covered up Mrs. L and asked her daughter again: *What happened?*

The response went something like this.

Daughter: She ate pizza in bed.

Me: Pizza? She ate pizza and now she has maggots?

Daughter: Last night she ate pizza.

Just then I heard an ambulance. I was relieved that the officer had called for one. The Emergency Medical Technicians (EMTs) came in and took vitals. I told them what I had seen and that I would need to take pictures as evidence for the case. They brought in a gurney and transported my client to the hospital.

I had phone calls to make, legal procedures to follow, and a chain of command protocol. I was able to file for a temporary emergency guardianship that the judge approved based on pictures alone. This meant that the state would assume the role of guardian to assist the client in her affairs.

Mrs. L was diagnosed with severe decubitus, which is skin breakdown. I was informed that even though the maggots were disgusting, they may have played an important role in keeping Mrs. L alive. It was explained that the maggots ate the dead tissue, which kept the gangrene from setting in and causing further complications. Mrs. L was stabilized after a week in the hospital. The prognosis from the doctor was good, and I approved a temporary nursing home placement to assist her during the healing process.

I was practically brought to tears when I went to visit Mrs. L. She was sitting in her wheelchair playing Bingo. The nursing home social worker commented on how well she had adjusted to the placement. She even said that Mrs. L wanted to stay at the nursing home on a permanent basis. I waited until the Bingo game was over and went to visit with Mrs. L. She was a woman of few words but still appreciative of my interventions. She did not wish to go home, nor did she want to see her daughter again. She said she had friends and a pension to pay for nursing home care, and she wanted to permanently reside at the facility. Since the client was no longer incapacitated, the temporary guardianship would expire and the state would no longer be the guardian, making the client responsible for her own choices and care.

The daughter was charged with a felony neglect case, for which she plea bargained and received a fine. She was clearly neglectful in caring for her mother and had fired every care provider who had attempted to intervene. She was also pending a federal charge of exploitation, since she misused her mother's Social Security check. She wanted nothing to do with her mother.

As terrible at this case sounds, not every case is this awful, and not every investigation or client leaves this sort of impression. Working as an Adult Protective Services worker isn't the job for everyone, but if you have an assertive demeanor with a strong stomach and ability to maintain a calm disposition in times of crisis, you may have found your calling. The intrinsic rewards are high and the personal satisfaction immense. You can be the key to making a difference in someone's life. You can maintain a person's dignity. Your education as a social worker will be valued.

Think About It

1. The roles that social workers play help tie knowledge to practice. Discuss some of the roles mentioned in the narrative and elaborate on other social worker roles not mentioned.

2. What is the role of a social worker in reporting elder abuse, neglect, or exploitation?

Chapter 3
Working With Immigrants in a Community Senior Center
• • • • • • • • • • • • • • • •

by Jinsheng (Jane) Qiu, Ph.D., LMSW

I am an Asian American social worker, working at a senior center in Flushing, New York, an area where Asian immigrants are concentrated. As the director and the social worker, I am responsible for the center's program planning, budgeting, statistics, fundraising, staff hiring/firing, daily activity implementation, and volunteer management. While taking an ongoing caseload up to 10, I supervise two full-time community workers, three part-time kitchen/maintenance staffers, and interns from disciplines of social work, nursing, and nutrition. I am also the site supervisor of two Title V workers from the New York City Department for the Aging (DFTA) and three Work Experience Program (WEP) workers sent by the city's welfare/job training programs.

Ours is one of the six senior centers in Queens under the auspice of our parent agency, which is a United Jewish Appeal associate and has a history of 70 years, providing services to Holocaust survivors, the homebound, AIDS/HIV patients, and elderly people in the community.

Our center is partially funded by the DFTA. For more than 30 years, it has been located in the basement of a Baptist church, which is our landlord. The building is not handicapped accessible. There are no windows and the air circulation is poor, which represents a typical setting of senior centers in metropolitan cities like New York. For quite a few years, there have been no occupancy permits or leases between the DFTA and the landlord, since the latter failed to meet the city's facility requirements.

31

We serve more than 200 elderly members on a daily basis, 95% being elderly Asian immigrants and the rest of Caucasian, African American, and Latino backgrounds. The average age of the clients is 75 years old, among whom, about 30% are 80 and over. It is our goal in general to help all members age well in the community. A specific task of ours is to assist the elderly immigrants better adapt to their new lives in the United States of America. For these purposes, we have provided multiple services, including nutritious congregate lunch, English classes, citizenship preparation classes, educational lectures, painting, dancing, singing, operas, crafts, all kinds of games, and field trips. We also provide a full array of social services, including but not limited to translation, entitlement applications, citizenship application, case assistance, counseling, cancer and Alzheimer patients' support, telephone reassurance, legal service liaison, advocacy, and referrals.

The following are vignettes of my work in one typical day of October 2006.

As usual, I started working at 8:30 a.m. After checking the voice mail, I turned on my computer to check e-mails. Here's one from Susan, daughter of 77-year-old Mrs. C: "I went to see my Mom today. She said that she liked the moon cakes your center sent for the Moon Festival. Recently, she has more smiles and occasionally goes out for a little walk." Mrs. C is a typical old style Chinese wife, following a Confucian doctrine: "Obey to your parents before marriage, to your husband after marriage, and to your son when widowed." After getting married at the age of 17 in Canton, China, she had been so dependent on her husband, an American veteran, that she was even unable to take buses by herself. One year ago, her husband died from liver cancer. If she were in China, she most likely would have lived with her son's family. But here, she stays alone. Obviously depressed and grief-stricken, she refuses to leave the house. We have been working with her daughter and friends, trying to bring her back to the center. Upon reading the e-mail, I was very pleased with her progress, which put me in a good mood for the start of the day.

Last week, our dishwasher was broken and I called the kitchen equipment contractor for repair. A technician came to check the 30-year-old machine and suggested a replacement instead of repair. I immediately reported this matter to my off-site supervisor and our DFTA program officer in hopes of getting some help. Yesterday afternoon, the DFTA officer came to inspect the situation. She asked me to submit at least three bids for a new machine. This was my top priority for today. So, at 9 a.m., I made several calls to equipment suppliers asking for quotes as soon as possible. Then, I wrote a reminder for myself to follow up.

Facility problems, such as a leaking ceiling, broken steam table, broken toilets, broken faucets, just to list a few, have been a constant harassment to the center's normal functioning. At times, I get very frustrated, because the problems often cannot be solved in a timely manner; sometimes they just remain unsolved. Currently, besides the broken dishwasher, another problem is on my mind. There has been no hot water in the four bathrooms for many years. Our funding sources claim that the repairs are the landlord's responsibility. The landlord argues that the church does not have the funds to make the repairs. Demographic changes have resulted in a declining church membership, which has limited parishioner contributions. The landlord further asserts that the rent DFTA pays is too low to cover the cost. When winter is coming, solving this long-standing problem has become more urgent. I have discussed this issue with our Policy Advisory Council, and a decision has been made to raise money to install heaters. I have already obtained the landlord's permission and cooperation. This morning, after calling for dishwasher quotes, I called the landlord and a plumber to schedule a meeting for tomorrow. Then I started drafting a letter to our community supporters to solicit donations.

Just after 9:30, an emergency was brought to my attention by a community worker. Ms. X, a cancer patient with metastatic disease, lost her Medicaid benefit for failure of recertification. As a consequence, her oncologist refused to continue her chemotherapy. For the elderly immigrants, the language barrier is the biggest obstacle in their daily lives. Clients may lose their benefits simply because they don't understand the government letters for renewals or other requirements. While comforting the distressed client, I instructed the community worker to contact the Medicaid office immediately for emergency assistance. Then, I called Mrs. X's oncologist to request her treatment be continued. When the doctor in private practice helplessly declined my plea, I turned to the American Cancer Society. With a referral to Queens Hospital Cancer Center, a public hospital, I called right away to make an earliest possible appointment for Ms. X and helped her sign a Health Insurance Portability and Accountability Act (HIPAA) form for her medical records' transfer.

Then I took a break from the office to walk around the center. Everything seemed to be going on in order, the cards/mah jong playing, billiards, Chinese opera. The daily English as a Second Language class was, as usual, over-crowded. More than 30 older students were in a small room packed like sardines. I felt frustrated, as we had been unsuccessful in advocating for a new site for many years. I saw the volunteer coordinator recruiting the lunch-line service volunteers and overseeing the ongoing coffee/cake service and silver wrapping. I thanked him and asked him to make sure that all volunteers put on hats or hairnets, gloves, and aprons to meet the city's sanitary standards. Partially as the initial design to promote volunteerism, and partially as the tight budgeting, senior centers are usually under staffed; only the very basic jobs are filled. Therefore, it is vital to empower, mobilize, organize, train, and supervise volunteers for the center's daily normal functioning.

Afterwards, I went to check the kitchen that prepares more than 200 meals Monday through Friday, a monumental task in itself. In one corner outside the office, the community workers, whose major tasks are to provide low-level case assistance from reading letters to entitlement applications to solving billing problems, were taking care of the walk-in clients. About 20 clients had already signed up on the waiting list for service, and more were coming in.

At the center's entrance, I spotted Ms. Y sitting alone and talking into the air. Years ago, her family abandoned her because of her mental illness. Since then, she has been living alone. On three occasions in the past five years, I sent her to the Asian Unit of the local hospital, where she had a diagnosis of schizophrenia. Her discharge plan included outpatient visits and counseling with a Chinese psychiatrist and a social worker in Elmhurst Hospital mental health center. Once, I tried to get her into a group home for the mentally ill, where supervision with medication was available, among other assistance. She refused. From time to time, she changed addresses and said that she did not have a home phone or cell phone when asked.

With greetings, I approached her and asked if she kept her appointments and refilled her prescriptions. She did not answer, but looked at me with anger and defiance. "They've come to get me but I'm not afraid. I did not do anything wrong." Realizing she might have another episode of recurrence, I coaxed her to the office while trying to persuade her to go see her doctor. She absolutely refused. I then called her psychiatric social worker. He asked me to send her to emergency right away and promised to handle the situation once she arrived. I called 911. When she resisted to cooperate, the police grabbed her arms with force and she cried with pain. I felt bad and informed the police of her heart disease, requesting that they treat her nicely. In the wake of the ambulance, I could not help pondering how to keep such psychiatric patients safely in the community. Despite the powerful anti-psychotic medication that makes deinstitutionalization possible, the fragmented systems have failed to provide a safety network for patients. Many lack affordable housing and effective monitoring and supervision.

This incident was followed by our daily lunch service at 11:30. After a brief announcement about the annual flu shot service to be held on October 31, the office staff helped the disabled members with their lunches. We also encouraged healthy members to help their needy friends.

At 1:00 p.m., I had an appointment with Ms. Z, my counseling case. About two years ago, she and her husband were baby-sitting their grandchildren in Arizona for their elder daughter, who was busy running a small restaurant with her husband. Unfortunately, Ms. Z was diagnosed with breast cancer, and the surgery exhausted all the family's savings. Under distress, existing family disputes escalated, culminating in the eviction of the elderly couple. They came to New York to stay with their younger daughter's family. When I first saw her, she was suicidal, feeling helpless and hopeless. After a needs assessment, our center helped her apply for Medicaid so that she could have the life-saving chemotherapy. I provided support through the treatment while conducting cognitive therapy and psychodynamic therapy to help her develop deeper understanding of herself and better communication skills with her husband and other family members. She was encouraged to set a goal of becoming a U.S. citizen. With only six years of schooling, she learned English from scratch. Recently, she passed the INS interview. We were all very proud of her. At today's session, we discussed the next steps of her plan: how to gain more self-confidence and independence through volunteerism and further improvement of family relationships.

After the session, I completed the case notes and work log. Documentation is always important to trace the progress of interventions, and to be accountable to our funding sources. Then I finished the revisions of the center's job descriptions. I planned to discuss the changes with staffers before submitting them to our central office. The new job descriptions will be used for the next annual staff appraisals. When the community workers finished serving the walk-in clients, I discussed the new assignments with them: organizing the Alzheimer's Disease caregivers to the Mayor's 13th Alzheimer's Conference on October 30 and preparing statistics for this month and new program for November.

Fifteen minutes before 4:00 p.m. when the center was closed, we did the routine safety check-ups to make sure that all file cabinets were locked and everything was ready for tomorrow. Ms. M, our 92-year-old office volunteer, made a surprise announcement: "I have decided to sell my house and move to the Flushing House," an assisted living facility in Flushing. Widowed for 20 years, Ms. M has lived by herself, having only a sister in New Jersey. In the past 26 years, she has been a full-time volunteer at our office with bookkeeping and phone answering duties. She regards this center as her second home.

Three years ago, she fell and was forced to stay home most of the winter. Last year, she battled breast cancer. Although she manages to go on, her deteriorating health has obviously taken its toll. She has more and more difficulties in managing chores like repairs, garbage, and cleaning the yard. As her social worker, I have been supporting her and working with her for a safer living arrangement. With understanding, I provided information, accompanied her to visit facilities she wanted to see, and listened to her complaints about being anxious, upset, frustrated, and even angry. She has been living in the private house for 75 years with memories of her parents and husband. It's really very hard for her even to think about leaving there. While resisting, she realized that she must make up her mind before the first snow. Among many alternatives, she preferred Flushing House for its good meals and its convenient location to our center.

I congratulated Ms. M, saying, "You've made my day! I am more than happy to see you're safer this winter." Her face beamed. This is the non-monetary reward of working with elderly clients, when I see the positive outcome of making a difference to better their lives.

Think About It

1. When and why did the worker feel frustrated?

2. How did the social worker juggle the multiple roles in direct services?

3. How could a social worker advocate effectively to improve the adverse physical conditions in the agency?

4. What ethical dilemma did the social worker face in working with Ms. Y, the psychiatric client?

Chapter 4

When the White Cane Comes in Handy: Helping Older Adults Navigate the Health Care System

● ●

by Karen Zgoda MSW, LCSW

Q*uestion*: When does a white cane come in handy?

Answer: At a town hall meeting when everyone rushes to get help with their health care.

I wish I could say I was joking. However, this joke is exactly what one older adult shared with me after she had attended a seminar on health care options. She claimed that the white cane was useful to get other folks out of her way so she could get individual help with her health care plan. Although I never heard about any actual violent episodes from that day, this woman certainly made her feelings about her health care vividly clear.

At 9 a.m., I arrive at the Veronica B. Smith Multi-Service Senior Center in Brighton, Massachusetts, where I am a senior advocate. The senior center is located in the heart of Brighton Center in Boston and easily accessible via four city bus routes. Since 2001, the senior center has operated as part of the Elderly Commission of the City of Boston. The senior center serves nearly 1,000 adults 60 and older each year. More than 75% of these seniors have low or very low incomes. Roughly 70% of the members are female. Services offered include health screenings, fitness programs, arts and crafts classes, ESL classes, community meetings with elected officials, educational workshops, and assistance with completing applications for government benefits and other community services. In addition, computer tutoring is offered in the computer lab. At a recent health fair, more than 150 older adults came to the senior center for free flu shots. The senior center also produces a newsletter (available online at *http://www.seniorpublishing.com/*) that is sent to members, local community centers, and local businesses to advertise special events and programs.

Throughout the day, I help seniors with any service needs they may have. These needs cover a wide range of issues, so I need to be prepared for just about anything. On a typical day, I might help a senior apply for housing assistance, apply for food stamps, find programs for home repairs, get fuel assistance, or obtain transportation. Sometimes a senior will receive a new card, explanation of benefits, or bill in the mail but cannot understand what it means, and they bring it to me to decipher. Lately, the bulk of my work has been helping seniors sort through health care and prescription options.

It takes a particular combination of knowledge and fearlessness to help people with their health care. The biggest fear I had to overcome was worrying that if I made a mistake, a senior would be without vital health care or medications. I find it helps to try and put the person's mind at ease. Seniors may feel scared, confused, frustrated, or angry after trying to navigate their health care or prescription coverage on their own. In fact, they may worry so much about making the wrong choice that they don't make any choice at all.

I have had considerable luck using the Medicare Prescription Drug Finder *(http://www.medicare.gov)* to help sort out and compare Part D prescription plans. On a recent day, Mrs. Murphy came to me for just this type of help. Together, we sat down in front of the computer, logged in to the site, and put in her Medicare number, Social Security number, birthday, ZIP code, her list of medications, and the dosage of each drug she needs per month. Once we plugged in this information, we received a list of plans available in her area to choose from. Plan options can be further broken down by the senior's preferred pharmacy. Be advised that not every plan will work with every pharmacy. A nice feature of this Web site is that you can compare up to three plans at once. Each comparison will be broken down by annual cost, expected costs for medications, and any annual fees. You can always choose three plans, compare them, and then choose three additional plans to compare them, and so on.

I found it helpful to suggest to Mrs. Murphy, as I have done with other seniors I work with, that she compare the process of selecting among various health care plans and prescription plan options to the process of buying a car. Most seniors have had some experience with car-buying or have at least been in a few different models and makes of cars. Seniors are now expected to go to the health care equivalents of Honda, Ford, and Chevrolet, comparison shop, and read *Consumer Reports* and anything else they can get their hands on to make the best decision for health care and prescription medication. In such a consumer-driven health system, where the responsibility to find the best deal is left to the individual, seniors are finding that correct and timely information is the key to making the right decision.

As I leave for the day, I am satisfied in knowing that, through the use of technology, Mrs. Murphy and other seniors will be more prepared to shop for the health care that will best meet their needs.

Think About It

1. How can social workers best help seniors prepare for consumer-driven health care and prescription medication choices? How can we help seniors make the best care decisions under these circumstances?

2. What new expectations and responsibilities are inherent in being a consumer of health care?

Chapter 5
Geriatric Community Care Management

• • • • • • • • • • • • • • • •

by Susan J. Harper, MSW, LSW, ACSW

The position of care manager (also referred to as case manager) is an entry level social work position, with an average starting salary of $25,000. A bachelor's degree is required for this position. Geriatric care management uses a strengths based model to assist consumers age 60 and older to remain in the community. The major emphasis of geriatric care management is matching consumers with available resources. Care management developed as a cost effective alternative to institutionalization in long-term nursing homes or personal care homes. The care manager must be knowledgeable about community resources in addition to services provided directly through the Department of Aging.

Each state's Department of Aging establishes how care management will be delivered. In Allegheny County in Pennsylvania, care managers are either direct employees of the Department of Aging or are employed by a contracted agency to provide services. When the Department of Aging receives a referral for services, the information is sent to the appropriate agency, and a care manager is assigned.

Consumers are divided into two categories: NFI or NFCE. NFI stands for Nursing Facility Ineligible. Loosely defined, this means that the individual is able to live independently in the community with very little in the way of formal supports. NFCE stands for Nursing Facility Clinically Eligible. This consumer is determined to be ill enough to be clinically eligible to reside in a nursing home, although the consumer's desire is to remain at home with support services. The care manager, a Department of Aging nurse, and the

41

consumer's primary care physician must all agree that the consumer is NFCE.

All consumers currently part of the caseload are reassessed and contacted for monitoring visits and phone calls. These phone calls and home visits are scheduled at regular intervals, based on the level of care (NFI or NFCE). Caseload size is recommended to be 50 consumers, but at times caseloads can be larger. In addition to currently assigned consumers, new applicants for services are at times assigned to the caseload.

My typical day begins at 7:30 a.m. The first activity of the day is to check voice mail messages, making note of those that require follow-up action. Next, I check my e-mail for any messages that require action. Finally, I check the mail folder for incoming mail.

I log onto SAMS (Social Assistance Management System), where a list of all of my consumers appears. Any actions that were taken since the last time I logged in are now entered into the computer. These might include phone calls not previously logged, visits at the end of the previous day, or completion of a Care Management Review and Care Plan.

I attend the weekly team meeting, at which time any new information from the Department of Aging is provided, as well as any information from the management. Also, this is an opportunity to request suggestions from team members about cases.

The majority of my day involves making phone calls to consumers, provider agencies, community resources, and consumers' family members. There is no "usual" number of visits or phone calls per month. All contacts are logged in SAMS.

On this day, one of my consumers, John, has returned home from the hospital. Another, Betty, has been in a nursing home for one month. I have a reassessment with Mary scheduled. I make a phone call to John to set up a visit this afternoon to assess for any changes. I contact the provider agency to authorize services to be restarted.

Next, I make a phone call to schedule a monitoring visit for Betty, the consumer in the nursing home, to make certain that she is doing well in her new environment.

My supervisor hands me a referral for a new consumer, Anthony. When a referral is received, the care manager is to contact the consumer by phone within 24 hours and complete the assessment within two weeks. A phone call to Anthony reveals that he wishes for his daughter to be at the assessment. Anthony gives me verbal approval to talk with his daughter, and in a phone call to the daughter, we schedule the assessment for the following week. I enter the contact information into SAMS.

At the intake interview, medical information, as well as functional abilities, other supports in place, and the consumer's financial information, is gathered and entered into a computerized questionnaire. The purpose of this is to determine if the consumer is NFI or NFCE and to find what medical conditions are limiting the consumer's ability to function independently. Activities of Daily Living (ADL), such as bathing, dressing, eating, and toileting—as well as Instrumental Activities of Daily Living (IADL), such as transportation, financial management, meal preparation, and shopping—are assessed. Also assessed is the level of support that the consumer is receiving from informal supports such as family members, neighbors, church members, and from formal supports such as the primary care physician, home nursing, or other assistance. By obtaining financial information, I am able to tell the consumer what he or she will have to pay for any services delivered. This is called Cost Sharing, and the amount the consumer pays for services is based on the consumer's adjusted income as compared to the poverty level.

With the consumer, I complete other forms, most importantly the consumer's decisions about who other staff members and I are permitted to talk to about the consumer's condition and services. I offer the consumer the opportunity to register to vote. Using a strengths based model, I work with the consumer to determine what resources would be helpful, and based on what the consumer needs, I am then able to assist the consumer with linking to resources in the community, such as food pantries, financial assistance, tax rebate information, LIHEAP information (Low Income Home Energy Assistance Program), home repairs, personal care services, and others, as needed. The care plan is developed and signed.

Following the assessment, I meet with a supervisor to review the consumer's circumstances and obtain approval for necessary services. If all services requested are not approved, I contact the consumer to explain the decision, and then contact agencies to set up services as approved. On this day, I begin the monthly phone calls to consumers scheduled for contact. Information gathered includes any medical changes, any problems with the services received, and any information that might be beneficial for the consumer. I log each phone call and conversation in SAMS. I make phone calls to schedule monitoring visits or reassessments that are due, and all calls are logged in SAMS. Other phone calls may be in response to e-mails or voice mail messages that were received earlier in the day.

My first visit of the day is to see John, who returned home from the hospital. Because a reassessment may be necessary, I take the computer with me as well as the care plan cover page for signatures. At the meeting, it becomes clear that there is no substantial change in functioning. Thus, there will be no change in services, and no reassessment is needed. Only a note in SAMS will be required.

Returning to the office, I log the visit into SAMS. Another consumer calls and reports that her heat is about to be shut off. With her permission, I make calls to the gas company to establish a payment plan for the consumer, and to Catholic Charities for assistance with the bill. I make a return call to the consumer to inform her of the progress and direct her to call the gas company to verify the payment plan. I also inform her about registering for LIHEAP when the program begins. She tells me that the problem is two broken windows and no money to fix them. I make phone calls to community resources for assistance with home repairs to locate someone to repair the windows. All of these calls are logged in SAMS.

The second visit of the day is a monitoring visit to see Betty, who has resided in a nursing home for 30 days. Betty tells me that she plans to return home following rehabilitation. I inform her that because she has been out of the home for 30 days, it is required that her case be closed. I explain how to reopen her case when she returns home, and I inform her that a letter will be sent confirming the case closure and explaining how to reopen her case.

The third visit of the day is Mary's reassessment. No changes are noted, and the care plan is reviewed and signed with no changes.

Evening visits and phone calls are discouraged, at times resulting in scheduling difficulties with family members who work and need to be at the assessment.

The most rewarding part of this position is the knowledge that consumers have been able to maintain their independence. Acceptance of loss that is due to death or placement is also part of the position and can be difficult. For this line of work, people skills are very important, as are computer skills (using software programs, typing) and the ability to multi-task. Being able to manage multiple pieces of information in action at the same time is vital. Patience and the tenacity to follow up with resources also are tremendous assets.

I have found support in this field through the NASW gerontology special interest group, SWAP (Social Workers in Aging Practice Council), and classes through the Professional Care Management Institute.

I graduated with my Master of Social Work in 1990. Since then, I have worked at many positions in two states, and all but one was in the field of gerontology. I find myself drawn to working with seniors. I feel that I receive as much from them as they receive from me. Care management that empowers seniors to participate in the decision-making process of service delivery appeals to my sense of fairness, and it is consistent with social work tenets. Even though this is an "entry level" position, I find the emphasis on direct contact with consumers over a prolonged period fits well with my personal goals.

Ethical issues that are inherent in this position include confidentiality, determination of Level of Care (NFI or NFCE), and safety vs. self determination. Maintaining confidentiality is difficult in a senior citizen apartment building where consumers know each other. However, it is imperative to maintain confidentiality.

When determining level of care, it is important that the primary care physician, Department of Aging staff nurse, and the care manager communicate and agree. There are implications for being deemed NFCE, such as being required to apply for PDA (Pennsylvania Department of Aging) Waiver. Explaining this program, exceptions, and limits of the program often falls to the care manager.

The safety vs. self determination issue is possibly the biggest challenge, because this is usually associated with a consumer who has been receiving services for some time. Over time, the consumer may become less able to manage independently, and the care manager must be objective, and may need to bring in other resources to assist in determining ways to maintain safety.

Individuals considering this type of work would do well to participate in a field placement with a care management agency. In this way, you will be able to experience the day-to-day workings of the agency, meet consumers on the phone and in their homes, and get a real "feel" for the work involved.

Think About It

1. What do NFI and NFCE stand for? What differences in services might you expect for consumers in each category?

2. What three people have to agree to determine that a consumer is NFCE? Discuss how a disagreement regarding level of care might be resolved.

Chapter 6
Community Senior Services

• • • • • • • • • • • • • • • • • •

by Debra Hartley, BSW, MSW

I am employed as a geriatric community development social worker for Seniors Services, the City of Calgary, Alberta, Canada. Today is one of my busiest days of the year. It is seven o'clock in the morning and I am driving to a local shopping mall where we are holding a Seniors Information Fair. This information fair is unique, as we are targeting immigrant seniors who face language barriers. Interpreters speaking eight languages will be available to accompany seniors to the displays so the seniors can access information about services in their own languages.

About four years ago, a team of community social workers and a geriatric nurse with the health region completed a community assessment of the east area of Calgary. As part of the assessment, we invited seniors, service providers, and other stakeholders from the area to a Town Hall meeting so we could learn about the community assets and identify concerns shared by the stakeholders. One of the issues that was clearly identified during the meeting was that seniors in the ethnoculturally diverse east area had challenges accessing information about services. After the Town Hall meeting, it became my role to focus on how information about services could be more accessible to seniors in the community.

The first task in addressing this issue was to form a planning committee of service providers and ethnoculturally diverse seniors to develop and implement an action plan. At times, it can be a challenge to engage seniors in the community development process. In order to do so, it is important for them to identify the issue to be addressed and then to engage them in the planning process.

47

Community development focuses on helping people identify and develop their skills and address their issues. As a community social worker, it is not my role to work in isolation to plan activities for the community.

After the planning committee met a few times to identify a strategy to address this issue, someone suggested holding an information fair. The question was how to plan it so it would meet the needs of the target population. First, the location of the information fair had to be accessible and well known throughout the east area of Calgary. Someone on the committee suggested holding it at a large shopping mall. Two of the seniors subsequently arranged to meet with the administrative staff at the shopping mall and spoke with them about the idea. They were delighted when they came back to the next meeting and reported that the shopping mall was supportive of the concept and would be prepared to rent tables and chairs for the event. Now the information fair is in its fourth year, and the planning committee continues to meet on an ongoing basis.

Upon arriving at the mall this morning, there is lots of work to do before the senior serving agencies arrive with their displays. Everyone from our planning committee arrives early to help set up for the event, including seniors and service providers. Some of the seniors are busy organizing the information table, where the interpreters will check in before they begin for the day. Other people are putting up signs and numbers on each table, so that every display table is clearly marked when the booth holders arrive. Soon, the booth holders begin arriving and committee members show the organizations where their tables are and answer questions. Today there will be 36 organizations with displays. The planning committee members worked together to decide which organizations should be invited to participate. There are many more senior serving organizations in Calgary, but since there is limited space in the mall, participating organizations are selected and invited to participate.

During the fair, I wander throughout the mall checking to see if a senior is trying to find an interpreter, making sure that our volunteers have a break, and answering questions. I also spend time visiting each booth. This is a great opportunity to network with other service providers. Relationships are important in community development and are an asset when you need to connect with someone at another agency. In community development, partnerships and collaborations are essential to our work. None of us can address the issues alone—we all have to work together.

As I walk through the mall, I note that the turnout seems to be good. All of the booths are busy providing information to seniors. A number of seniors have an interpreter with them. At the beginning of the morning, we distributed evaluation forms to all of the booth holders. Evaluating our work in community development is important, as we are always looking for ways to improve. If the agencies at the booths do not think this is a worthwhile initiative, they will not return next year. Each year, the planning committee uses feedback from the participating organizations, seniors, and interpreters to improve the information fair.

A reporter from a local television station has come to the mall and interviews me, as well as some of our other planning committee members. It is great to have an opportunity to highlight some of the good work that Seniors Services is doing in the community in partnership with others.

At two o'clock, the Seniors Information Fair ends. It always seems to be busier in the morning, so the planning committee decided that the fair should end in the early afternoon. As the booth holders start to pack up, we gather all of the evaluation forms and assist the booth holders to their vehicles, if needed. The members of the planning committee briefly meet and concur that the day has been a great success. We will be meeting in a few weeks to review the evaluation forms and to have a celebratory luncheon. Everyone is tired. There has been a lot of running around throughout the day.

I go to the mall's administration office and thank the staff there for all of their work and for hosting the information fair again. Rarely do we find a partner in the business community that so willingly supports our initiatives. I work hard to maintain the relationship with the staff at the shopping mall so we can continue with this event on an annual basis.

Now I have to go on to a meeting! My meeting this afternoon is with a group that is focusing on transportation issues that affect seniors. This concern was identified by many individuals in Calgary when we conducted a series of community consultations with seniors and service providers. Despite the fact that we have a good transit system and handibus service available to those who cannot access the transit, time and time again we hear that transportation is a major barrier for seniors when they want to participate in the community. The lack of accessible transportation can lead to isolation.

The meeting I am attending this afternoon is being held in one of the smaller seniors' centers in Calgary. My role is to facilitate the group, to conduct research about the transportation needs of seniors, and to identify best practices in other communities. The Transportation Planning Table has eight members, including five seniors, one service provider, and two members of the business community. I enjoy working with this group because the members have diverse backgrounds and different points of view. All of them are very committed to improving transportation services for seniors in Calgary.

Everyone has arrived, and the chair calls the meeting to order. I am pleased that a senior volunteered to be the chair of the Transportation Planning Table. I support him in his role by drafting the meeting agendas and minutes for his approval. It provides him with an opportunity to utilize and develop his skills. He always keeps the meeting moving. If people get off topic and go off on tangents, he is able to bring them back to the focus of the discussion. Of course, I could have assumed the role of chair, but that really would not be conducive to the community development process. I try to lead from behind, to build community capacity, so after I move on to new projects and communities, seniors and other stakeholders will be able to continue with the initiative. If I, as a professional, appear to be the leader, then other stakeholders may assume little ownership of the project and may not feel as committed to the process.

The Transportation Planning Table has been meeting for more than a year now. Once the Planning Table was formed, the members agreed that they wanted to gain a better understanding of the barriers that Calgary seniors face when trying to access transportation services. We had the opportunity to work with a sociology class at the University of Calgary, and its research focus for the semester was on seniors and transportation. The students conducted an environmental scan of transportation services for seniors in Calgary and interviewed more than 150 seniors to learn about their concerns and issues. The Planning Table also conducted focus groups with seniors, so they could gain a clear understanding of the issue. In community development, research is extremely important. It is essential to speak with people and to learn about their concerns and priorities. The research and information gathering process is also an opportunity to begin developing relationships with people in the community and to engage them.

Today, the focus of our meeting is to plan a transportation stakeholders meeting. We are inviting service providers from the nonprofit and for-profit sectors and also from Calgary Transit and the handibus system. We need to clearly establish the goals and objectives of the upcoming meeting. The Transportation Planning Table members have heard from service providers that often they do not know what services are offered by other organizations. This meeting will be an excellent opportunity to share and exchange information about services. We also want to facilitate a discussion about how the stakeholders may be able to work together to improve transportation services for seniors in Calgary. We plan the agenda for the upcoming meeting. The chair has agreed to act as the chair for the stakeholders meeting. Each Planning Table member will have a role to play, so each person knows that he or she is making a valuable contribution. Some will act as greeters; some will help facilitate the conversation. I will offer support by making arrangements for the lunch to be provided, photocopying agendas, and helping to set up for the meeting. I have drafted an evaluation form for the stakeholders to complete. We want to know if the meeting was valuable and if they would like to meet again. At the conclusion of our meeting, the members of the Planning Table agree that they feel well prepared for the stakeholders meeting and are looking forward to it.

The day is over and I have not even stepped into the office!

As a social worker for the municipal government, I am registered with the Alberta College of Social Workers (ACSW). To practice as a social worker in the province of Alberta, it is now mandatory to be registered. For annual registration, a number of educational requirements must be fulfilled. The ACSW also ensures that all social workers act in an ethical professional manner or disciplinary measures can be taken. In community development work, social work ethics are just as important as in clinical social work.

In Calgary, there are very few geriatric community development social workers; the focus continues to be on clinical social work. To be successful in this type of social work, it is essential that you have excellent interpersonal skills and the ability to develop relationships. However, this is true of all areas of social work practice. A good understanding of the community development process and of the aging process is required. I would highly recommend this field of practice to anyone who enjoys working with seniors, service providers, and other stakeholders as partners. In community development, seniors have a strong voice in all of the work that we do.

Think About It

1. How can the work of geriatric community development workers support the roles of clinical geriatric social workers?

2. What common skills and knowledge are required in the roles of geriatric community social workers and clinical geriatric social workers?

Chapter 7

Best Practices in a Community Setting

● ●

by Karen V. Graziano, MSW, LCSW

Each leaf on every tree has a different hue and strikes me as remarkably beautiful on this early autumn morning. I know that the leaves will fall soon and winter will be upon us, so I organize my immediate and short-term priorities, recognizing that there is a good deal to accomplish in a limited amount of time. My long-term goals hover and mingle in my mind, as they will be realized in a tangible tomorrow.

In geriatric care management, inclusive in the Naturally Occurring Retirement Community (NORC) Program, my foundation and basis for the "hub" of the "wheel" of services is understood as "safety." With the crisis in aging emerging as this unique population increases exponentially, there is a groundswell of response on many levels. Bringing needed services on site, ensuring one of the most important aspects of program development, accessibility of resources, helps to maintain older adults at home with dignity. Today, in fact, the small staff (professionally challenged in various respects, which is in part due to the limitations of underfunding)—an experienced R.N. (in-kind staff); the bilingual caseworker; the poorly educated, brash, but brilliant assistant; and myself—will brainstorm an upcoming health fair.

Since this is a low-income, public housing population in New York City, there is an overwhelming degree of chronic illness. Diabetes, including severe complications, hypertension, renal dialysis, cancer, and arthritis are some of the conditions that make up the mix. The caseworker counsels a diabetic client discussing Medicaid benefits in her rather makeshift office, as it is a complex issue. He is non-English speaking, uneducated, being from a rural town, and may be illiterate in his own language. The caseworker approaches me, as the supervisor, stating that this elderly man was in the grocery and noticed that free chickens were being distributed. He was told to sign on the dotted line, and therefore, was now, unwittingly, an HMO Medicaid recipient. I instructed her to expedite his disenrollment, since straight Medicaid, which offers enhanced freedom and flexibility of services, is preferable.

I am appalled by the irresponsible and underhanded tactics displayed by the HMO in its outreach efforts. Realizing that this is an advocacy issue, I report it immediately to the Attorney General's office. Now I rest easier, since I know that this is one of the most responsive agencies in the field, intervening on behalf of the most vulnerable of our society. Unfortunately, in direct service, frustration can reign as good intentions are met with bureaucratic underpinnings, staff burnout, and a "benign neglect," therefore underscoring the importance of contacts, networking, and the invaluable resource directory. You will be amazed, quite unexpectedly, that the "key to the city" lies in your ownership of best practices, and you will become empowered.

Okay, staff, can we all get together now? The nurse is caught up in a blood pressure check, alerting me that the client's pressure is dangerously elevated, yet the client is not amenable to medical intervention. This is no time to mince words, as even though we respect self-determination, a concerned judgment has to be instituted while barriers of resistance are broken. We briefly discuss her valid, but vague concerns and with the power that comes with position, as the director, I am able to state that it is now my responsibility to ensure her best interests, and I will call the ambulance, as well as her daughter. She seems to feel relieved with her sense of well-being intact.

After the ambulance leaves, we do plan our health fair with the purpose of education, networking, marketing, and outreach. We decide to invite local providers and partners to staff informational tables, enable a doctor from the local hospital to discuss a diabetes PowerPoint presentation (networked through the nursing organization), introduce a cooking demo illustrating the benefits of "special diet" compliance and nutrition, and present a role-play regarding the hidden but pervasive issue of elder abuse. This crowd, our target group, does not respond well to lectures, as some other socioeconomic groups do, whereas interactive programming seems to make a meaningful impact.

The afternoon is approaching at light speed as we all grab a bite at our desk, as usual. The nurse left for the day after EMS transported the client, ensuring that she will follow up with her contact at the hospital later in the day. Hmmm, what's pressing? There is that referral to Adult Protective Services that needs a follow-up today and, of course, the food pantry has to be distributed. The assistant has been trained to disperse the food bags in an equitable way, which is quite a challenge, if you can understand the mindset of this particular population. She has trouble absorbing this, but as a social worker, my mantra to staff and some seniors who take issue with the complaining, sometimes ranting, is that aging is all about losses. We see the loss of friends, loved ones (sometimes even grown children—a tragedy from which one can never recoup completely), isolation as the community and world change. We see ageism perpetrated by perhaps even their own doctors, and we see the loss of their faculties, such as hearing, mobility, vision, and/or memory. Then, to complete the scenario, emerges the culprit of the downward spiral, depression. Dependency needs are rocketing, as would be expected, resulting in a spectrum of response ranging from fierce independence (reaction formation to an increasing state of dependency) to a ball of putty (feelings of inadequacy, loss of self efficacy) in what might be the wrong hands. Neediness and emptiness are at the fore.

Yes, the bags of groceries are free, including the fresh vegetables supplied by a grant from the United Way. Of course, proper nutrition is vital to good health, and since it is available, there is an increased probability that Sally will eat a nutritious meal, as contrasted to grabbing fried chicken at a local fast food chain or earmarking the money to pay her granddaughter's cable bill. Sally, however, is irate as, after inspecting the bags, she realizes that her friend received apples and she received oranges. She confronts the food pantry assistant in a rather rude and demanding manner. The assistant, Myra, "loses it" for a moment and is relegated to her bullying mode. I intervene: "I'm sorry you did not receive the apples, but instead the oranges. We had to alternate baskets for the sake of fairness, since apples were sparser today. Sally, it's unlike you to handle yourself in such a manner. Is there something else going on?" I conclude by setting a limit in stating that we cannot have these outbursts. Myra goes outside to get some air.

I speak to Myra, eliciting the frustration that comes with the "helping professions" (or, more precisely, the "empowering professions"). I reiterate that not only are these clients perhaps physically and emotionally challenged, but their inadequate coping skills need bolstering. However, I add that I will not allow anyone to be the target of abuse, whether client or staff, and if this episode is repeated, further action will be taken. This holds true for both Sally and Myra.

Wow, this day really flew, as it has been particularly busy. I have made an impact. I may not have changed the world as much as I first aspired to when new in the field, but I have never lost perseverance, and I find comfort in feelings of competency. In seeking out this profession, I yearned to be superior to those models that were merely going through the motions. They are still ubiquitous, and I still aspire to high ethical standards with sincere concern for the client system as my core value. On the contrary, there are exceptional social workers in this vibrant and relevant field, where opportunities for making change abound, but there is a need for visionaries who will sculpt our world and act as social architects of our dreams.

Winter is just around the corner, which brings contemplation about the changing of the seasons. Some mourn the loss, and we acknowledge this, while never losing sight of the promise of tomorrow.

Hmmm, let me make that call to Adult Protective Services before I leave for the day.

Think About It

1. Strategize treatment approaches to deal with depression in older adults while including them in the treatment process.

2. What is your reaction to ageist attitudes expressed by colleagues, intruding into the professional realm? How would you deal with the blatant ageism? What could you accomplish on other levels?

3. Elder abuse often takes the form of financial exploitation by family members. A senior would have to pursue action via family court for any formal protection, leaving most of them powerless. Their dysfunctional family members are usually perceived as "needy" or "threatening." What options do seniors have, and where do they find the strength to extricate themselves from the secondary gains/co-dependency social trap? Is there a program response you would develop to address this unmet need for service delivery?

Chapter 8
A Day in the Life of a NORC

• • • • • • • • • • • • • • • • • •

by Man Wai Alice Lun, Ph.D.

Before working in a Naturally Occurring Retirement Community (NORC), I had never heard of this type of service for senior citizens, funded by both New York City and state government contracts. However, as the aging population continues to boom and more elderly people prefer to stay in their neighborhoods to "age in place," this kind of community-based senior service is becoming more crucial to daily life. Indeed, NORC can be tailored to fit various regions, locations, cultures, settings, and delivery modalities.

Working in the NORC senior services program in Lower East Side Manhattan was very challenging, because I was serving an educationally, linguistically, and culturally diverse aging population. In this low-income housing complex, we estimated 30% of the residents to be age 60 and older. They moved in as young newlyweds immediately after WWII, and were now retired, desiring to age in place with their friends and neighbors. Being new in the position of program director, I was gradually picking up the operations of the program, and I had gotten to know some really wonderful people. Although the office was set up on the first floor in one of the traditional, unmodified apartments without fancy or formal furnishings, we provided a wider range of social services than many traditional models of senior services, including case assistance, case management, counseling, referrals, and recreational activities, with a small staff consisting of two case workers, some senior volunteers, and me. Also, another part of my job was to coordinate health providers in the community to come to the NORC center to provide health services. Indeed, this program was to be funded at one time by United Hospital Fund as one of their "aging in place initiative" grants and the Isaac Tuttle Fund. Currently, the NORC is funded by the New York City Department for the Aging.

My busy schedule started at 9:00 every morning with elders lining up to seek every kind of help imaginable. Sometimes, I translated English letters for Chinese seniors. Although translation is generally an easy job, the difficulty lies in being patient, because some elderly people do not understand the content of the letter. The more you explain to them, the more confused they can become, not realizing the broader scope of issues that cannot be conveyed in simple "yes" or "no" answers. And sometimes, there can arise larger, systemic justice issues, as I will illustrate. Another difficulty is developing trust with elderly people. Unless they trust you and you respect them, they will not open up to you their hidden issues.

One day, facing many walk-in cases and scheduled appointments, I needed to manage my time well, be organized, and somehow manage to be flexible at the same time, never knowing who or what would come up next. Today, it was one of the older Italian ladies, Ms. Veritas, who came to my office and asked me to help her with her phone bill, because she misplaced the bill and was afraid she might miss the payment. She wanted me to call the phone company to explain her situation and direct her as to what she should do. It sounded like an easy task. But the more I looked at the bill, the more confused I became. What confused me was that on her phone bill, there was an item about renting a phone for which she was charged $30 per month. First, I did not know that the phone company rented phones to people (we all buy our own phones); second, $30 for renting a phone was exorbitant. Since I first needed to understand the situation, I asked Ms. Veritas if I could go to her apartment and take a look. Ms. Veritas was a very private person and she hesitated with my request to do any home visits. She usually just came for our lunch program and refused any other kind of assistance, service, or fun activities. So, such hesitation and distrust was to be expected. But because she thought her phone did not work, and she was afraid, she let me go to her apartment. I told her I would like to come at 2 p.m. (knowing as a proper Italian American hostess, she would want some time to prepare for my visit).

I arrived at her apartment at 2 p.m. It was a small, sparsely furnished apartment: a small, old TV set, a couch, and an all-purpose table on the other side. A lot of letters and papers were stacked up in piles on the table. She showed me where her phone was. I was surprised that her phone was an old rotary phone hanging on the wall. The fashion was from the '60s or '70s. I found out that she had been renting this phone for more than 20 years, and she did not know that phones were very affordable nowadays. After I took her case to the staff meeting, my supervisor suggested that we could buy a phone for her from our small emergency funds. As a result, I bought her a big-button phone for $10 and just plugged it in for her the following day. To ensure the phone was working (thereby reducing her anxiety about this new and "advanced" phone), I went back to my office and called her. When everything was set up, I suggested that she stop renting the phone and not pay that portion on the bill, thereby saving some money. I assisted her in calling the phone company and told them to cancel the renting service. Guess what! The phone company was resistant, but finally caved and asked her to ship back the old phone! Who would use that phone again?

The next day, she came to our office with a bag of bananas and cupcakes. What a sweet and special treat! You know, after building up a trustful relationship with a client and completing the whole process of social work practice (engagement, intervention, and ending), the reward is great—the deep joy that you know you are helping someone who is more vulnerable to society's wiles.

During the week, we had a regular staff meeting to discuss different cases and issues with colleagues, which became crucial to NORC functioning. On this day, we met after lunch and talked about cases for an hour. My colleague, Amy, talked about her client, Mr. Guzman, a 63-year-old with a chronic drinking problem and mental impairment. He came to her attention because he expressed that he had insufficient money to buy food and necessities. He lived by himself and was not eligible for other financial aid. Sharing with us her preliminary action plan, Amy indicated that she would meet with him and address that his smoking habit ($50 per week) was one of the factors contributing to his not having enough money to buy food. She would help him outline a weekly budget based on his pension and Social Security, to help him manage his spending. I reminded her that she needed to help him actually put into practice any plan of action to reduce spending on cigarettes. For instance, Amy might need to ask him to come to see her weekly and show her a form of "journal" that he jotted down for all expenses.

Another colleague talked about her transportation project, which would start in two weeks. The purpose of this project was to use a newly purchased paratransport vehicle to take elderly people, who had difficulties in using public transportation, to places they wanted to go. For instance, they were planning to have a short trip to a shopping mall and to have a nice lunch in a famous restaurant nearby. These elderly people used to go shopping and enjoy meals in this restaurant in their younger days. However, since some of them became home-bound or needed to use wheelchairs and other assistive devices, they could not enjoy their lives in the same way anymore. This project had socialization and recreational purposes, as well as re-motivating them to identify new meanings in their lives. Since they were also involved in the planning of trips, their involvement really increased their self-esteem.

Indeed, having various activities in the senior services program offered different kinds of social work interventions to elderly people in supporting them to improve their activities of daily living. And as social workers in the community, we played all kinds of roles, such as enabler, facilitator, educator, coordinator, and empowerer, to achieve the goals of promoting the well being of elderly people and strengthening the quality of their lives. And we believe through the active elder volunteers and staff at the NORC, that elderly people are able to have success aging gracefully.

Think About It

1. Discuss the importance of providing care to elderly populations in their communities and lingual-cultural context.

2. Discuss the needs of elderly people who are aging in place.

Chapter 9
Gas Masks, Self-Affirmation, and War in Israel

• •

by Patricia Levy, Ph.D., LMSW, ACSW

T he sirens had gone off the night before. I had spent most of the night in our "sealed room" at home with my husband, children, and the dog with her specially improvised cloth "gas mask" over her snout.

At the Daycare Center for the Chronically Ill Elderly, where I worked, we had been preparing for more than a week for the coming Gulf War, orienting the elders on what to do if we came under attack. The staff had instructed the elders that if they wanted to spend the day at the Center, that they were to come with their gas masks in hand, and be prepared to wear them should the siren sound that one of Saddam's missiles might be coming our way.

The director, nurse, care workers, and I as the social worker had met as a team. All of us had been through prior wars, our husbands and sons called up to serve in the Israeli Defense Forces. Our elders had also experienced these events, many of the men in the past having also served with sons and grandsons in the army. We were worried, however, about being ready to cope with any of the spontaneous reactions that our elderly population might have during the coming conditions of war. All had chronic illnesses and were in various stages of mobility. Some needed personal hygiene care and medications. Family members had been contacted about their loved ones' attendance and participation at the Center during the coming period of time and the anticipated stress. An emergency contact list was also updated should anything happen.

As the social worker, I had a professional relationship with all of the 60 residents who were transported to the Center on a daily basis. Having carried out a thorough intake, I knew each of their personal stories. All of my clients were former immigrants from a variety of regions, including Europe, North Africa, and Yemen. Many had come through the Holocaust during World War II as survivors from the Nazi concentration camps, starting their lives and families all over again in Israel.

Because I was particularly experienced in groups, the staff asked if I could conduct a series of groupwork meetings with our elders regarding their feelings and thoughts about going through another war. In addition, all staff would watch for signs of tension and illness. I needed to be ready to intervene immediately should any of the elders seem to be experiencing emotional and psychological discomfort. We also planned to listen for conversation about family members who might be on combat front lines, and we needed to be ready to provide aid and comfort.

That first morning after the war started, traveling from my town of Ashdod to Rehovot, a half hour's drive, I tried to keep my eyes on the road while at the same time keeping an eye out for a falling bomb. There's something very beautiful about a Mediterranean sky—a special kind of light turquoise blue. Of course, a siren would sound first, but I still watched. Luckily, by the time I pulled up to the Center, I hadn't had an accident.

This Daycare Center for the Chronically Ill was a particularly attractive building, built in the round out of white stone, with light shining through the artistic designs of the stained glass windows. I met Chaim and Suzanne sitting outside on the bench together, holding hands. Both were Russian immigrants and had Alzheimer's. Suzanne loved to dance to the "Balalaika." She would twirl gracefully, with her arms up in the air, smiling at the world.

I said "good morning" to them both and entered the Center ("Mercaz" in Hebrew). Care staff was busy, getting breakfast to those who had arrived, their boxed gas masks next to them in plastic bags. Traditionally in Israel, when coming to work, people expect everyone to say "good morning," and to ask how each person is. Personal contact is expected within professional functioning. It was not unusual for staff to also tell me, as the social worker, what was going on in their lives.

After greeting staff, I noticed that there were fewer of our elders present. I hurried to my office to prepare for the two groups that I'd be running that morning on their initial response to the war and self-affirmative coping techniques. I had titled this morning's first session "My Coping Ability."

Having finished breakfast, the Yemenite group of elders, men and women, came together. Most of the members of this group had come as children to Israel as part of Operation Magic Carpet (1949-1950), in which the entire community of Yemenite Jews was flown to Israel, congruent with their community belief that they would return to the "Promised Land" on "wings" (Book of Isaiah, 40:31). As Orthodox Jews, some of the men wore side locks, yarmulkes on their heads, and beards. The women were also attired modestly, some with traditional burnt brown henna marriage markings on their hands. They spoke Hebrew with a strong Arabic accent. I had found in speaking with these elderly that often, rather than directly answering, they answered my questions with stories of life events and biblical metaphors. Many of the elders were small boned people with a colorful sense of humor. They seemed to smile with their complete bodies, gesturing vividly with graceful hands and bright, expressive, dark eyes. The thought that they were most likely a very ancient community from Middle East origins always impressed my Westernized mind.

In speaking of what they did to cope with their fears and thoughts while in the sealed room in their homes during the sirens, they related that they had prayed the prayers that they had learned as children. They spoke about taking stock of their responsibility as elders for the welfare of the extended family, including their relationships with their children, even adult children. They felt that these roles were God-given and that, in return, their children were obligated to care for them in their old age. Thus, a continuity of family and community roles, values, and beliefs would be passed down from one generation to another.

The second group of elders was of European origin. Most had immigrated to Israel as refugees in the early years of Israel's existence. One old man wore his beret proudly as he explained that he had been a member of the Partisans fighting the Nazis during World War II. When speaking of coping with stress, the men spoke with some anger about how strong they used to be and what they did before they became ill and aged. Unlike the Yemenite group, they expressed an intellectual response to the war, talking politics, social philosophy, and the cultural implications of language. Both men and women stressed the importance of concrete decision-making as a means of maintaining control of oneself and one's internal coping dynamics in response to out-of-control external events that affected one's life.

As the social worker, I helped to weave the themes of aging, ability, and sources of meaningfulness together for both groups. As it happened, a siren went off at the end of the meeting with the European group. As another staff member and I put on our gas masks, to our dismay but respect, the group refused to put on theirs. As they explained, this was their choice. They had survived the Holocaust. What more did they have to fear? They took life as it came at them. When the siren was over, they went to eat lunch.

Later in the day, I passed a group of the most Orthodox religious men from the European group. Every day, they sat in a circle, leaning back in their chairs, conducting philosophical and ethical debates. When I first passed by, I heard them telling the story of a father and a son in one of the concentration camps. They were starving. The child held a piece of bread in his hand that the father took from him and ate. *Question: Was the father right to take the piece of bread from his son to survive when the frail child would probably die anyway?* I did not hear the answer as I was meeting one of the families whose father's Alzheimer's disease had worsened and would need a referral for intervention.

Later, I passed the group of old men one more time. They were debating whether in Hebrew, the word God was masculine or feminine. On my way home, I said "shalom" to all, both staff and the elders who were waiting to be transported back to their homes. As I drove home, I thought about what had occurred that day, about the courage and the richness of the personal meanings and wisdom that I had learned from the elders.

I rode home feeling peaceful and grateful for being a social worker with these opportunities of learning. I didn't glance at the sky as often as I had on the way to work.

Think About It

1. What were the differences in world views of the European and the Yemenite elderly?

2. What was the coping mechanism of the Holocaust survivors? How might their experiences during World War II influence the coping behaviors that were displayed in the story?

3. What was the role of the social worker with the elderly populations described in the chapter during war time?

PART 2:
Health Care—
Hospitals,
Home Health,
and Hospice

Chapter 10
Firsts: Mrs. Blue Visits the ER

● ●

by Gary E. Bachman, MSSW, LSCSW

I'd first noticed her in triage, patiently sitting with her hands folded in her lap, wearing a pink house dress with embroidery at the neck and thin-soled shoes with rhinestones arranged in a pattern across the toe. Her hair, recently styled, reflected a soft bluish gray that must certainly have come from a bottle. And in the busy and frantic pace of the trauma center, she shined like a diamond errantly dropped in a bucket of coal. Her soft smile reflected a contentment that belied the torn bodies that had whisked past her on gurneys and the railing drunks cuffed to wheelchairs impatiently waiting for gapping lacerations to be drawn tight prior to their transfer to the county jail.

Working with so many nameless souls transported from violent car collisions and bloody crime scenes, my observation skills had evolved to take in such typically insignificant details quickly and without much thought. Initial identification often hinged on such details, and such knowledge is frequently central to the timely delivery of wrenching truth and on occasion hope, to desperate families, loved ones, or the investigating detectives.

I had also observed that this elderly woman wasn't likely to be one of mine. She was, you see, too calm, too clean, too orderly, too nice, and in retrospect, too old. My public was generally the young and the active. They were the people who drove fast, disdained seat belts and helmet laws, drank, snorted, and smoked "recreationally," hit their children, hit one another, stayed when they should have left, quit taking their meds, "saw things," had decided they were done with life, or were so unlucky as to have been at the wrong place at the wrong time. And in life's demolition derby, the ER was a pit stop where interventions were strategic, short, simple, and certain. Usually.

The date on my master's degree was hardly a year old when I'd taken this position on the evening shift at the city county hospital. Among my peers, I'd been considered widely experienced, as I'd worked in a variety of social work positions with my bachelor's degree. I'd even been so fortunate as to have received advanced mental health training for working with children and families, and I had trained and supervised volunteers at a mental health/substance abuse "crisis center." I may have known a lot, but in retrospect, I knew very little. The ER was to become the place for many of my "firsts," even if at the time I was proudly proclaiming my broad and thoroughly professional preparation. There was the time, early on, when Dr. P. looked me straight in the face and referring to the raging angry psychotic I'd just seen, asked, "What do you think we should give him? And how much?" (Certainly he was just testing me. Right?) There was my first "overdose," a man with panicked eyes suddenly spewing a volume of unimaginable and frightening blackness onto the floor—a potion that I later learned was just a mixture of powdered charcoal and water administered to absorb the acetaminophen still in his gut following an intentional overdose. My first fatal child abuse case arrived when a four-year-old girl was suddenly thrust into my arms by her father as I took a break from the ER out on the ambulance dock. (Sometimes the lessons learned are as simple as where not to take your break.) That same event would lead to my first trip to the witness stand in a criminal prosecution. There was my first death notification, and my first "really bad" burn. There was my first broken neck with certain paralysis, and the first time a patient took a swing at me. There was that first "battered woman" who later went home with her abuser, and the first who said, "Once is enough," and entered a shelter on what was her first wedding anniversary.

Scattered among all the ugliness there is also the beauty: the first cries of a totally new person, Mom smiling through tears and Dad looking like he'd just won the lottery. There was the first of what would be many thank you notes from people whose lives we'd touched: people who remembered the most fleeting details of kindness and compassion that had suppressed their own fear and pain. And then there was that first little lady with blue hair.

Some of those we encounter in our work will inevitably stick in our minds with remarkable details remaining clear and fresh. And while we may be inclined to share such stories, caution must be taken to assure the individuals and families privacy. Thus, wishing to share this story, I have cautiously chosen to reveal this individual to you as I have to other students of social work, medicine, and nursing, as "Mrs. Blue." She has for so long now been "Mrs. Blue" that although small details remain, her true name has been thoroughly erased. But I assure you she did have one, and through that evening she would proudly and patiently repeat it for an endless series of helpers.

The police had been the first to question her after motorists had called 911 to report an elderly woman walking alongside a busy 4-lane traffic way. Next were the paramedics who had brought her to the ER, then the nurse, and then me. Without waver, her answers were clear and consistent: name, address, telephone number, family we could call, good friends, and neighbors. All of it was politely and faithfully provided in a manner worthy of Rod Sterling's assignment to a place in *The Twilight Zone*. For this lady, it was as if time had stopped, or perhaps just gone away.

The home address she'd given was in an area that had been redeveloped into a shopping center a decade prior. The phone number was that of a family who'd had the number for six years and who knew nothing of our dear guest. There were perhaps four families of the same last name in the phone book, but none of them knew our guest. Next I tried our widely acclaimed, expensive and newly computerized medical records system, which even as we tempted confidentiality by keying in each and every name she'd provided, failed to offer any insight. A call to the police department's "missing persons" division was yet another dead end. Letting my fingers do the walking, I launched into the yellow pages, identifying and calling nursing homes, retirement centers, and other hospitals in an increasingly large circle out and away from where she'd been picked up by the medics. All of this would be without even a hint of success.

As the night drew on, I would occasionally slip out to see other patients, but Mrs. Blue remained my constant challenge. I suspect that part of my initial—and I'll admit it now—discomfort was the simple fact that my work with the elderly had been remarkably limited. I was truly treading lightly armed into no-man's land. Most of the elders that came through the ER were there with medical conditions warranting a direct admission or a quick tune up and return home. Most were also accompanied by family members or certainly a thick packet of records from the nursing home, topped with a "face sheet" containing all that we could ever want to know about who to contact and under what circumstances to do so. These were not patients that I ever had any dealing with. But this was so different. Entirely and totally.

At one point, Mrs. Blue asked me if I'd like the hamburger from the hot meal that had been ordered for her. She actually called me sweetie and expressed concern that I seemed so awfully busy that perhaps I hadn't taken time to eat my supper. I don't recall that a patient had ever asked about my well being before, or for that matter offered to share a meal with me. This was not life as I knew it. How could this wonderfully sensitive woman worry about my well being yet remain so totally unfazed by the chaos about her or the very simple reality that she herself was somehow lost?

The ER doc, whose signature would eventually go on the medical record, spent only a moment with her before declaring his diagnosis, "Dementia. Probably Alzheimer's type," and asking of me as he passed behind the next curtain, "What are you going to do with her?" He was with the next patient before I could even begin to form my response.

Dementia? Alzheimer's? But she does remember. She has details. And she's calm and patient, and polite and so apparently well cared for. None of this fits with what little I know of such things, and frankly, I'm a guy plagued by the things he doesn't know. Taking advantage of a relationship fostered in the ER just the night before, I called the psychiatry resident physician "on call." And over the phone, I got my first lesson in dementia. Although there are different types, it most commonly begins with small impairments of "short term memory," things like where you left the keys or where you parked the car. These are things that happen to us all, but in dementia there is an intrinsic cause and a sometimes gradual, sometimes rapid progression of such impairment. The ability to learn and retain new information gradually erodes, and as life goes on, the gap widens between what is current and what is past. With some, the time line is clear and constant, while for others remote or distant memory is progressively erased with the most recent going first. Through this process, long established social skills often emerge to dominate social interactions, thus disguising or hiding cognitive deficits. Individual identities are blurred, and new characters on the stage are cast in generic terms of endearment or familiarity. Dear and sweetheart are interchangeable with the gender specific names of familiar loved ones: a brother, husband, or perhaps a grown child.

I also learned not to confuse dementia with delirium or depression. In the elderly, acute mental status changes such as confusion and disorientation may be the result of treatable and reversible medical conditions, and such symptoms are referred to as delirium. Similarly, I learned that when elders are depressed, memory problems may be more reflective of not wanting to remember rather than any neurological defect.

As Mrs. Blue appeared neither confused nor depressed, dementia indeed was the likely diagnosis, and the doctor asked me to administer a Folstein Mini Mental Status Exam. (Another first!) The exam is a very simple instrument designed to preliminarily assess an individual's capacity to process and remember new and unique information. And while the exam may not have helped me find where she belonged, it certainly provided me a learning opportunity as well as a manner to formally document her level of functioning. I retrieved a copy of the test from the file cabinet and, after briefly reviewing its simple questions, I returned to Mrs. Blue's realm with thirty more questions. What is today's date? What is this place? What are these items? Copy this line drawing. Write a sentence. Follow these instructions. Spell a particular word, backwards. Other questions were those already asked perhaps a dozen times, yet each was again answered with thoughtful consideration and a pleasant reassuring smile. Essentially a simple structured interview, unrushed and without undue pressure, its results were starkly apparent in spite of polite assurances and apologies for inattention: twelve points of a possible thirty. After hours in the emergency room, she believed that we must be in a busy shopping mall and I was certainly Greg, the son of a dear friend. And there was certainly no cause for alarm, as her husband would be along shortly. It had never remotely occurred to me that she didn't recognize our location as anything other than a busy ER or that I was just one of a dozen different people asking her the same questions over and over. She didn't know. And neither was she being uniquely warm and sensitive to all my efforts on her behalf. To her we were all one giant "sweetie," an amalgam of someone she should be nice to.

My shift was nearing its end when I finally approached the charge nurse. I was no closer to finding Mrs. Blue's home or family, and it was apparent that we would need to admit her overnight. In the morning, the inpatient social worker would again reach out to the police for any missing persons reports, contact adult protective services, and repeat each of the dozens of calls I'd made through the evening. Someone out there loved and cared for this sweet woman, and certainly they must have missed her by now. I imagined their frantic search and willed them to our front door. That was all that was left for me; I'd done my best. I reviewed my notes on a half-dozen patients, being sure that the important details were documented, and gave my report to the night social worker. With that I was done: I walked back to our office, hung up my scrub coat, washed my hands of the day's challenges, and left through the front door.

Outside, I briefly encountered a woman emerging quickly from a just-parked car. She called to me, "Is this the way into the emergency room?" and without waiting for a response turned to her companion still behind the wheel and exclaimed, "Hurry, Greg, the paramedics said they brought her here!"

I stopped briefly, pointed the way, smiled, and walked on.

Think About It

1. Who are those people and/or "populations" that you may regularly encounter in your daily experience, but never really "see"? How do people get lost, either on the streets or in the system? And what can you do (at any level—individually, agency-wide, systemically, or in the larger society) to give some direction?

2. What does your workplace (or you, for that matter) look like through the eyes of others?

3. How do you handle unanticipated or unexpected situations at work?

4. How do you handle "firsts," particularly ones you're not prepared for? Think of an example of one of your professional firsts. What did you learn from that experience that may either serve or hinder your future practice?

5. What is a "learning experience," from your own professional education or practice, that you will *never* forget?

Chapter 11
Social Work in Outpatient Rehabilitation

• • • • • • • • • • • • • • • • •

by Karen Horwitz Rubin, MSW, ACSW, LCSW-C

I am employed in an outpatient rehabilitation department of a metropolitan teaching hospital. We have a wide variety of patients coming for physical therapy, occupational therapy, and speech therapy. Many of the patients are over 65. They have had amputations, orthopedic surgery, strokes, and other neurological problems. Some are facing problems related to living with debilitating illness. Others are having problems with getting the help they need for financial reasons. Many are experiencing changes in family relations and social relations that are related to their chronic conditions. The department is large (about 25 on the staff), but even in such a large department, it is unusual to have a full-time social worker.

The department director wanted to have a social worker on her staff and used the argument that having a liaison between inpatient and outpatient rehabilitation (the hospital has a 50-bed inpatient rehabilitation unit) would increase the number of patients referred to the outpatient department. She also knew that the Commission on Accreditation of Rehabilitation Facilities (CARF) was encouraging follow-up care. She was able to make a case for having a full-time social worker, and I was lucky enough to be hired for the job in March 2001. It was a "new" job at the time, so I have been able to use the director's guidelines to create the job and then to add other facets as time and need dictate. My monthly statistics always reflect the number of patients with whom I have had contact who subsequently come to outpatient rehab, so the director has been able to continue to justify the position. The therapists are happy to have a social worker on the staff. It is a relief for them to be able to refer a patient who is expressing concerns about his or her home situation, finances, transportation, and/or family situation to a social worker.

My day begins with inpatient "modules." These are team meetings on the inpatient rehabilitation units to discuss individual patients, their progress, and discharge plans. Several patients are highlighted and then the rest are reviewed quickly. I alternate between the two teams that meet at 8:00 a.m. Another team meets later in the day, and I attend that meeting when I can. In the team meetings, I learn about patients who will be discharged and who might benefit from a call two to four weeks after discharge. I have worked with the inpatient teams (which include social workers and nurse case managers) for a long time, and they often tell me which patients can use my services. My presence at the meeting makes it much easier for them to make referrals to me. Today, two patients sound like ones I should add to the database I maintain of patients to be contacted.

One patient is a 71-year-old man who has had a stroke. He is making progress and will be going home with his wife. He is being referred to our home care agency for services at home, but is expected to recover enough to come back to us for outpatient therapy. He has significant speech problems, and I know that our speech therapists would like to know more about the patient before he returns. I make a note to tell them about him, so they can talk to the inpatient therapists. I also decide to stop by his room later in the day and tell his wife that I will be calling in a few weeks. I will give her my card at that time and ask her to call me if I can be of any assistance with making the transition to outpatient therapy.

The second patient is a 66-year-old woman who recently had a below-knee amputation because of circulation problems related to diabetes. Our hospital has an amputee clinic where patients with amputations are fitted for prostheses, as well as an amputee support group that I co-lead. Many of our patients with amputations come back to our outpatient therapy department for prosthetic training. I will call this patient in about a month to talk to her about the support group and to help her with any issues she may be having in regard to getting to clinic or to therapy. Although the inpatient social worker tells the patients about the groups we have available at the hospital, many of them are not ready to hear about them while they are hospitalized. The onset of disability can be shocking, and often denial is the first response. Lengths of stay in the acute hospital and in inpatient rehabilitation have gotten much shorter than they were in the past. There is not much time for the patient to come to terms with his or her disability. This is another way I can help; I am available to patients and families after they are at home and have had time to live with their changed life situations for a while.

After the module, I return to my office. Today, I see Mrs. Sheridan in the waiting room. Mr. Sheridan is back for more physical therapy. He is an above-the-knee amputee and has been fitted for a new prosthesis. He is now receiving therapy to learn to use the new prosthesis and so that adjustments can be made to it to make ambulation easier. Mrs. Sheridan and I have become very close over the past two years. Mr. Sheridan was originally referred to me by an inpatient nurse case manager on a surgical unit. He had recently had surgery for circulation problems in his remaining leg and told the case manager that he could not get the prosthesis for his left leg (which had been amputated in April 2004) because he could not afford the co-pay. Mr. Sheridan was 72 years old at the time and had Medicare, but Medicare only pays 80% toward a prosthesis. In Mr. Sheridan's case, his co-pay was about $4,000. He had had Medical Assistance to supplement his Medicare at the time he was initially seen by the vendor. This was because of his very high medical bills. However, after he was discharged from the hospital and his medical expenses returned to normal, he was no longer eligible for Medical Assistance. Mr. Sheridan and his wife live on a fixed income and are unable to individually pay for co-insurance. I met with Mr. Sheridan at that time (March 2005) and told him that I would look into the status of his prosthesis.

Little did I know at the time what a complicated process helping Mr. Sheridan obtain his prosthesis would be! The vendor refused to release the partially completed leg without a co-pay. I tried to intervene with all the systems involved. Mr. Sheridan was no longer eligible for Medical Assistance and they would not pay for it retroactively. I contacted a local charitable organization that can help with medical equipment not covered by insurance and learned that the fund does not cover prostheses. I also referred Mr. Sheridan to the State Department of Rehabilitation Services, as it sometimes assists with medical equipment that enables recipients to maintain an independent lifestyle. I contacted a worker I knew at the agency and, with Mr. Sheridan's written consent, sent the requested information.

Despite their frustration about not receiving the prosthesis, Mr. and Mrs. Sheridan followed up on each of my suggestions. They also attended our amputee support group regularly and obtained advocacy information at one of these meetings. In September 2005, Mr. Sheridan called to tell me that he had heard from the vendor and was told that he could come in for a fitting for his prosthesis. He never did receive "official" word from the Department of Rehabilitation Services about funding, but that was apparently the source. When he came in for therapy with his new prosthesis, he was able to walk. It brought tears to my eyes and was one of those moments that make a medical social work career rewarding. Because of my advocacy and Mr. and Mrs. Sheridan's patience, hard work, and determination, he had achieved his goal. He could now learn to walk with his prosthesis. He is back now because of some modifications that were made, and he has switched to a new vendor.

After talking with Mrs. Sheridan, I return to my office to plan our outpatient rehabilitation CVA (stroke) team meeting. I am responsible for planning several outpatient meetings a month. In the midst of my work, a physical therapist stops by to ask me if I have time to see her patient. She is working with a woman who has had a cyst on her lower back and is having difficulty with balance and walking. The patient is 74 years old and widowed. Her children live out of town and are employed full-time. She is European and says that she lived a life of diplomacy and foreign travel. She is now very limited in her activities. She actually wanted inpatient rehabilitation, because she does not think that she can manage independently at home. However, she is able to walk independently and does not meet Medicare guidelines for an inpatient hospitalization. I try to help her with her feelings about her situation and to make a few suggestions. She is not interested in Meals on Wheels or other options to make her home life easier. However, she leaves my office in a better frame of mind and later tells her therapist that I was "a big help."

Sometimes the "easy" referrals surprise you—an elderly woman referred for assistance with transportation turns out to be a social worker and a member of the first graduating class at Howard University School of Social Work. You never know with whom you will be working when you work in an outpatient department. This is one of the things that I like about working in medical social work. Each day is different, and each situation is a little different, as well. I have been a medical social worker for over 35 years but find that I still enjoy the challenge of the work. Much of my work has been in the area of physical rehabilitation, and many of my patients have been older adults. I feel that I have learned more from my patients over the years than they have learned from me. It is rewarding work, because I am helping people to get through what may be the worst crisis they have ever faced. My presence as a helping person can really make a difference. Sometimes the "little things" like helping a patient to obtain a needed piece of medical equipment has a big impact on the patient's life. Many of my current patients thank me profusely for enabling them to use the local transportation system for people with disabilities. For these patients, being able to travel independently makes a huge difference in their lives.

My days are varied. I always start out with a plan to work on some project—planning a meeting, my statistics, making follow-up telephone calls, and entering data into my database. However, there is usually a new patient to be seen or an existing one who calls with a new problem. The days go quickly. I usually leave work with the feeling that I have accomplished something and have been of some help to others.

Think About It

1. Why do you think it is helpful to have a social worker contact a patient and/or his or her family member two to four weeks after discharge from the inpatient rehabilitation service?

2. Why do you think that denial is frequently a response to suddenly becoming disabled?

Chapter 12
Hospital Social Work: A Fast-Paced Environment
• •

by Dara Bergel Bourassa, Ph.D., MSW, LSW

I t is a Tuesday morning. I am sitting in my car and notice that I have about 30 minutes until I have to be at work at the hospital. I hope traffic won't be too terrible, here in Baltimore, MD, but you never know. As I drive, listening to my favorite morning talk show, I think about what I have to do today.

I work at a suburban hospital on the west side of Baltimore as a hospital social worker. I got the job about two years ago, immediately after getting my MSW at the University of Pittsburgh in Pittsburgh, PA. Actually, I was hired before I graduated, and I started my first day of work the Monday immediately after graduation.

The units I am responsible for are the orthopedic unit and the renal unit. I really like these two units, and I enjoy the fact that there are many diverse social issues and people that I get to interact with on a daily basis. I was never interested in working with the elderly population until I started working at this hospital. Approximately 75% of the patients I see are older adults, and I "fell in love" with this population, just by working with them and their families.

I get to work around 8:30 a.m. and immediately enter the main office to collect my mail, my unit census, and any social work referrals. I then go to my office, which I share with three nurse case managers, and check the e-mail and voice messages. I look at the new census to see if Mr. Jones left last night. Mr. Jones is a 78-year-old African American married male who is receiving dialysis for end-stage renal disease (ESRD), which means his kidneys do not function anymore on their own. He receives dialysis as an outpatient at a facility that is near his home. He is on the first shift, meaning that he must be at the dialysis facility at 6 a.m., every Monday, Wednesday, and Friday.

His dialysis port became infected (which is very common for dialysis patients), and as he was in the hospital, lying in bed all day, he became debilitated. His wife told me that she had just had surgery and did not feel that she could take Mr. Jones home, as Mr. Jones would be relying on her because he was feeling very weak. I asked the doctor to order physical therapy, and yesterday it was decided that Mr. Jones could benefit from some additional therapy. One of the ways that Medicare will pay for rehabilitation is for a physical therapist to verify the need for therapy at least one hour per day. Medicare will pay 100% of the cost of an inpatient rehabilitation stay for the first 20 days, and will only pay 80% of the cost for days 21-100. Luckily, Mr. Jones had a secondary health insurance plan that would cover the 20% that Medicare would not pay, if his stay extended past the twentieth day. I was given permission by Mr. Jones and his wife to refer him to sub-acute rehabilitation. Sub-acute rehabilitation is usually located in a nursing home, and the patient "lives" there until he or she is physically well enough to return to his or her prior living environment. This was a way for Medicare to cut down the cost and overall length of hospital stays.

So, I referred him to a rehabilitation facility, located in a nursing home, that has dialysis in-house. He was accepted, but they could not admit him until 7 p.m. I notice that his name is not on the census, so I am glad that everything went smoothly last night.

As I continue to check the census, I copy my notes from yesterday and those for previous patients that are still on both of my units, and highlight the new social work referrals for the day. I then go out onto the unit and meet with my case manager for case management rounds. Since I have both units, I will attend two sets of rounds. At rounds, I learn that Mrs. Kramer's family is having a difficult time dealing with the fact that she may need hospice care for end-stage renal disease. I discuss this issue with the doctor, case manager, and the nurse, and we all decide that a family meeting should be organized so everyone is on the same page. I make a note of this and will call the family in to meet, after rounds.

There are seven people scheduled for discharge today, just on the dialysis unit alone. I ask the case manager if any of them need rehab placement (since arranging this is one of my major roles as a social worker), and I find out that three of them need placement! However, only one of them needs a rehab facility with dialysis on-site. Phew! I note this on my list and hope that the orthopedic unit is under control! But this is what it is like in a hospital, and I love it.

Also, during rounds, I am alerted that an older woman was admitted last night and needs a psychiatric placement. Mrs. Brown is experiencing extreme paranoia. The psychiatrist has already been in to see her and feels that she needs inpatient psychiatric treatment. *Oh boy,* I think to myself, *this is going to be a busy day.*

Next, I go upstairs to the orthopedic unit and meet with the case manager there. Since it is a Tuesday, we have many scheduled surgeries for the day, meaning that we will not have many discharges. I am relieved to know that the orthopedic unit is somewhat under control, and update the case manager about the issues that are going on in the unit downstairs. She says that I should spend my time down there, and she will page me if she needs me.

It is around 10 a.m. and I make a quick call to the psychiatric hospital that I know has a special unit for geriatric patients. I keep my fingers crossed, hoping they have space available, and they do! So I quickly fax over all of the required information from Mrs. Brown's medical chart and contact her doctor at the hospital so she can begin her discharge summary and medications that she will need upon discharge. The psychiatric unit will page me when they reach a decision to take her or not. I inform my case manager and the patient's nurse, and then I note all of this information in Mrs. Brown's medical chart, in the social services section. That way, if any staff members want to know what is going on, they can read my note.

Now it is 10:45 a.m., and I pull the chart for Mrs. Kramer. I review her social history and note that she is a widow and lives alone in a one-story home. She seems to have been exceptionally independent until this most recent hospital admission, and I feel a little sad knowing that her doctor has finally recommended hospice care. I have known Mrs. Kramer from many past hospital admissions, and I know that this is something she has thought about for some time. I go in and talk to Mrs. Kramer, and she gives me permission to call her two children. We will all have a family meeting about hospice care. Her adult children, who are in their 50s, will meet with me and their mother in her room at 4:00 p.m. today to discuss the options within hospice. I make a note of this meeting in the patient's chart and alert everyone who is involved with her care on the unit. I am really glad that her children are able to make it in so quickly, because I know that they work.

My stomach starts to rumble, and I notice that it is 1:00 p.m.! I can't believe how fast time has flown. I really enjoy lunch time, not because it is a break from the units, but because it is a time when I get together with some of the case managers and other social workers, and we just talk and laugh. We sit in the lunch room and take up an entire table and just gab. During lunch, I get paged. I recognize the number as the phone number of the psychiatric hospital. Thank goodness the lunch room has a phone. I ask the hospital operator to dial the number, and I talk with the admissions coordinator. Mrs. Brown has been approved, and they would like for her to arrive at 4:00 p.m. I thank the coordinator profusely and quickly finish my lunch and head back to my office.

I check my e-mail (no messages there) and my voice mail. The case management department's secretary has alerted me to some new social work consults. I run down to the main office and collect those before heading back to the dialysis unit.

I quickly set up ambulance transportation for the woman going to the psychiatric hospital and notify her nurse, and leave a message on her primary contact's home answering machine about her discharge plan. Afterwards, I meet with the three patients who need rehabilitation. They are all agreeable to go to rehab and would like facilities that are close to their homes, so their friends and family can visit. I give them each a list of facilities that are near them, and they all decide on their individual facilities. I then proceed to make the referrals. I have a good working relationship with the admissions coordinators at the rehabilitation facilities that my patients most often go to, and I enjoy calling them and just chatting. I have never met any of these coordinators, but I feel as if they are family, because we talk so much. The facilities will get back to me with their decisions on whether or not to take the patients.

I look at my watch and see that I have 15 minutes until the hospice meeting. I have a stack of hospice information, but am missing a list of hospice providers. I quickly run up to the fourth floor (I am on the second floor—good exercise!) and briefly talk to the oncology social worker about this list. She gives me her only copy, and I make a few more copies in the fax machine, since the only photocopier is in our main case management office, and I do not have the time to go to that part of the hospital.

Now that I am prepared, I go into Mrs. Kramer's room and see that her children have arrived. The children, their mother, and I discuss all of the various options that Mrs. Kramer has available to her. Everyone decides that Mrs. Kramer would be better off in an inpatient hospice facility. They choose this option because they want to spend as much time as they can with her and feel that this is the best option for them. I provide some comforting words to Mrs. Kramer and her children, because they are all visibly upset at having to make such an important decision. I then proceed to make the referrals. Since it is 5:00 p.m., she cannot be discharged today, so we make plans for a possible discharge tomorrow. I alert the doctor to dictate a discharge summary, tell her nurse about the plan, and make the notes in Mrs. Kramer's chart.

I cannot believe how quickly this day has gone. I feel as if I completed a lot of tasks today and am happy about my progress, because some days these situations do not work out as well. I check my e-mail and voice mail one last time and make a list of the patients I definitely need to see tomorrow, as well as the discharges and other issues that need a response.

I thoroughly enjoy this job and know that if I were anywhere else, I might not be as happy. I love the different types of people I meet, learning about the different medical diagnoses, belonging to the hospital environment (which I have always found fascinating), and knowing that I am making a difference in patients' and families' lives.

Think About It

1. Why do you think the social worker talked with Mrs. Kramer first, before talking to her family?

2. In the hospital environment, which of the NASW *Code of Ethics* issues do you think applies the most?

3. End-stage renal disease is a life-threatening illness. When someone, especially an older adult, is diagnosed with this, what issues do you think affect them the most?

Chapter 13
Welcome to Geriatrics! Life as a VA Social Worker

● ●

by Denice Goodrich Liley, Ph.D., ACSW, BCD

L ike many people, I never planned to become a geriatric social worker. It just sort of happened—much like the aging process itself.

As a graduate student in social work, I had already determined that I wanted to do medical social work. When I explored my final year social work practicum options, the field practicum director suggested I visit the Salt Lake City Veterans Administration Medical Center to check out the field practicum opportunities available there. I needed a summer block placement, and the VA Medical Center was the most likely place where I might be able to secure one.

I did not know any students who had been involved in placements with the VA Medical Center. The mere mention of the VA turned my nose up. I envisioned a huge military bureaucracy of soldiers, or at least people working there who acted like soldiers, and would order me: Do this. Go here. Go there. And worst of all, I visualized men...and more men...no women and no variety...an assembly line of male soldiers in hospital gowns, in all likelihood designed to resemble uniforms.

Now, at that time, in my mind's eye, I visualized myself as a creative, fun-loving, young female who was flamboyant, and definitely NOT soldier material.

Being the compliant graduate student I was at the time, I reluctantly scheduled an interview with the VA, with the expectation that I would be returning to the field director to solicit an alternate choice for that placement. Conveniently, the Salt Lake City VA Medical Center was right across the street from the university; it wouldn't consume much time for me to follow through on the dreaded deed.

My scheduled interview was the first time I had ever stepped foot into this VA Medical Center, much less any other VA. The buildings did not appear to be too institutional. In fact, they were much like other hospitals I'd visited, and where I really wanted to work. Amazingly, the VA employees neither saluted nor made commanding statements to me! They actually looked like regular people. And surprise of all surprises, the coordinator of social work students was a woman! She gave me a tour of the hospital.

The only opening for a summer block placement happened to be on the geriatric unit. The student office was an old patient room—complete with its own bathroom and a window. Not too bad! All in all, it looked pretty good. Everyone I met was friendly, and the patients resembled other patients at other hospitals. People visited with one another. The VA facility did not even resemble the men's club I had anticipated, with me being the only female present.

On a fluke, I decided "why not" and accepted the placement. I stayed there more than twelve years, leaving only to complete my doctorate in social work with a focus on aging. Amazing what one reluctant visit can do for a career!

It is very common for a social worker with the Veterans Administration to become acquainted with the facility by being a student there. The Department of Veterans Affairs, a.k.a. the VA, is one of the largest training programs for graduate social workers across the United States. Many stipend placements are available for second-year Master of Social Work students in a wide array of areas. It is very common that, following a positive social work practicum experience, students seek employment with the VA upon graduation.

The VA is one of the largest health care systems in the nation. It not only provides inpatient medical care, psychiatric admissions, and outpatient follow-up support services, but it also addresses areas of social concern, such as homelessness and aging. The VA provides direct services to individuals who have served in the military; however, collateral services are provided to many family members. The wide variety of social work opportunities, the many different locations of VA programs across the United States, good salaries, and a good benefit program make employment with the VA an attractive option for many social workers.

I worked as a student an entire summer and was hired two months post graduation in early fall as the social worker for the Geriatric Evaluation and Treatment Unit (GETU), when first hired, which later was renamed the GEM (Geriatric Evaluation and Medical Service).

The Salt Lake City VA Geriatric Unit is a sub-acute inpatient medical unit of 27 beds. Patients come to the geriatric unit in a variety of ways. Upon discharge, patients are followed through an outpatient clinic. Those individuals may be experiencing problems at home and need admission. Some patients transfer in from another medical or surgery service for further workup of a medical condition or require a longer recovery period before discharge can occur. A nurse practitioner holds regular outpatient clinics throughout the week, where a previous patient's family member can call to request an appointment for the veteran. The patient might be admitted from this visit. Some patients are admitted as planned and scheduled respite admission to provide a break for their caregivers, so they can continue living in their home environment.

The only requirements for admission to the geriatric service are that the patient is a veteran of military service, with an honorable discharge, and be at least 70 years of age. The majority of patients are well into their 80s. Some patients are in their 90s, with a few at 100 years of age.

The VA Geriatric Unit is a part of a teaching hospital. It is not uncommon that, at times, students and staff outnumber inpatients. An attending physician oversees the medical care, making rounds with the medical students, interns, and at least one resident daily. Nurse practitioner students, nursing students, physical therapy students, pharmacy students (both undergraduate and graduate), occupational therapy students, psychology students (Ph.D. interns), and social work students (second-year master's students) rotate through the facility on a regular basis.

As a "teaching unit," the VA expands education and practice with older adults. Some individuals choose to be in the service of, and hold a high commitment to, the patients and families there. Those individuals—myself included—stay day after day, week after week, month after month, year after year. We get to know many of the patients and families well, and work with them until the time of their deaths.

Of course, student placement with the VA is not for everyone. Some students there experience a lesser degree of enthusiasm— some medical students, interns, and residents will not be excited about their rotations. Others come with more positive and open attitudes. It is a matter of preference. Teaching hospitals have variety, and some prefer other services to routine ones. People do make generalizations about aging, hold unrealistic expectations of older patients and their family systems, or approach their assignments to "just get them off my service." Quicker and sicker discharges don't work well for those individuals who must see the patient later.

No day is typical on the Geriatric Service Unit. Each day holds a skeleton structure of some activities. Interdisciplinary team rounds take place on Monday afternoons, with a representative of each discipline staffing patients. It provides an opportunity for personnel from a variety of disciplines to see the various aspects of this patient, rather than just from the perspective of a medical diagnosis. Staffing serves to lay the groundwork for the team to strategize and prioritize the patient's needs and to discuss discharge concerns. The game plan for the week is laid out during the staffing meeting.

Some patients remain on the geriatric unit for weeks, while others may be there only a few days. The nurse practitioner clinic occurs on Tuesdays. Patients arrive for check-ups, medication testing, or evaluation of an unexpected non-urgent change. Wednesday is the large outpatient clinic, where patients who reside in the community can be seen, preferably once every six months. At this clinic, the allied disciplines are available to families and physicians. This clinic runs all afternoon. The social worker frequently holds family meetings on Wednesday evenings, if needed. Another nurse practitioner clinic takes place on Thursdays. Support groups are held on Thursday afternoons. Typically, Thursday is the biggest discharge day of the week, because if a problem arises, it gives the staff another working day to address it. Successful discharges are a cornerstone of the geriatric service. Geriatric personnel want patients and families to be prepared and ready for discharge, lessening the likelihood of sudden readmission. The patient and family system involved in geriatric patient care is, by nature, complex and fragile.

Fridays in VA geriatric care typically mean another nurse practitioner clinic, phone calls, and home visits. Medical rounds occur daily; nursing report happens three times each day. Patients are seen, some new ones admitted, and other patients might be discharged. A lot of time and effort goes into each of these activities.

As the social worker on geriatrics, I began each day before I ever arrived at the VA. I read the obituaries. I needed to be aware of any of my VA patient/client deaths prior to arriving at work. It helped me to feel prepared when I arrived and lessened my shock should a family member call before I became aware of someone's passing. I routinely worked 7:30 a.m. until 4:00 p.m., with variations. I attempted to be on the unit one evening a week to meet with working family members, to spend time with the evening shift, and to hold support groups. On my late day, I generally didn't report in until about noon. The unit and social work department allowed for flexible hours, as long as the needs of the unit and patient concerns were met. Flexibility is an imperative asset for a teaching facility, where staff and students constantly rotate. For patients and families, staff flexibility often provides the greatest benefit.

The one downside to such flexibility is that sometimes people—both families and staff—expect the employees to be available "whenever." It is vital for social workers to have firm boundaries about when they will take phone calls, come in from home, and make changes in work hours. During my early years, I was more flexible, until I realized how little time I took off for myself. A supervisor advised me about the need to be consistent and that others (such as the emergency room social worker in the middle of the night) could cover for me when I was not there.

My day began much the same each day, with new admissions. Some admissions are scheduled, and others occur at various times of the day and the week. The chart (there may be three volumes from many admissions) was my first source of information. Often there may only be a brief period of time between the present and the most recent social history. A patient "new" to the VA could provide the opportunity for a thorough social history, evaluation of at-home social support network, and resources. The most frequent question was, "Can this individual return to the same environment?" The highest level of functioning at the safest level of care is the most common goal. I would need to assess short-term versus long-term concerns, explore what resources the patient and family had, determine whether all benefits had been explored for the patient and family, and determine what, if any, concerns were not being addressed or looked at. I would always ask whether the patient and family were able to meet their needs.

I would query the nursing staff to see if anything unusual had transpired since I left the day before. Typically, the staff nurses are the pulse of the unit and bring forward patient concerns, family issues, or possible discharge questions. If the doctors were around, I checked to see whether anything new or urgent needed to be addressed. I preferred a quick chart check of the doctor's orders from the day before to see if tests or plans were being made that could affect the patient's discharge date or disposition. Then I did a quick walk through the unit to greet patients and family members, if they were there.

I would then prepare for the Monday team meeting. I might be following up on a family resource, or support services, or meeting with a patient or family new to the service. I spent a lot of time on phone calls, attempting to connect with family members or agencies. A social worker commonly has an "A" plan and a "B" plan, dependent upon the patient's condition at discharge, family resources, and what appears to be the best outcome given this situation. I strove to be highly visible to the staff and to the patients. Maintaining visibility helped others to perceive me as a resource up front, rather than getting referrals when there was little I could do to help...or being summoned to the dreaded "discharge now" crisis.

I functioned as a resource to the outpatient clinics held by the geriatric service. I would meet with families to check out how everything was going, whether in-home services were needed (either through the VA or through other community sources), and just how the family was doing. Were there any concerns about risk factors for caregiver fatigue or injury? Did compliance issues about medications exist? Were any other services (alternative therapies, for example) being used? Why or why not? I was frequently asked to meet with families and patients who had possible depression, dementia, or other psychosocial issues. I could be asked to talk to patients and families to explore a possible upcoming decision, such as home nursing, residential care, or nursing home placement. It was very helpful to broach these difficult topics well in advance of having to make a final decision. Giving families and patients some time to think out the "what if" was helpful. I had to learn that the patients and families needed to be thinking about those taboo topics, that they often were waiting for someone else to bring them up, or more often than not silently hoping no one would bring them up. This was one of the nicest advantages of the geriatric medicine service. We got to know many of the patients and families for quite some time. Building those relationships helped in the assessment and treatment of the patients and their families.

A caregiver support group was regularly held in a six-week series, with a month or two off, and restarted. I ran the group, along with a social work student (if one was available in the unit) and a nurse practitioner. Typically, we didn't hold the group during the worst winter months, as it was difficult to get out and many caregivers lacked community transportation. The group had open membership to any caregiver of a veteran. Sometimes, family and caregivers from other VA programs participated. This helped some of our geriatric families to gain perspective on their own circumstances, as well as to serve as a resource to other families. The support group provided opportunities for the social worker to learn about problems in the home and to suggest an outpatient clinic visit, or possible respite admission. Attending the support group afforded family members the opportunity to connect with people in similar circumstances. They sometimes developed close friendships with one another and continued to meet informally after the group disbanded. Over the years, the nurse practitioner and I learned that if we didn't disband the group, then it was difficult to bring new members into the group.

As the geriatric social worker, I routinely visited patients at home or made a visit to check out the home environment prior to patient discharge. The nurse practitioner and I made the home visits together. Sometimes we took along a medical, physical therapy, social work, nursing, or pharmacy student to talk with a homebound relative to assess whether discharge would be feasible or to assist in an outpatient evaluation of a patient. It is always enlightening to see patients and families in their own homes—the normal versus the medical world—the shoe on the other foot—being a guest in their world, rather than being in the medical arena. The home visit facilitated discussion of the care plan for the patient, given the home environment.

Another major area of my work as a VA geriatric social worker was to listen. Family members of patients frequently called me to discuss something they felt was not working well, or to explore another option. I might stop by a nursing home where a VA patient was placed, to meet with the patient and family to discuss whether the patient would be able to return home. I had the option to have community agencies call to relay news about patients and families. Sometimes, patients would call just to say everything was going well, or that something planned for home care was not there, or that they were not doing well and needed to come back to the VA for a while. Most typically, each call meant my making another call to check in on some equipment or community service that was not where it was supposed to be.

Each day ended with a to do list, follow-up, finish up, or check out. One day's list varied, not only in patient and/or family name, but also in the individual needs. There were very few days when I could say, "All is done." Most tasks carried over, waiting to see how the patient was doing, what the family thought, and whether resources could be found to ensure that the patient was being cared for with the highest level of safety. Every day or so brought an emergency, something unexpected, either with the patients on the unit or at home. I got to reprioritize my list and help in some crisis. A common crisis was a change in the medical condition of a patient, with the family being unsure about what to do. Someone might have needed transportation getting a nursing agency to make a visit, or I might have needed to go out to provide support as a patient was dying at home. No day was ever dull or routine.

The joys of the VA! Some maintain the notion that the Department of Veterans Affairs is a male-focused, military bureaucracy. Those early thoughts of mine! My experience was that nowhere else could I have had the opportunities to learn what I did while with the Veterans Administration Medical Center at Salt Lake City. During those early years, I met veterans from World War I who had experienced some of the most horrific circumstances. I had the opportunity to work with veterans who had been prisoners-of-war during World War II and the Korean Conflict. Over the years, I met many female veterans. The variety of individuals, the unique family constellations, and varying human conditions could not be matched in any other environment.

I credit my skills today to my years of geriatric social work practice with the VA. I experienced one of the greatest gifts as many patients and families let me be part of their journey in aging. I had the opportunity to learn about many different resources in communities and families. I learned about resiliency, coping with loss, and dignity of caring for others. I learned about commitment. "Till death do us part" became one of the hardest vows to break when I tried my best to convince others about the necessity for nursing home placement. I had the most unique opportunities to share the intimacy of the end of life issues with many families—the celebration of lives well lived.

Think About It

1. What do you think is the hardest part of being part of an interdisciplinary team as a social worker?

2. Have you ever ruled out working in a certain area as a result of preconceived notions you have about it?

3. Do you have any stereotypes or notions about geriatric families? What are they?

Chapter 14
Do Unto Others: Life Lessons Learned as a Medical Social Worker

• •

by Marian Swindell, Ph.D., MSW

I received the "911" page to call the home health care agency where I worked. I returned the page, and the Director of Nursing explained that one of the home health aides had been bathing Mr. Lambert and had noticed severe burns and bruising all over his body. I told the Director I would be in the office shortly. I arrived about 15 minutes later and discussed the situation with the home health aide. The patient, an 88-year-old man, had been with our agency for about four weeks. We all enjoyed seeing him but dreaded seeing his wife. She did not want us in her house, messing with her things, interrupting her day, spoiling her routine. She grumbled continuously while we were there and often made us stand outside the house for several minutes before letting us in. The aide explained that she had seen severe bruising and small burns over Mr. Lambert's legs, chest, and back and that while she was bathing him, he cried in pain as the water touched the new burns. Up until this week, the wife had supposedly been giving him sponge baths. Through tears, the aide asked me to stop everything I was doing and go see him immediately.

Investigating abuse was one of the most difficult aspects of my job. Seeing or hearing that patients had been beaten, starved, burned, hit, scratched, cut, left to sit in their own feces, or abandoned in basements tied to cots always sickened me and broke my heart over and over again. I could never understand, and still do not, how or why people abuse others. Yes, my education and training provide me a framework to process the abuse, but I still do not understand how, with all the social work programs, community outreach, television and radio commercials on domestic violence, support groups for domestic violence, respite care, financial assistance, and church support groups, that we still have people abusing others.

My heart was breaking as I got into my car, called Mr. Lambert's number from my cell phone, and explained that I was in the area and was hoping to stop by. I also explained that one of the home health aides had requested I make a visit. Mrs. Lambert said "sure" and hung up the phone. I drove to the house, rang the doorbell, and waited for what seemed like an eternity. Mrs. Lambert finally opened the door and told me she had "forgotten" that she had heard the doorbell. This "forgetting" to answer the doorbell happened almost every time one of the agency workers went to visit the patient and was quite frustrating, especially in the heat of the noonday sun.

I stepped into the house and walked over to Mr. Lambert. He was sitting in his wheelchair and looking out the window at a large open field in the backyard. He turned and smiled at me. I knew that he knew why I was there. I also felt that this was not a good time to talk about what had happened as his wife was standing right next to us. I began to think how I could talk to my patient alone and (a) find out what had happened, and (b) consider how he wanted me to handle the situation. As if reading my thoughts, my patient told his wife he had to go to the bathroom. She huffed and told him he would have to wait until the nurse or aide came back that day. I explained that I had been trained in proper lifting techniques and that I could take him. She said "great," and she would use the opportunity to hang her clothes on the clothesline.

I wheeled him down the hallway and into the bathroom. He asked me to run the water to help him "go" and I obliged. I lifted him from the wheelchair and leaned him over my shoulder as we pulled down his shorts and underpants. I placed him on the commode and he started crying. "I know why you are here. I don't want to leave her. She just gets mad with me. I don't want to leave her. She has no one else. My children don't like her and I'm all she has. It's been going on for years because she doesn't think I'm a man because I'm in a wheelchair and all." Through tears, he just kept saying he didn't want to leave her. I examined his burns and bruises, all the while looking at scars of scrapes and scratches up and down his arms and legs. On his back, I noticed bruising in the shape of a large round object, a pan I presumed. I asked about the bruise and he said nothing. I counted more than 40 bruises and 10 burns. I lost count of the cuts and scratches. I explained that it was my job as his social worker to protect him and provide a safe and caring environment for him to live in. I remembered my struggles with the *Code of Ethics* during my master's training. I wanted to take this man home with me, somewhere safe, somewhere secure. I knew I would not leave him alone with his wife that night, and I also knew he did not want to leave the house.

I sat on the edge of the bathtub, water still running, looking at Mr. Lambert. During my initial assessment on my first visit with this patient, he told me they had been married close to 30 years. They had no children together, but he did have two sons and one daughter from his first marriage. He explained that he counted on his wife for assistance around the house and for companionship. With her around, he was never alone. I remember thinking that he had chosen the word "alone" after a second or two of hesitation. I looked up and asked him about his friends and family. "God has blessed me with three healthy children, a roof over my head, and a long life filled with goodness and love. I'm old now, though. My spirit is strong, but my body is weak. One day I will walk away from this place, but probably when I am dead and my spirit walks away from my body."

My mind was processing through this problem. I wanted him out of the house, or I wanted his wife out of the house. I knew he was in danger. He was aware that he was being abused. He knew I could remove him from this house. As I processed through my options, I was aware that he was studying my face. He could see my mind working. Placement in a nursing home? Placement in an assisted living facility? Removing the wife? Will he be safe tonight? My mind began to race. I knew the wife would come back from hanging her clothes any second now. I was filled with panic. What if she had come in already and had been standing outside the bathroom door? Could she hear over the running water? Fear led to anger, and I thought, "This is enough. Enough abuse for this man, enough pain, and suffering. Enough is enough."

I turned the water off, asked Mr. Lambert if he was "through," flushed the commode, dressed him, placed him back in the wheelchair, and wheeled him out to the living room. I was mad and frustrated with this situation but reassured my client that things were going to be okay. Out in the living room, I looked through his medical chart, found the "contacts" section where his children's phone numbers were listed, and asked if he would be willing for one of his children to stay with him in the house for the next few days. He looked at me and smiled: "She'll never go for that." Then he looked away, out at that field, and began to cry.

I walked over to the phone, called the first son listed, explained the situation, and asked if he could come to his father's house right away. "I am on my way," he said. I looked at Mr. Lambert and said, "He's on his way. Everything is going to be okay." He looked up at me and said, "She's never going to go for that." He looked away again, out at that field, but this time he did not cry.

A few minutes later, as he and I sat together looking out the window at that big open field, his wife walked in. I then stood, placed my hand on my patient's shoulder and calmly said, "Perfect timing. I have a few things I would like to talk over with you. When I was helping your husband to the bathroom, I noticed a lot of bruising and burns on his arms, legs, and back. He would not tell me really, exactly what had happened, but some of the cuts and bruises are quite old and are beginning to heal. I am concerned for your husband's well-being, safety, and recovery. In cases such as this, I often remove patients from the home, placing them in a nursing home or with a relative. It is important that he, as a patient of our agency, focus all his mental and physical energy on recuperating. If he is being abused, as I have confirmed, his energy is being focused elsewhere. I have made a record of my findings in my file and I am considering placing him in a nursing home or with a family member." She tried to interrupt me. I proceeded without missing a breath. "If placement is successful, you may have to find another place to live. I have contacted your stepson, and he is coming over right now. I also have asked him to stay here with his dad for a few days until we can explore these options." She demanded I reconsider. "No, ma'am. Reconsideration at this point is not an option." My patient smiled. It was at that precise moment that my patient and I knew he was a free man.

I remained standing, turned to Mr. Lambert, and gently smiled. We waited in silence for his son to arrive. A few minutes later, the son walked into the house, past his stepmother, and knelt down before his father on the floor. The son was visibly upset and had broken out in huge red splotches all over his face and neck. He told his dad that he knew all along what had been happening, that his dad had told him never to speak ill of his stepmother, and that if he couldn't say something nice, to say nothing at all. The son then begged his dad to come live with him and his family. He had built a guesthouse, just for the dad, a few years earlier. The son explained how much he needed his dad around to help with the grandchildren, fix things around the house, and oversee the place, especially while the son was at work. The son explained that he would feel his family was safe if he knew his father was living there with them. The son then turned to his stepmother and explained that she could come visit once a month, on Sunday afternoons from 1:00 p.m. to 2:00 p.m., just like she had allowed him to come visit his father once a month, on Sunday afternoons from 1:00 p.m. to 2:00 p.m. Mr. Lambert's smile was brighter than the Florida sun.

The son, his wife, three grandchildren, and I moved the father into his new home that weekend. I am pleased to report this family is still together, healthy and happy. Except the stepmother. She did attempt to visit her husband one time. The family, however, "forgot" to answer the doorbell after she rang it.

Think About It

1. What do you think are some of the contributing factors to elderly domestic violence?

2. If you were the social worker in this case, what would you have done if there were no children to contact?

3. What lessons did you learn from reading this story?

Chapter 15
A Typical Day in Home Health

• • • • • • • • • • • • • • • • • •

by Gary B. Schwartz, MSW

It's four o'clock in the afternoon and time to start the plan for tomorrow's visits. As a medical social worker in home health practice, I receive referrals daily to see patients. The offices I work for on an as-needed basis call with basic information on the patient. Then they fax a complete face sheet and any other data I may need. Generally, I plan to see three to four patients a day, mostly new assessments and some follow-ups. I see from my faxes that there are three assessments for tomorrow and I also have a revisit. Right now, I will call the case managers of the new patients and have them give me their assessment of what they feel the patient needs. What are their greatest challenges, what physical condition they are in, and who else in their support groups will I need to contact?

The first patient is Mr. W, age 82, and he has Parkinson's disease. He had a recent fall in his home, and after a short hospital stay, he is very weak. He is wheelchair bound and lives with a supportive wife, who is becoming overwhelmed with his care. The next patient is Ms. X, age 72, who lives alone, has chronic pulmonary disease, uses oxygen 24 hours a day, is faced with financial issues, and has a supportive son in the area. The third referral is Mrs. Y, age 82, who recently had a hip replacement, lives alone, was independent before her surgery, and needs some resources on a temporary basis. And last, I will see Mr. Z, who has a recent history of falls. He has had trouble getting his medications, nutrition challenges, and a messy home.

Thinking back to how I got started, I was working as a counselor in an addiction treatment center when I was encouraged to get some courses to pursue a certification in addictions therapy. One of my professors told me that she felt society and I would be best served if I worked for and received a master's degree in social work. After much consideration, I applied to the university, got accepted, and began this interesting profession. As an intern, I worked in a transitional care unit at a local hospital, where I was exposed to elder care, case management, assessments, community resourcing, and hospice counseling. This was exciting and positive for me. After graduation, I worked at the hospital, in an assisted living facility, and then a nursing home.

I was later approached to work in home health, which is a perfect match with my experience in elder care and my commitment to and knowledge of the local community. There are times when there is a decrease in the amount of work, but it all works out for me to make a good living and help others. The rate of pay for visits is $50-$100 in this area. This type of work is good for me, as I am an independent person and do not need the structure of an office environment or close supervision. There are many state and federal guidelines that must be followed. The agencies I work with have constant training to make sure that all professionals meet the policies set down by governmental agencies. This is a great line of work for those interested in elder care.

It's now about five o'clock and time to call the patients to make appointments for tomorrow. I schedule one hour in the house for each patient and fifteen to thirty minutes travel time between appointments. Ms. X is available at 9:30 and Mr. W at 11:00. Mr. Z has a morning doctor's appointment, so I will see him around 2:00 in the afternoon and Mrs. Y at 12:30. I tell the patients that I may be up to an hour late and will call if I will be any later than that. Now I set up my briefcase with the files and appropriate forms for reports and take care of personal duties for the rest of the day.

Now I'm headed for my appointments and get to Ms. X on time. She comes to the door with her oxygen and is a little apprehensive about the visit. We sit at the kitchen table and begin talking about her health today. Her apprehension begins to lessen. I listen to her as she talks about her health, before I ask what she feels are her greatest challenges. Having had a recent hospital stay because of extreme weakness and an asthmatic attack, she is presently unable to drive her car and get to the doctor or the store. Also, having diabetes, she needs to have a special diet, and her nutrition is suffering. She has a supportive son in the area, yet he is quite busy and cannot always come help her. Ms. X has Medicare and Medicaid and a reverse mortgage on her home to help with bill paying. I suggest a local ride service to help with appointments, but she does not want to use it. Ms. X tells me that she can get a friend to give her a ride to the doctor next week. She agrees that she is not the best at her diabetic diet. I ask if she thinks she would benefit from a few cans of Glucerna, a diabetic supplement. She states that she will accept anything that is free, and I begin to see that she may be a bit of a system manipulator. Often we see this type of behavior with patients who are chronic with lung disease. I continue trying to be helpful and nonjudgmental. Ms. X. states that her portable oxygen tank is too heavy and asks if I can find out if there is a lighter type. I am aware that many durable medical equipment companies have a liquid oxygen delivery system that is available. I tell her that I will have to call her provider and her doctor to see if we can get this system for her. After going back to the office, I call her doctor and he says that when he sees her next week, he will discuss this with her. I ask her permission to contact Meal on Wheels for meals that have sugar-free desserts and will help with her nutrition. She states that she cannot afford these meals and the intake coordinator at Meals on Wheels agrees to send her the meals for free for a few weeks. Having addressed all of her stated concerns, I ask if she has a living will, and if not, I can help her prepare one. She states that she does and that her son is her surrogate. Asking if there is anything else that I may have missed, Ms. X assures me that we have covered everything. I have her sign an agency form that lets the agency and Medicare know I was there, and I thank her for allowing me to visit. Giving her my card, I tell her that if she is aware of anything we may have missed, to please call the agency and I will contact her.

Next, I drive to see Mr. W and his wife. He has just arrived home from the hospital where he stayed for seven days after a fall. He is also quite weak, and has advancing Parkinson's disease and advanced dementia associated with his Parkinson's. His wife is overwhelmed with his care and needs help in the home. He presents very poorly and is unable to communicate very well. He is aware that he is quite ill and that his wife may become ill, too. We agree that some help is needed in the home. I speak with his wife about the possibility of hospice care and let her know a little about what services they may provide. She agrees that this may be a good thing and gives permission to speak with the doctor about an evaluation. She has shown me her husband's power of attorney for medical decisions. I also speak with her about a program called long-term care diversion. This program is designed to allow a patient to stay in the home with a lot of help. This would allow her to have some time for herself and give Mr. W excellent in-home services. Mrs. W gives me permission to facilitate the application for this program. Some paperwork has to be generated by the MSW, nurse, and doctor. When I return to the office, I start this paperwork. I fax the doctor the request for a hospice evaluation order and the paperwork for the long-term care diversion program. Thanking the patient and his wife, I move on to the next appointment.

Mrs. Y slowly comes to the door with her walker. I am glad that she is using it. She has had a recent hip replacement. She lives alone and her home is tidy. Her daughter, who lives three houses down the street, helps Mrs. Y with much around the house, including nutrition and cleaning. However, her daughter works and cannot help Mrs. Y get to her doctor's appointments. I discover that Mrs. Y broke her hip as a result of a fall in her home and that she is a fall risk of late. We talk about the possibility of placement in an assisted living facility. She insists that she wants to stay in her home. I suggest that she get a LifeLine, so if she falls again she can immediately get help. Mrs. Y agrees, and I make a call to set up this service. Her mood is good and she is aware of her limitations. We talk more about transportation to medical appointments, and she agrees to allow me to get her into the Dial-A-Ride program. I call them to set up a ride for next week's appointment. As we talk, she elaborates that her daughter does not help with meals for the daytime and asks if I am able to help her in this area. I explain and suggest the Meals on Wheels program. She agrees, states she can afford them, and allows me to call and get this service started. She does not have a living will in place, and after I explain exactly what a living will is and does, she states that she does not wish to have one. I assure her that this is okay and she is glad to know that she is being affirmed in her decision. I thank her for her time and move on to my next patient.

Four weeks ago, I visited with Mr. Z. At that time his home was in great disarray. He did not have all of his medications filled, because of financial concerns. He also has a history of recent falls. On the last visit, with his permission, he was signed up for the Medicare D program for medication assistance. I also referred him to a local church that helps people who cannot afford their medications. Mr. Z also allowed me to call the local senior help line and get him started for services for housecleaning. With Mr. Z's permission, I called the local LifeLine service to obtain services for him.

I am returning on this visit to see how all is progressing with Mr. Z. Upon entering his home, I note that it is neat and the bathroom is sparkling. It is apparent the senior help line admitted him into its services. All of his medications are laid out on the table. He states that he feels much better now that he is able to take them all. The dementia medications he is now taking are beginning to help, and with the pillboxes that our nurse has set up, he is taking them as prescribed. He has a LifeLine in place, but he has not been wearing it. I encourage him to put it on, reminding him that it doesn't help if he falls in the bathroom and the button is in the living room. He agrees and puts it on. We talk about how he feels about these changes. His mood is much more positive than on the last visit. This is evident by the smile on his face and his body language. Thanking him for allowing me to visit, I say goodbye and leave.

This concludes my visits for the day. Now, it's back to the office to write reports and speak with the case managers. They are glad that there have been some positive results. They will follow up with these patients and let me know if more visits will be needed. I now will go home and check my faxes, make calls, and schedule appointments for tomorrow.

Think About It

1. What more could this social worker have done for any of these patients?

2. What other resources are available that could benefit the patients?

3. Could you suggest assessment tools that would benefit the social worker and patients?

Chapter 16
A Day in the Life of a Hospice Social Worker
• •

by Sally Hill Jones, Ph.D., LCSW

Driving to work Monday morning, as my thoughts move to the day ahead, I wonder if Mr. Valdez made it through the weekend. He was slipping into a coma when I saw him Friday, and his wife was as ready as she could be. However, his son was holding onto hope that his Dad would "beat this" yet. It is my day to do admissions, and I hope there will not be too many. Although I love getting to know new patients and families, there is so much paperwork. Ten years ago when I applied for a hospice position, I only knew I wanted to help families with end-of-life choices because of how lost I felt when my father was dying, in a year-long vegetative state, kept alive by the feeding tube. I learned there was much more to hospice work than I knew, including the paperwork. I love it, though. Sometimes there is only a little help I can offer patients and families, or that they will accept. Other times, I know the team I am a part of has made a real difference in the patients' and families' quality of life toward the end and in having some control over their deaths.

At morning report, where we are updated on weekend developments, I learn Mr. Valdez died last night. The son was able to say goodbye to his father not long before he died, and everyone seemed okay when the on-call nurse left. I make a note to check in with the family. I feel a little sad, but quickly push on with the day's work. I touch base with team members on the needs of patients we share, and my day begins to fill up. Rosie, the nurse for Mrs. Patterson, expresses her frustration that Mrs. Patterson has not made funeral plans and does not have a DNR (Do Not Resuscitate) order. I explain that Mrs. Patterson is still uncomfortable making these decisions. Rosie says that Mrs. Patterson needs to face that the ovarian cancer is worsening and begin to make plans. I agree to talk to Mrs. Patterson again, but remind her that the patient has the right to make decisions the way she sees fit, and that facing the severity of her condition is a process that takes time. Rosie rolls her eyes and walks off, muttering. She is new to hospice nursing and wants the "good death" for all her patients. It is a learning process to accept that our ideas and the patients' ideas of a good death are not always the same. Even when they are, the reality does not always match the expectations.

The admissions nurse has scheduled two admissions, for 1:00 and 4:30. I mentally redo my schedule and realize I am much more flexible than when I first started at hospice. I head out to see the Stone family. Mr. Stone is an 89-year-old man with Parkinson's disease. My main concern today is his wife, age 87, who has been taking care of Mr. Stone for several years and has her own medical problems. The Stones' children help, but Mrs. Stone insists on doing most of the care herself, stating repeatedly that she vowed "in sickness and in health." Everyone has talked to her, to no avail, about the need to take care of her own health so she can continue to care for her husband. Today when I arrive, she looks particularly tired and says it has been a hard night. After hearing about the night's difficulties, I ask about her recent doctor visit, and she reluctantly tells me her doctor is threatening hospitalization because of her worsening diabetes. Sensing this may be a critical opportunity to work with Mrs. Stone to accept more help, I explore further. She says she did not realize it would get this bad. She believed she could handle anything and feels she is failing Mr. Stone. Although I have asked this before, I ask again whether Mr. Stone would see it that way. She cries a little and says she knows he would not. I then ask what she would want Mr. Stone to do if the situation were reversed. She says strongly that she would want him to take care of himself. I ask her if she would be willing to let someone come in to help her, so she can be there for Mr. Stone instead of being in the hospital. She agrees. I feel hopeful, but she agreed to this before and did not go through with it. I need to set up the help right away.

I am paged to go to Ms. Thompson's home because she is dying. Ms. Thompson, a 72-year-old woman who lives alone, cared for by paid caregivers, has suffered from severe, painful arthritis for many years and now faces terminal cancer. She has refused pain medications for the cancer, saying she can handle the pain. When I explored this, it became clear that she was using the coping methods that had allowed her to live with pain for many years. It has been difficult for the hospice team to see her in pain when relief was available. She lives in a very small trailer home, filled to the brim with newspapers and magazines and various other collections. I tried to get help clearing out the place, but she wanted it just the way it was. As I approach her home, a sense of calm comes over me that it's going to be all right. When I arrive, Ms. Thompson's dog is in his protective place on her bed and she is in a coma. I sit beside her bed and think about her life. There is no family to call. The nurse and I sit with her as she dies. It is such a relief for us to see the pain leave her face, replaced with peace. I feel privileged, as being present at the moment of death does not happen often. The nurse pronounces her death and begins to prepare her body, while I call the funeral home and the neighbor who agreed to adopt the dog.

While we are waiting, Ruth's husband calls. Ruth is a 43-year-old woman at the end of a long struggle with metastatic cancer. She is extremely thin, in a coma, very close to death. Her family has been gathered for weeks, because all indications were that Ruth was going to die any day. Patients and families understandably want to know "how long." Accuracy is usually not possible until the very end. Even then, as in Ruth's case, there are so many individual factors that prevent accurate prediction. Ruth's family wants to figure out why Ruth is hanging on. Ruth has been a patient for several months, so I have established a good relationship with them. I feel comfortable suggesting the usual possibilities: that she is waiting for a loved one to arrive, or to tell her it is okay to go, or to tell her they will be all right, or for a certain meaningful date. I also suggest that sometimes people find it too difficult to allow themselves to let go when loved ones are present, pulling them back. Her husband agrees to discuss these ideas with the family members and call me later.

After a quick lunch in the car on the way to the noon admission, I review the information on the prospective patient. Mrs. Baldwin is a 65-year-old woman who was diagnosed with aggressive stomach cancer a week ago. Her family has given strict instructions not to mention death, cancer, or hospice. I begin to build rapport with her two daughters and gather admission information. They are clearly distraught about the diagnosis and want hospice to provide comfort and personal care, but have a strong belief that the healing power of the pastor's and congregation's prayers will cure her. In exploring this further, it is clear that the doctor has discussed the prognosis with Mrs. Baldwin and the family, but for them to discuss these things would mean a lack of faith. I assure them that I grasp the importance of their beliefs and will share this with the team. I also explain that we will do our best to describe our services to Mrs. Baldwin without using those words, but that if she wants to discuss these things, the hospice workers will honor her wishes. They assure me their mother will not want to discuss these things.

The daughters insist on being in the room when I visit with Mrs. Baldwin, who is bed-bound and appears to be in pain. I introduce myself and explain that I am from an organization that provides many services for people in situations like hers. I tell her that her daughters have told me how important her faith is, and she nods. I ask if she can tell me what the doctor explained to her about her condition. She says the doctor told her she has something terminal, but she knows her faith will see her through. I explain the services we provide, including nurses, certified nursing assistants (CNAs) who help with personal care, chaplains, social workers, and volunteers. We go over the kinds of services provided by each discipline, the usual number of visits, and how long the services will be provided before the need is reevaluated. I skip over bereavement services, thinking I can explain them later. I explain how Medicare will be billed for all services related to the diagnosis the doctor explained to her. I ask Mrs. Baldwin if she is in pain, and when she nods yes, I explain that if they decide to use our services, a nurse will be able to help with that, and that her doctor will still be involved if she wishes. It is evident that Mrs. Baldwin is tiring, and so I describe patient's rights and that our services are designed to address her needs the way she wishes.

She indicates that she wishes to talk to me alone. Her daughters seem surprised but respect her wishes and leave the room. Mrs. Baldwin tells me that her daughters cannot handle any talk of dying and asks me to refrain from discussing death with them. We talk frankly about her desires for her own death, should it be her "time to go." She also wants her daughters to take care of her personal needs instead of the CNAs, as she is a very private woman. I explain her wishes for personal care to the daughters, who are relieved to hear this was her concern.

I know I have some work to do to with the Baldwin family to offer them the opportunity to discuss her death together, if we get to that point. We go over the paperwork and get signatures on all the forms. I will share with the team members the delicate line we need to walk with the Baldwin family to respect their wishes at the same time we offer opportunities to move toward acceptance of the death as well as they can, and perhaps even talk together about it. As I leave, I call for a nurse to see her soon for pain assessment.

I then head toward the nursing home to visit two patients, Mr. Garcia and Ms. Dayton. The nurse informs me that Mr. Garcia has gone home! I am amazed, because the last time I saw Mr. Garcia, a man in his 40s with cirrhosis of the liver, he was showing signs of being very near death. He was not alert, he was indicating that he saw angels and deceased family members, and his stomach was extremely distended from the fluid buildup. The nurse said that reducing the fluid helped him to the point he felt well enough to leave. Mr. Garcia did not have family in the area and likely returned home to another city. I had no way of reaching him, because he refused to share family contact information. Mr. Garcia was not our patient very long, and this ending feels incomplete. I knew he was dependent on alcohol and feared he would return to drinking. Yet, perhaps this would be a turning point. I would not be able to discuss this with him or refer him to AA. I will deal with that later.

I head off to Ms. Dayton's room. She is 86 years old and in advanced stages of Alzheimer's. She was widowed and had a loving son and daughter-in-law who cared for her at home many years until their own health began to suffer. Her great niece is a CNA at the nursing home. Ms. Dayton is bed-bound and responds very little to others. Her facial expressions indicate if she is uncomfortable or in pain. Her family has placed beside her bed a book of photos and descriptions of her life for visitors and staff. From this book and talking with the family, I have a sense of who she was before the Alzheimer's took hold. I sit and talk softly to her and stroke her hands. She cannot understand words, but most likely registers voice tone and emotion as well as touch. I turn on her favorite music. I find myself slowing down and becoming calmer as I talk to her. There is sometimes doubt that my visits make any difference to her, but I am usually convinced as I talk to her that she is taking in the caring tone in my voice and touch.

As I leave for the 4:30 admission, I get a call that the patient I was going to see has died. Sometimes the referral to hospice comes too late for us to provide much, or any, service. This could be due to reluctance on the part of the patient, the family, or the doctor. Misconceptions about hospice are still believed, and acceptance of hospice services sometimes brings the reality of death closer.

Back at the office, I make calls to the Valdez family to offer my condolences and see how they are doing. I also call several agencies to set up services for patients—some in-home help for Mrs. Stone, and following up on referrals for other patients for legal services, Meals on Wheels, veterans' benefits, and a low-cost funeral. I work on the paperwork for Mrs. Baldwin's admission. Ruth's husband calls to say they are thinking Ruth is waiting for Christmas, three weeks away. They want to celebrate Christmas sooner so she can go if she is ready. I agree to visit tomorrow to discuss this.

As I drive home, I listen to some music that helps me unwind. Even though I don't have time, I make a quick stop at the park to sit and "release" the day's concerns as I learned in self-care workshops. It does not always work, but it has helped me to take my work home less than before, since I want to continue in hospice social work. I silently thank Mr. Valdez and Ms. Thompson for what they taught me and for the privilege of being part of their last days. Then I say good-bye. I go through what I would have liked to do for Mr. Garcia, let go of that, and wish him well. I drive home and let the music lift away the concerns of the day. Just as I'm falling asleep that night, I remember I need to talk to Mrs. Patterson about her DNR and funeral plans.

Think About It

1. What social work values and ethical principles do you see in operation in the hospice work described?

2. How should the social worker help Ruth's family decide whether to celebrate Christmas ahead of time?

3. What are some of the skills required when working in an interdisciplinary hospice team?

Chapter 17
The Need for Hospice Social Workers in Skilled Nursing Facilities

• •

by Renee R. Adams, MSW, LCSW

I believe that I have one of the most misunderstood positions in the field of gerontological social work. I work for a nonprofit hospice agency as a medical social worker on the skilled nursing facility (SNF) team. This means that 100% of my clients live either in a nursing home or an assisted living facility and have a terminal prognosis with a life expectancy of six months or less.

My typical day starts around 7:30 a.m. I review messages on my BlackBerry, which provides important updates about activity that has occurred the night before. This information typically includes deaths, new admissions, and transfers. I remember the first time that I was notified of a death on my pager, about seven years ago. The true impact of the loss was nearly overwhelming. Now, however, receiving this news daily has become a very routine part of my day—not in a cold, uncaring way, but in a way that is absolutely necessary to succeed in this field and to be helpful and supportive to clients. Once I receive the updates from the night before, I am ready to schedule and begin my day.

My first order of business is to see a new patient with Amyotrophic Lateral Sclerosis (ALS), which is better known as Lou Gehrig's disease. After working with many patients and many diseases, I believe this is the most insidious of all diseases. ALS patients typically remain cognitively intact, but at end stage, the disease affects the ability to utilize their muscles. This not only affects communication, but also affects their ability to swallow, use their hands and feet, blink, and even breathe.

Mrs. Singer, at age 73, is younger than my typical client. She recently moved from living at home with her family to a skilled nursing facility. She has a soft, difficult to understand but still intelligible voice. She is afraid and wants to go home. I re-explain what hospice is and what we can provide to her and her family. I tell her about communication devices that exist and encourage her to allow me to make a referral to the ALS Association, which she somewhat reluctantly agrees to do. She also consents to having a volunteer, but declines a chaplain, as she is an agnostic. We also discuss advanced directives. She has completed a health care power of attorney and living will, but she has not made any specific mortuary arrangements. This is something that we, with the support of her family, will work on together. We then just spend time getting to know one another and hopefully establishing a good rapport, which will be essential over the course of the next few months. Following our visit, I check in at the nurses' station, give an update to the facility social worker, and complete the necessary paperwork. Then I call her family to introduce myself and provide support and education regarding the services our agency offers and to offer to meet with them. I decide to see Mrs. Singer three times per month, with the option of seeing her more frequently if desired by her or her family. I will focus on supportive counseling and assisting her and her family with anticipatory grieving and finalizing mortuary arrangements.

My next visit is with Ms. Hamilton, a 94-year-old widowed female with dementia. This visit typically is more companionship than anything else, as she is minimally responsive verbally. Upon my arrival, she is sitting in the common area with her eyes closed. She does not immediately respond to hearing her name but eventually does open her eyes. I have brought a tactile stimulation bag that our agency provides with sing-a-long CD, book, lotion, balls, and aromatherapy. I give her a hand massage and talk to her about her son who lives out of town. At the close of our visit, I take out the lemon aromatherapy, which I haven't done before, and lightly spray the air around her. She smiles and starts to talk fluently about how it reminds her of Girl Scout camp. Amazing, you just never know what it will take to connect with someone. Also, what works today may not work tomorrow. I close our visit and call her son to tell him the exciting news. He thanks me for the call but seems less than impressed. I leave feeling a great sense of accomplishment and only wish that her son felt the same.

On my way to the next visit, I receive a page. One of my long-term patients who lives at an assisted living apartment has requested a visit as soon as possible. I have been working with Mr. Washington for a little over a year. (Hospice patients can be re-certified if they continue to show decline.) He is an 86-year-old widowed male with chronic obstructive pulmonary disease (COPD). He requires oxygen, smokes (when not on the oxygen), and has been declining rapidly over the past couple of months. I have been encouraging him to consider alternate placement, and I suspect this is why he requested a visit today.

I arrive to find him visibly weaker and disheveled, which is out of character for him. His apartment smells of cat urine, and he has dishes piled up on the counter. I assist him in straightening up the kitchen and changing the cat litter while making small talk. During one of our previous visits, we put a plan in place for his cat after he passes away. This is about the extent of advanced planning that he has been willing to discuss. We finally sit down to discuss whatever it is that he has called me for. After an awkward silence, he blurts out, "Can you help me get Viagra?" I immediately refocus, as this clearly is the last thing I was expecting to discuss during today's visit. I am also thinking of the "important" visits that I had to cancel or reschedule to respond to his call. I then realize that this is important to him, and he deserves my time and respect while researching his options. I place a phone call to his nurse to find out if this type of activity is possible from a medical standpoint. I learn that it is and that she is going to contact his physician to obtain an order. This particular medication is not covered under his hospice benefit, as it falls "out of the plan of care." He is so relieved to have this concern addressed. Apparently, he has had his eye on the "home delivered meals gal."

My visit portion of the day is coming to a close, and I decide to stop by the office to finish up some phone calls and complete the paperwork that is required with each visit. I also plan to contact the appropriate team members and provide them with an update on my visits. I try to end the day on time, as I will be on call this evening for emergencies. Needless to say, death is not confined to 9:00 a.m. to 5:00 p.m. Therefore, it is crucial that an effective social worker establish clear boundaries, in order to prevent burnout and continue to be able to provide top notch care. We receive pages 24 hours per day but are strongly encouraged to shut off our BlackBerries during off hours. The agency is staffed with after-hours and on-call staff to handle emergencies. All e-mails and pages will be saved and can be retrieved the following morning, so no information is lost. It is essential to separate yourself from the world of terminal illness, death, and dying to maintain a sense of peace and provide good self-care.

As usual, I feel a great sense of accomplishment at the end of the day. The work is challenging, bittersweet, frustrating, and rewarding, but never boring. This may come as a surprise to many when they hear about nursing home patients. The perceptions that many have about this population are simply incorrect. It is not one of the "easier" practice areas for social workers. In fact, it is just the opposite. It requires an enormous amount of creativity, patience, and skill to engage patients, SNF staff, and families who may be, for whatever reason, unwilling or unable to be active participants in the patient's care.

It is easy to forget during the day-to-day rush of seeing patients in skilled nursing facilities that they are not only patients, but individuals. They are people like us with loves, losses, dreams, ambitions, desires, passions, regrets, and fears. They have good days and bad. They get angry, jealous, lonely, and happy. They fall in and out of love. They are grieving the loss of their mates, family, friends, abilities, identities, and freedoms. They are so much more than what they appear and need to be reminded of not only who they were but also who they are. That is the role of a social worker in this setting. In my opinion, it is one of the most valuable social work roles there is.

This field, in my opinion, is more of a calling than a career. It takes someone with extreme patience to work with this population. Although most areas of practice within social work are not glamorous, this area of practice is even less so. The facilities are at times less than desirable, although many facilities have come a long way over the past decade. In fact, many facilities have set a new standard of care that others are striving to achieve.

One of the main reasons that I believe facilities can benefit from utilizing the hospice team is that of staffing. Hospice staff can supplement the care that they are currently providing patients. For example, a social service office may be staffed with an individual who is not necessarily a degreed or licensed social worker. This person is typically charged with providing support services to nearly 200 patients. Clearly, it is not humanly possible to provide in-depth counseling or support to each and every person, given those numbers. The role for a facility social worker often becomes more crisis management and risk management with a focus on an enormous amount of government-required documentation. Individuals on hospice care have very unique and often time-consuming needs. They need to learn about the disease process, complete or update advanced directives, choose treatment options, complete estate planning, mend relationships, complete a life review (if desired), and perform many other tasks too numerous to mention. A hospice social worker can be invaluable throughout this process. We have the necessary time to spend with each patient, as our caseloads are significantly lower than those of SNF staff members. Some believe that having a hospice team within a skilled nursing facility is a duplication of services; however, once the patient, family, and SNF have the opportunity to benefit from the supplemental services, they usually agree that the support is invaluable.

One of the areas that can be a challenge in this field is the large amount of driving that is typically required. In addition, you do not have a personal office, which means you either have to be extremely organized or your car becomes a collection of resources, paperwork, phone numbers, and files. Most of us fall into the latter category. One of the biggest benefits to not being office-based is the flexibility. It is very nice to be in charge of your own schedule and be able to coordinate your day. However, you must be flexible, as you may get called to a death visit on the other side of town when you had your entire day booked with other, equally pressing visits.

The salary range in my area is approximately $40,000 to $60,000 per year, with bi-lingual MSWs being highly sought after and compensated accordingly. One of the biggest challenges to breaking into this area of practice is that of experience. You need hospice or medical experience to get into the field, which, of course, presents the usual dilemma of somehow getting the experience without working in the field. The way around this is by way of internships. Our agency, as well as many others, accepts second-year MSW interns. We train them for an academic year and typically, at the end of the internship, they are offered a position, assuming that the experience was mutually beneficial. This has given many new graduates a great opportunity to enter into a field that others may not be able to enter for many years. Our agency benefits, as well, by having well trained, young, enthusiastic professionals wanting to work in this capacity.

You also need to appreciate working independently. For the most part, you are part of an interdisciplinary team; however, you may only see your fellow team members a few times per month. Otherwise you are on your own, seeing patients, and communicating the results of your visits with the team via voice mails or e-mails. I happen to enjoy working independently, but this can be quite an adjustment for someone who is accustomed to conferring with fellow employees numerous times throughout the day for both professional and personal support.

One of the most common misconceptions that I hear is that working with nursing home patients is not challenging enough. Some of the more challenging aspects of my job are finding ways to connect with patients who are non-verbal or have dementia; discovering ways to involve family members who find it too difficult to visit; balancing the importance of not only providing excellent care to the patient and family but to the staff at the facility; teaching staff the importance of honoring patients' wishes and not forcing their own will regarding care; identifying ways to promote choice, self determination, and validate self worth in settings that often allow for limited choices at best; educating staff, patients, and families about the critical difference between euthanasia and palliative care; and explaining to sometimes very disappointed patients that we don't have a "pill" for them to take to end their suffering.

As you can see, being a hospice social worker on the SNF team definitely utilizes those skills acquired in undergraduate and graduate school, as well as many that are not taught in the classroom setting but only learned through experience in the field.

A favorite quote by an unknown author best sums up our roles in many practice areas. "A social worker is a professional who knows where you have been, understands where you are, recognizes where you want to go, and always invites you to grow."

Think About It

1. How does your spirituality affect your practice with clients? How would you comfort someone who believes in a hereafter? How would you comfort someone who does not?

2. How do you differentiate, and attempt to merge, the wishes of the family and the desires of the patient? How do you do this when the patient can no longer speak for himself or herself and has no advanced directives? How do you manage conflict within a family when it negatively affects the patient?

3. What would you do if a family asked you not to mention "hospice" to a patient? Is it the patient's absolute right to know he or she is on hospice service? Explain why or why not.

PART 3: Nursing Homes

Chapter 18
Social Work in a Nursing Home

• • • • • • • • • • • • • • • • • • • •

by Heidi Hovis, BSW, LSW

As I drive my fifteen-minute commute to work, I'm making a mental "to do" list. I know that in several hours this list will be obsolete and the priorities on my current list will be replaced with immediate problem solving, crisis management, and a plethora of resident needs I have yet to anticipate. I pull into the local coffee house and get my mandatory skim latte. As I stand in line with the other caffeine addicts, I am still adding to my list and shifting priorities. I can pretend for a few more minutes, with my hot coffee in hand, that I have some control over the day ahead.

In the past year as a licensed gerontological social worker in a long-term care facility, I have honed many of the skills I learned in my undergrad social work classes. I have also learned many skills not listed on any index of my social work textbooks. I have learned medical terms, what dementia really does to a senior, and the joy of Google.com when looking for resources. I have learned that Elderly Waivers are additional funding sources for seniors and CADI Waivers are the same but for those youngsters under 65. I have learned that Meals on Wheels food is "bland and tasteless" (according to many who have dined on the cuisine) and that when it comes to charting, the mantra stands true, "If it's not charted, then it wasn't done." I have learned how to write behavior plans for "non-compliant residents" and what every Axis I diagnosis on the DSM looks like. I have learned that my (HIPAA-compliant) stories of work at dinner are unlike any of my friends', all of whom work in the corporate world.

Taking the last sips of my latte, I sit at my desk and open my Outlook Express e-mail. My eye catches the e-mail I'm looking for: the daily MDS schedule. I open the e-mail and scan the list. Three due today. The MDS, or Minimum Data Set, is a requirement for all the nursing home disciplines, such as nursing, dietary, occupational therapists, physical therapists, speech therapists, and recreational therapists. The results of the assessment by the different providers are used to determine the payment rates for a patient and to bill Medicare, Medicaid, and insurance companies accordingly. As my nursing home is for-profit, there is constant pressure to comply with the time requirements and to complete the necessary accompanying paperwork.

I always attempt to finish my MDS early in the day to best clear my schedule for the anticipated unexpected.

I click on my last "OK" for my final MDS and glance up at the clock. It's almost 9:00 and time for the facility's morning "stand up" meeting. The facility where I work has 220 beds, six different wings, and six nurse manager/social worker teams. These pairs are at the morning meeting as well as the executive director, the director of social services, director of nursing, two assistant directors of nursing, three MDS nurses, one Medicare nurse, the business office executive, the director of dietary, the director of maintenance, and the admission coordinator. We discuss census with admissions and discharges, clinical indicators such as patient falls, pressure ulcers, and elopements (runaways). We talk about family or resident concerns and room changes. Our census is on target at 214 and no major concerns today.

After the meeting, I have a care conference planned with a recent admission. Mrs. Edith Joup's daughter Amy is coming to meet with the interdisciplinary team of nursing, dietary, therapies, and myself to discuss her mother's care and long-term goals. I blush as I remember my first encounter with Mrs. Joup. Armed with my stack of photocopied admission forms, I met with Edith to complete her social history form, her Folstein Mini Mental form, her Geriatric Depression Scale form, and my psychosocial assessment form. My goal was to assess Edith's cognitive state and determine any interventions for her possible mood or potential behaviors. I remember Edith was slumped in her wheelchair and appeared disengaged from the commotion of the unit around her. "Edith?" I asked, "I'm your social worker, Heidi. Do you have a minute?"

I really should have asked for an hour, considering my staggering amount of paperwork, but I learned long ago, social workers couldn't focus on the minute details. Edith looked up and remained silent. I proceeded, "I'm here to get to know you a little better, so our team can best meet your needs." Silence.

As I flipped through Edith's history and physical sent by her hospital doctor, I saw the diagnosis of CVA followed by a diagnosis of dysphasia and then a diagnosis of depression. Great. I was asking verbal questions to an 84-year-old woman who couldn't speak as a result of a stroke. I sat down. I looked at Edith and explained my role. I stated that next time I visited, I would bring a picture board.

I called Edith's daughter in Chicago, Amy Yellig, who was the Power of Attorney for Edith's health care decisions. Amy shared about Edith's love of crosswords and chatting with friends at the local senior center. Amy described her mother as a "fiercely independent" woman who had been a community volunteer and Bible School teacher, although she had slowed down in past years, since Amy's father's death. After a pause in telling me about her mom's pre-stroke life, Amy asked, "So, when do you think my mom can go home?" I swallowed. This is the least favorite part of my job.

"Amy, your mom had a pretty severe stroke. As a result of the stroke, your mom has brain damage. The therapists and doctors here are working hard to improve functioning. However, the brain damage will never be fully repaired. She may never be able to go home and be as independent as she was before."

Amy was quiet. Finally, she spoke. "I just wish I could be there. I live so far away, and Mom can't talk on the phone."

I brainstormed quickly, "Perhaps you could e-mail me greetings and I could print it off and read it to Edith."

I could hear relief in Amy's voice. "Thank you. That would be great." I smiled at the two words so rarely heard by a social worker's ears.

I took an e-mail from Amy and a picture board to my next visit with Edith. She refused to even look at it. Edith refused to use a word board and would only raise a polished thumb for "yes" and down for "no." Edith was obviously frustrated she could no longer form the words that flowed so freely before the stroke. Cognitive testing was inconclusive because of the speech barrier, but it became obvious to staff who worked with Edith frequently that the majority of Edith's cognition was intact.

I remember I spent an entire afternoon searching the Web for possible resources and finally called a friend at the Courage Center, a nonprofit that served people with disabilities. My friend said if I could get a referral from Edith's doctor, Edith could see a therapist at the Courage Center and be assessed for a Dynovox. My friend explained that primarily those with ALS used the Dynovox as a communication device. A person would type into the portable machine, and an electronic voice would speak from the box the typed words. Edith would have a voice.

After consulting with Edith's daughter Amy and getting a "thumbs up" from Edith and a written order from her nurse practitioner, Edith traveled to the Courage Center for her training. It went well, but the Dynovox was not covered by Medicare and was quite expensive.

Today, I entered the care conference with Edith's daughter Amy and the rest of the interdisciplinary care team. I had met with Amy earlier in the week to discuss the option of applying for Medical Assistance when Edith's Medicare coverage had ended. I knew Edith had a meager income and was close to meeting the $3,000 asset limit to be eligible for MA, but I wasn't sure how close.

After the nurses and therapists gave updates regarding Edith's progress in the few months she had been at the facility, it was my turn.

"Edith has really been adjusting well to her stay here. She's interacting well with other residents and appears to have a great sense of humor," I stated.

At this point, Edith gave me a "thumbs up." I explained how the in-house psychologist had seen Edith and reported that Edith's depression was directly related to her loss of independence. I shared that the in-house psychologist encouraged staff and family to recognize Edith's cognitive abilities and allow her to have choices in her daily routine. I paused at this moment and then launched into Edith's visits to the Courage Center and how the Dynovox would fit the in-house psychologist's recommendations and further Edith's ability to form relationships at the facility. Then I brought up the cost. Edith's daughter looked at the other family members gathered and then at Edith. She asked her mom, "Is this what you want?"

Edith gave a spirited "thumbs up."

"Well, we do need to spend some money for the Medical Assistance eligibility," Amy said, "I think that's just about the amount."

Edith still uses a wheelchair. She still puts a polished thumb up for "yes" and down for "no." She carries her Dynovox around and types phrases like, "Hello, good lookin,'" and, "Any new e-mails?" Her outlook is positive and she attends every activity in the facility. Her electronic voice warms me more than my daily latte. Some days, after all the stress, list making, and paperwork, I can genuinely admit I enjoy being a social worker.

Think About It

1. Like many other social workers, this social worker juggles many different responsibilities. Does this surprise you? What is your reaction to this aspect of social work?

2. What are your attitudes toward people with physical and mental disabilities?

Chapter 19
The Mount

• • • • • • •

by Laurie Silvia, BSW, MSW, LCSW

I t is 8 a.m., as I walk through the front entrance of the Mount St. Francis Health Care Center. "The Mount," as it is affectionately named by staff and residents, is a private nonprofit nursing care center. Located in Woonsocket, Rhode Island, the center is an old converted brick building that is home to approximately 180 elders. My heels click briskly along the linoleum floor as the aromas and sounds of nursing home life surround me. I smell the breakfast trays of bed-bound residents and hear the first floor nursing station busily beginning morning rounds. Mrs. A. in room 101 is crying out for someone to come and help her, and her soft moans follow me down the corridor. I mentally prepare my day, as I recall the phone calls that I need to return and the two residents down on the independent unit that have come back to us from the hospital. I will need to "re-admit" them to the unit, and my mind is already rebelling at the amount of paperwork that will require.

I came to the Mount fresh out of college with my bachelor's degree in social work. I had put myself through school working in the field of human services, with the developmentally delayed population. I was eager to put my new skills to work on a managerial level. Because I had previous experience in the field, I was aware that a career in social work would never make me rich, nor would it give me status in the community. It is important to note that what the profession lacks in prestige, it makes up for in opportunities.

In gerontological social work, you are given the opportunity to be a vital part of an individual's life, in a way that most professions do not allow. The decision to work in the field of gerontological

125

social work gave me the best experience in my undergraduate career. I have yet to find such a rich and rewarding population to work with as America's elderly community.

I am almost to my office when I hear the chattering voice of Mrs. C.'s youngest daughter. Mrs. C. is one of the fortunate residents who have family that are very involved with her care. Her two daughters visit her daily and try to be present for her mealtimes. Lillie bounds out of her mother's room, nervously chewing her fingernails to the bone. She is "wondering" why Mom has not been given her strawberry Ensure with her meal. Mom is on a very stringent diet, and Ensure is crucial to keep her weight up. I readily agree with Lillie that Ensure should be on Mom's tray, and assure her that I will help her with this.

As I enter the room, I greet Mrs. C.'s roommate and move on to her section of the room. Mrs. C. does indeed have Ensure on her tray, but it is vanilla and not the strawberry that Lillie insists that her mother prefers. It is sometimes the smallest details that will trigger a family member to find the social worker. Then, there are other families that would not blink an eye at the most crucial of moments. There will be situations when you know that the presence of a son or daughter would be so appreciated by the resident that you are serving. It is important to keep in mind that we, as gerontological social workers, are seeing the end of the picture. There are so many other scenes that we have missed along the way. You will learn to piece together the resident's life story, and some residents and families will have rich histories that they will want to share with you. Others residents will come to your facility with nothing but the clothes on their backs and a vague recollection of their life.

I sit by Mrs. C.'s bed as we talk and take her hand in mine. Mrs. C. has advanced senile dementia, and she rarely talks these days. She is happy to have someone sit with her and will seek your hand to pat if you get close enough to her. I review Mrs. C's morning regime with Lillie and reassure her that I will speak to the dietician to determine why her Ensure was not the flavor that Lillie recommended. I dig through my briefcase to write a note to myself before leaving the room and Lillie goes back to feeding her mother. I walk out of the room in the hopes of getting to my office before I am stopped again. I hear Lillie talking to her mother, and her cadence is bright and cheerful. It occurs to me that perhaps it is not such a bad thing that the social worker's office is at the end of the hall. I am forced each morning to remember what I am really there for, and it is to meet the needs of the residents and their families. The paperwork will get done in time.

Upon entering my office, I see the neat pile of paperwork that I left yesterday, along with my endless list of phone calls, room visits, and requests from the nurses. This is one thing that you will learn as a gerontological social worker; it is a rare day when you will get everything done and be fresh for your next day of work. You will need to learn to prioritize the needs and make sure at the end of the day that everything that cannot wait until morning has been attended to. There is a wary lesson that we all learn in our field. In order to ensure quality care for elderly residents, the state will require you to do an inordinate amount of paperwork to chart each resident's psychosocial needs. You will find yourself writing so many care plans that you will be challenged to spend quality time with the residents that you serve. As I was new to this amount of charting and psychosocial care planning, it took me a few weeks to catch my breath. Soon, I was steadily keeping pace with each resident's written requirements and was "charting" along with my co-worker. Just two weary social workers at the end of the day, cramped in our office and plugging away at care plans.

I begin the morning by sitting at my desk to read my notes from yesterday. I review everything that needs to be done for the day and start returning my phone calls. Then I am off to my floors to meet with residents, consult with the nurses, and deal with the issues of the floor. The nursing facility consists of four floors. There are two social workers, each responsible for two floors. We will trade our floors every couple of years, as a way to avoid burnout. It also gives us the opportunity to hone our social work skills with different experiences.

Currently, I am in charge of the independent unit, located on the ground floor, and the first floor. The first floor is for residents who are not alert and oriented enough to be considered "independent." They are usually ambulatory and cognizant of their surroundings. They have senile dementia and require more care to meet their needs. This is the largest of our four floors. The independent unit is for residents who are alert and oriented to time, place, and person. Most of the residents on this floor are ambulatory, although there are a few in wheelchairs. These residents are very lively in the activity department, serve on the resident's council, and can complete their personal care regimes with minimal or no assistance. The third and fourth floors consist of the skilled nursing unit and the Alzheimer's unit.

I have no sooner gotten down the stairs to the ground floor when I am met by Mrs. B., a large, robust woman who has been a resident at the Mount for years. She is a character and is loved by all for her feistiness and overly dramatic antics.

"OH Dahling, I have been waiting for you to come down. It seems I am in TROUBLE again." She laughs boomingly, as she draws out the word trouble and expertly rounds me into her room. I laugh along with her and sit by her "throne" of a bed, as she makes herself comfortable. It seems that Mrs. B. has conveniently "forgotten" that her diabetes does not allow her to eat chocolate. She "knows" that her roommate can't eat it, either, but sometimes a woman needs a little chocolate to get through a day. She goes on to regale me with tales of nursing home life on her floor and the dramas I have yet to hear of. I listen for a while, realizing the need for a resident to have some one-on-one attention, then remind her yet again that a "little" chocolate will put her roommate into a diabetic coma and will harm her, as well. She knows the drill by now and will sheepishly grin and give me her stash of sweets.

I head toward the nursing station with a couple of chocolate bars, reminding myself that I will need to call Mrs. B.'s family again to remind them that she cannot have candy in her room. I hear Mr. M. swearing loudly down the hall and know his will be the next room to visit. Before I have a chance to ask what is happening, I am paged by the first floor. The ground floor nurses have heard my page and they are eager to keep me downstairs. They begin talking to me about Mr. M., as I get to the phone to return my call. I am now surrounded by the ground floor charge nurse and two nurse's aides, who are angrily eyeing me. I listen to a first floor nurse's concerns over a family who has come to sit with their loved one as she is dying, while nodding assurance to the nurses next to me. I hang up the phone and take a minute to hear what is going on with Mr. M.

One thing about working with the elderly—it is never dull. On any given day in the life of a gerontological social worker, you will be met with a myriad of distractions and details that need your attention. There will be the funny moments when you sit with a resident, such as Mrs. B., to hear her tales of woe, and then there will be the very serious and critical moments with residents like Mr. M. There will be times when you will need to call upon all you have learned in your college career about your profession and sound social work practice. In a nursing facility, you will be challenged, encouraged, and sometimes saddened by the experiences and stories that you will hear from your residents and their families. What is positive about gerontological social work is the opportunity you are given to make a difference in the life of an elder. You will become a page in the last chapter of their lives. The difference between a great gerontological social worker and a good one is what the residents will recall on that last page.

I begin my ascent to the first floor with some trepidation and a small amount of unease. Although I am comfortable with death and the cycle of life, it is never easy to be present in a professional capacity as a resident is dying. Death will be a part of your job and something that you will deal with regularly. There will be some clients who have all of their affairs handled. They will be admitted to your facility with a Do Not Resuscitate (DNR) order and the support of their children and family. Then you will have an elder who comes to the facility with severe senile dementia and no DNR orders. In many instances, these elders will not have family or a loved one to attest to their last wishes.

Ms. R. is one of the lucky ones. Her family and children have surrounded her bedside, and they are gently speaking with her, assuring her of their presence. I quietly enter the room, and one of her daughters spots me immediately. She is holding herself together, but I can see the strain in her eyes and posture. I am asked to join the circle and I do so. I notice out of the corner of my eye the open window, where there is a warm breeze that enters the room. Many of the older nurses have kept the custom of opening a window when a resident is dying. They explained to me that it is done so the spirit can freely leave and find its way to the afterlife. As always, I am touched by their gesture and humbled to be present during such an important part of a resident's life. There are not many areas of social work that allow you to be so intimately involved in the cycle of death.

Ms. R. did not have a lot of money in her life. She was divorced from an abusive husband and raised her children as a single mother. Her life was wrought with dysfunction, childhood abuse, and alcoholism. Yet, as she died, her children surrounded her. They remembered her sacrifices and lovingly whispered their good-byes to her as she passed from this world. How powerful it was for me to stand among this family during her death and further assist them in the details that accompany a funeral and burial. In gerontological social work, the opportunities for personal and professional growth are endless.

Eventually, I return to the ground floor. Mr. M. is a new admit and is finding it difficult to deal with mealtimes. He has recently lost his wife and will fondly recall her cooking skills and how they enjoyed their spiced foods and wine with dinner. Although he is aware of his dietary restrictions, he is adamant that "nursing home food sucks," and to prove his point, he has smeared feces on his walls. I recall his screaming earlier in the day and now understand why the nurses' aides were so upset. I enter Mr. M.'s room and he glares at me moodily. He is aware of why I am there, and before I can say a word, he shouts, "Well Laurie, the FOOD here tastes like SH**, so why not put it on the walls?" I wait him out, a silent presence in the midst of his anger and grief. He begins to talk about his wife and how much his misses her. As I listen, his breathing begins to even out. I move the discussion toward his outburst and talk about how he can communicate his anger in a more productive and "appropriate" manner. Eventually, he promises to apologize to the staff that he fought with. I bid him good night and begin walking to the door when he calls my name. He doesn't speak as our eyes meet. Slowly, he inclines his head to me in a gesture of thanks. It is the best he can do, and I accept it gratefully.

It is now the end of the day, and I am in my office with my associate, returning more phone calls and writing my care plans. We talk together of Ms. R.'s death and I begin to unwind from a long shift. We can laugh, in the privacy of our office, at some of the residents' behaviors and seriously discuss how to approach some of the more grave issues that are facing the residents and their families. There are matters regarding nurses, dieticians, activities, clients' rights, and referrals from outside agencies. I will need to prepare the paperwork for a resident who is being transferred back to an assisted living facility, following his recovery from surgery. I am also steadily paged back to the floors despite the arrival of the second shift of nurses.

As I do at the end of every day, I neatly arrange my papers on my desk. The care plans, telephone calls, and requests will all be there waiting for me in the morning. Fortunately for me, so will the elders who reside at "The Mount."

The author would like to thank Dr. James T. Decker, her advisor and former director of the MSW Program at Bridgewater State College, for forwarding the call for papers, as he believed and supported her passion for this work.

This chapter is lovingly dedicated to Laurie Silvia's late grandparents, John and Gloria Rapoza.

Think About It

1. How do you feel the American culture views the elderly? Do you believe it is different from other countries and societies?

2. As social workers, how can we respect the elders we serve and honor their life stories?

3. How can our profession assist the community in meeting the needs of the elderly?

4. How would you feel if someone told you that you were not allowed to eat the foods you loved (such as candy or spicy foods)?

Chapter 20
Life as a Nursing Home Administrator

• •

by Erica Holman, LLMSW, LNHA

I often think about the systems that have interacted, intertwined, and directed me to my current position as a nursing home administrator. My MSW training and education are clinical, and yet I work in one of the least understood positions in the medical care field, in a host environment, and in an organizational position!

I worked as a social services director in a nursing home for a few years before joining a consulting firm and becoming a licensed nursing home administrator. Dually licensed social worker-nursing home administrators are a rarity in the long-term care industry. I have been fortunate to fill a niche market of being resident centered while drawing upon human resource skills and good customer service to ensure ongoing success for the residents living in the nursing home, as well as success for the families, employees, and facility owners.

When I applied to graduate school, I thought I was finished with long-term care. I had been consulting troubled facilities for several years and I felt tired and burned out. I wanted to get my MSW and go into private practice. Fortunately, I maintained my nursing home administrator's license and continued working, albeit part-time, in long-term care throughout graduate school. Upon graduation, I realized I was in a perfect position to help revolutionize the long-term care industry! The face of the nursing home industry is changing, and I believe we are seeing the last few years of life of the "traditional" skilled nursing facility. I put my clinical training to use from an organizational viewpoint, and I have been extremely satisfied and successful with my decision and my career.

I am the administrator of a 115-bed skilled nursing facility. Running the facility entails adherence to all state and federal guidelines for resident care, health, and safety; managing 125 employees; having a working knowledge of Medicaid and Medicare regulations as an approved provider of services; working with attending physicians; oversight of resident care; maintaining good family and visitor relationships; participating on committees at the health care association and at the university; managing a multi-million dollar budget; and participating in activities that serve to empower and improve the health and well-being of the residents.

My day begins the minute I enter my office and hang up my coat. I look through the assortment of messages and notes that have arrived since I left work the day before. If there is a critical message, I address it immediately. Otherwise, I make rounds. Rounds are a great tool for "managing by walking around." I greet residents, families, and my staff and get a sense of how the day has been going. Quite often, residents will stop to tell me their concerns or give compliments to the staff. Making rounds keeps me visible not only to the residents, but for my staff. I try to give out more compliments than criticism, and when I do find a problem, I address it with the responsible person instead of waiting until it becomes serious.

After rounds, I have an 8:45 a.m. "stand up" meeting with my management team. We review the 24-hour reports, which are brief nursing notes that provide an overview for individual residents. Today as we read through the notes, we discover Mrs. Melvinson has been asking for more pain medication and has started to engage in attention-seeking behavior. We quickly strategize a behavioral approach and move through the rest of the 24-hour reports. The management team informs me of its plans for the day, gives me the heads-up on residents in critical or life-threatening status, and provides a list of the daily care conferences.

Immediately following the stand-up meeting, the clinical staff (nurse managers, physical therapist, activity, and social work staff) reviews the accidents and incidents from the previous day. We've been patting ourselves on the back, because our fall rate and accident rate has been decreasing since we've extended evening activities. This morning, we have two accidents to review. One is a minor bruise on the resident's hand, which we determine was the result of a blood draw. The second accident is more involved. Mr. Alton has had a fall, and we can't be sure of what's going on. He has a history of falls, and the therapists have worked with him extensively. As we review the clinical record and talk about him, we discover he has been refusing to attend recreational activities, because he has been napping more during the day. The labs are reviewed, his lifestyle preferences are reviewed, and we look at his Medication Administration Record. Mr. Alton has a history of back pain, and his physician recently ordered a pain medication that has a potential side effect of daytime drowsiness. We contact the physician and explain the situation. The medication is changed and the care plans are updated. Everyone on the team feels satisfied with our work on this resident.

I leave my office and go to the dining room for a cup of coffee. Housekeeping is just finishing the morning clean-up, and residents are filtering back into the dining room. I chat with several residents who tell me about the volunteers from Michigan State University. The residents love the college students' visits, and they describe the visits with a mixture of glee and semi-shock at the way the kids dress. I touch base with the housekeepers, saying "good morning" and thanking them for how great the building looks this morning.

It is quickly approaching 10:30 a.m., and I have a daily census report that is due to the corporate office. I swing by the front office, pick up the staffing and overtime reports, and return to my office to prepare my daily report. This usually takes no more than 10-15 minutes to complete. While I am preparing my report, a family member calls needing to talk about her mother.

This family member is on my weekly call list. Even though I am the administrator of the facility, I am still a clinical social worker and this has been essential in ensuring the well-being of the residents. I have a list of families that I call or touch base with weekly. These are families identified by my staff as chronic complainers or being needy. The nursing staff cannot safely manage resident care and spend 20-30 minutes on the phone with one family each day! The licensed nurses are responsible for about 25 residents, and they handle multiple phone calls daily from the lab, pharmacy, physicians' offices, and families. The chronic worriers and complainers are my domain. I've explained to my staff that there is (almost) always a kernel of truth in the complaints and that we cannot take them personally. Families feel tremendous guilt and sadness over having a family member in a nursing home. My calls and visits have drastically reduced the frequency and voracity of complaints.

I talk to the daughter as I run through the report. She wants to go away on vacation and wonders if it is a good idea. I smile. Her mother is one of the healthiest, albeit fragile, residents! We discuss the pros and cons of going out of the country for vacation, and I assure her that I will personally check on her mother daily and keep her informed via e-mail. I finish the report as we hang up, and I feel intensely grateful to have a job that allows me to help people like her.

I return the paperwork to the front office and make rounds for a second time. It's getting close to lunch time, so people are up and down the hallways. I look at the Medication Administration Records as I make rounds, flipping through to make sure all medications are marked appropriately. I knock on a couple of residents' doors and ask if I can look at their rooms and bathrooms for cleanliness. I talk to the nursing assistants about some of our behavioral interventions, and then I return to my office to pick up messages.

I check out with the front office as I leave the facility to attend a luncheon meeting at Michigan State University. I am a community participant on a committee to train gerontological social workers. This year, I am supervising four MSW students at the facility. It has been wonderful. Two are clinically oriented and are working directly with the residents, and the other two are organizationally oriented and are working on culture change and behavioral interventions.

The meeting is interesting, and we discuss various issues that routinely come up for our graduate students. Are they receiving appropriate supervision? How are they managing stress? What is their understanding of use of self and transition? We explore the dynamics of growing old in a culture that worships youth. I network at the end of the meeting and return to my facility.

As I walk into my office, my social worker and activity director follow me. They ask if I have time to discuss the Senior Companion and Volunteer Programs, as well as review our ongoing Quality Assurance plan for activities and social work. They have brought data for me to review. The activity component is going well. The volunteers have been assigned to residents and tasks that are pleasant and reinforce the reason they became volunteers. The activity program has been extended into the evening, and we have noticed a reduction in our accidents. We are not sure yet if it is a result of the extended activities. The social work component is more difficult—we are working on training the staff on individualized behavioral interventions, as well as reducing psychotropic medication dosages and use.

We haven't been able to reduce the use of psychotropic medications as much as we had originally planned. The social worker notices there is a pattern of nurses who routinely notify the physicians for increases in psychotropic medications without attempting behavioral interventions. I call the director of nursing to help problem-solve, since her staff is prominently involved in the issue.

The director of nursing points out that one of the graduate students has been working closely with the nursing staff to educate them on the purpose of behavioral interventions. We decide the best course of action is to individually address this issue. We will provide one-on-one education to the nurses most frequently requesting increases or use of the medications regarding the requirements of the regulations for use of psychotropic medications. The social worker is glad we are addressing the problem and takes the lead on planning the one-on-one sessions. She is relieved the problem seems so easily solved.

When everyone leaves my office, I check my e-mails. The Senior Vice President expects us to check our e-mail at least three times daily and acknowledge his requests on a daily basis. Today's e-mails are not too intense and it only takes about half an hour to respond. There are some marketing questions I answer and a couple of questions about our census.

The change of shift has occurred, and I go out to make rounds again. The afternoon crew is a great group of self-motivated workers. They truly embody the mission of our facility to provide care in a way that respects the residents' individual preferences and abilities while drawing on the residents' strengths. The crew is upbeat and jokes around with me during rounds. The residents are perked up by their arrival.

During afternoon rounds, the maintenance director meets me in the hall and takes me to a room that is being remodeled for one of our married couples. We have worked closely with the ombudsman, the licensing officer, and our family and resident councils to provide rooms to married couples. There is a potential dignity issue if a resident shares a bathroom with someone of the opposite sex. All the stakeholders worked together to decide how to cope with this potential dignity issue. The solution was relatively simple—lock the bathroom doors to prohibit anyone from walking in.

The daily conference call occurs at 3:00 p.m. Depending on our budget and our census, we may not be on the call. Unfortunately, this is one of our below budgeted days, and I have to make the call. The corporate marketing director discusses the push for increasing the census and gives marketing tips. Each facility on the call reports recent admissions and discharges, predicts the next week's census, and sets a weekly goal.

One of the graduate students comes into my office after the conference call. We discuss the one-on-one education for the nurses and how to approach it without seeming punitive or blaming. We spend about 50 minutes in supervision, which is a welcome change of pace after such a busy day. This intern is very motivated and enjoys all aspects of long-term care. She is preparing to graduate, and we discuss networking and how to find a job. I suggest she have her résumé ready and begin sending it out before graduation.

Finally! I am reaching the end of my day. I know that tomorrow will be very busy, because we will be orienting new employees and having a quality assurance meeting. I pull the quality assurance data that will be discussed by the interdisciplinary team and the medical director. I check my e-mails and return the last phone messages of the day. I quickly walk through the facility to make sure things are going smoothly before I head home.

I will be brutally honest. Nursing homes are vilified. No one wakes up and says, "I'd love to go to a nursing home today." The decision to enter a facility is agonizing, especially if there is limited potential for rehabilitation and return home. When people visualize a nursing home, they think of bad odors and death. Disabuse yourself of these notions! Those are not the sole determinants of a nursing home. Our society is sanitized, and we rarely experience the reality of bodily fluids, chronic illness, or the active dying process.

I love the nursing home industry. I have the pleasure of working with residents and families to improve their quality of life. I have seen family members rise to the highest level of love and empathy as they help their loved ones through the dying process. Chronic pain and management of it often forces estranged families to reach deep inside to help their mother get through the ordeal. Of course, these factors drive many families apart, but one component of life is seeing it for what it is—life isn't always perfect—my job and my staff members' job is to help residents and families come to terms with the life-changing events they are experiencing.

The long-term care field is a wonderful career choice for me, but it is my training as a social worker that allows flexibility in my career. Salaries for nursing home administrators vary across the nation, but in Michigan the average annual rate of pay is in the $75,000-$120,000 range. Nursing homes as we know them are a dying animal. Baby boomers will not tolerate small rooms, institutional food, and shared bathrooms. The future is limitless as we recreate long-term, improve care delivery, increase independence, restructure Medicaid and Medicare, and enhance in-home care services.

Think About It

1. What are some ways the administrator of a nursing home can keep in touch with the day-to-day clinical issues faced by the staff and residents?

Chapter 21

Investigative Social Work: The Nursing Home Surveyor

● ●

by Kimberly McClure Cassie, MSSW, MA

Nursing homes are one of the most highly regulated industries in the United States. The federal government has regulations in place concerning almost every aspect of resident life and facility practices. I am a nursing home surveyor. My specialty is social work, but I am part of an interdisciplinary survey team consisting of two nurses, a dietician, a pharmacist, and me. Our job is to inspect nursing homes for compliance with federal and state regulations. We typically visit every nursing home in the state for an annual inspection and more frequently if complaints about the facility reach our attention.

Today, we are finishing up an annual survey at Shady Acres Nursing Home. Our office also received complaints about the care and services provided in the facility during the 11 p.m. to 7 a.m. shift. To investigate that complaint, we started our survey three days ago at 4:00 a.m.

The facility was locked when we arrived, but through the glass door, we could see a young male nursing assistant sleeping on the sofa in the lobby. Of course, that in and of itself is proof of nothing. The staff member could be on a 10-minute break, but it was enough to arouse our suspicions. Our knock got the attention of the employee sitting behind the nurse's station and a confused resident who was standing at the nurse's station, but the sleeping staff member was undisturbed.

The employee who answered the door was the nursing supervisor in charge during the night shift. Our team leader gave our card to the nursing supervisor, explaining who we were and what we were there to do. The nursing supervisor asked us (over the gentle snores of the sleeping staff member) to wait in the lobby until she could call the administrator, but our inspection began the moment we entered the facility.

Each member of the survey team had been assigned a specific area of the nursing home to investigate. I was assigned to monitor the 100 hall. With my survey forms and pen in hand, I began my initial tour of my area.

I was first struck by an odor of urine. It seemed to be concentrated around the rooms at the end of the hall. I tapped lightly on the door to room 120, not loud enough to wake a resident up, but loud enough to alert an awake resident to my presence. Both of the gentlemen in the room were asleep, and as I crept into the room, I noticed a dried brown ring on the bottom bed sheet of one of the residents. A dried brown ring is indicative of urine that has had enough time to dry. I wondered how many other residents might be in the same condition. As I continued my initial tour, I found four residents in a similar condition at the end of the hall.

At the front of the hall, I noticed a nursing assistant putting soiled linens on a cart and the confused resident we had seen at the nursing station when we arrived. The confused resident was walking in and out of different rooms. In one room, she took a hairbrush off of a bedside table. In another room, she woke up a resident who began screaming at her to get out of the room and go back to where she belonged. The confused resident raised her arm with hairbrush in hand and spoke in a loud, defensive voice to the resident in the bed, but she didn't strike the resident. After leaving that room, the confused resident wandered into yet another room and crawled into bed with a sleeping gentleman who didn't respond to her presence.

I approached the nursing assistant, introduced myself, and began to ask her a few questions. I learned that her name was Tasha. She had been with the nursing home for two years and said that she really enjoyed her job. "I like it here," she said, "but I feel like I have to do all the work. John is supposed to work the hall with me, but this is a second job for him. He is supposed to help me with the men at the end of the hall. They are too heavy for me to lift by myself."

"Where is John?" I asked.

"I have no idea. He takes a nap in the lobby sometimes. I don't blame him. He works all the time, but if he is too tired to work, he shouldn't come in. I can't do it all by myself. Can you get us some help in here?"

I told Tasha we would do our best to make sure the residents were well taken care of. "By the way," I asked, "who is the little lady that is wandering up and down the halls?"

"Oh, that's Miss Margaret. Margaret Miller. She has Alzheimer's and she walks around a lot at night. Sometimes she goes into residents' rooms, but she don't mean no harm. She's just confused."

"What do you do when she wanders into other residents' rooms?"

"Nothing really. If the residents don't want her in their room, they will yell at her and she leaves."

"Okay, thanks," I said, as I went off to find the sleeping staff member I saw when we arrived. I thought he could be the John fellow Tasha was telling me about. I went back to the lobby, but no one was there.

I asked the nursing supervisor to introduce me to the staff assigned to work my hall. She introduced me to Tasha, but she couldn't find John. She went off to look for John and returned with him a few minutes later. I asked the nursing supervisor to stay with us for a moment. Before I could start to question John, Margaret came up to us and babbled at us incoherently before wandering into another resident's room. Neither John nor the nursing supervisor said anything to her. I noticed Margaret taking a drink of water out of a water pitcher in the resident's room before she wandered back out into the hall.

I turned my attention back to John and asked him to identify which residents he was assigned to care for. Not surprisingly, all four of the residents found in a bed of dried urine were his responsibility. Then I asked John and the nursing supervisor to accompany me into the four residents' rooms. The odor of urine was still evident as I brought the brown dried rings of urine to their attention. John was quick to tell me the rings were there when he arrived at 11 p.m. When I asked him why he had not changed the residents at that time, he didn't have an answer. The nursing supervisor said she would get the residents taken care of right away. I left to meet up with my teammates.

I was the only one of the team to find dried urine stains indicative of inadequate incontinence care, but as the survey progressed, Margaret was seen by several surveyors wandering on other halls and in other residents' rooms. We interviewed a number of residents who told us Margaret had stolen things out of their rooms. One resident told us that she was afraid of Margaret, because she would awaken in the middle of the night to find Margaret standing over her. The resident was afraid Margaret might push her out of the bed or hurt her in some way. After reviewing Margaret's medical record, I found that her wandering behavior had been addressed in the care plan. According to the care plan, staff were to redirect Margaret away from other residents' rooms when she began to wander. No one on the survey team ever saw a staff member redirect Margaret. Margaret's wandering in itself is not a problem, but when her wandering results in the theft or damage of other residents' property or when it affects the psychosocial well-being of other residents, it becomes a problem that the nursing home must address.

Our survey was very thorough. We examined the handling of resident funds with the business office, the bed hold policy with the social worker, and the activity plans with recreational staff. We observed staff interactions with residents, the cleanliness of the environment, and the handling of food in the kitchen. We found several problems during the survey. In addition to the failure of the facility to provide timely incontinent care on the 11 p.m. to 7 a.m. shift and the failure to protect other residents from Margaret's wandering intrusions, we found that food was not served to residents at the proper temperature, a female resident's breast was exposed as staff transported her to the shower room, a preventable pressure sore developed as a result of poor care, a few inaccuracies were found in resident assessments, a prescribed medication was not administered to one resident as prescribed, and some residents were not adequately groomed.

We will spend the next several days writing up a deficiency report that will be sent to the facility, and they will have about six weeks to correct these deficient practices before we return to follow up with another brief inspection. If the facility fails to correct deficient practices in a timely manner, its management faces a variety of potential repercussions, including monetary penalties, suspension of admissions, directed in-service training, or in extreme cases, facility closure. The facility will have an opportunity to dispute our findings at an informal dispute resolution meeting. Fellow surveyors who were not involved in this survey will determine whether or not our findings were validated after hearing both our side and the facility's side of the issues.

I find the life of a surveyor to be very rewarding. I ensure that vulnerable, frail elders receive proper care and services in nursing homes. If I find a deficient practice, facilities must correct the problem and put measures in place to ensure the deficient practice does not occur again. While the job can be personally rewarding, it can also be challenging. I find myself regularly in the midst of conflict. With complaint investigations, for example, if I find evidence to substantiate a complaint, the nursing home staff is angry, and if I don't, the complainant is angry. A mentor once told me that in this job, if half the people are angry with me, I'm probably doing a good job.

Surveyors are well trained for their jobs. I underwent six months of on-the-job training by my state agency before being sent to a week-long federal training workshop. Before surveyors can begin to investigate a facility without direct supervision, they must pass a two-day written examination that covers medication management, proper food handling, resident rights, nursing care, and other areas. Even though my specialty is social work, I had to demonstrate knowledge in all aspects of nursing home care to be a surveyor.

The ideal candidate for a surveyor position would be an individual who is not averse to spending time in nursing homes. You must be able to tolerate the sights, sounds, and smells that can sometimes be found in nursing homes. Social work surveyors may be asked to investigate complaints involving resident abuse or death. It takes a special person to be able to deal with the emotions that surface in this type of complaint investigation. Surveyors must have a keen eye to detail and be willing to complete a large amount of paperwork. Everything a surveyor hears, sees, and does during an inspection must be documented clearly. Three years after an investigation, you could be called to court to testify about your findings. Finally, a surveyor must be willing to travel. In my job, I travel two to three nights a week. Many surveyors have a hard time juggling the responsibilities of family and work when on the road, but for those who do, the gratitude of residents, their families, and caring staff is worthwhile.

Note: For confidentiality purposes, this chapter does not describe one specific survey experience, but a compilation of experiences I had as a nursing home surveyor.

Think About It

1. Why do you think Tasha was so forthcoming with information that validated a deficient nursing home practice?

2. What are some strategies a nursing home could employ to constructively manage the wandering behavior of some confused residents in order to protect the rights of all residents without physically restraining residents?

3. How can a surveyor balance the responsibilities of work and family when traveling two to three nights a week?

Chapter 22

A Day in the Life of an Ombudsman

• •

by Della Govea Sanchez, MSW

L et us begin by defining the word *ombudsman*. Ombudsman is a Swedish word that means a person who oversees the interests and legal affairs between the government and its people. As a state certified ombudsman, I am an advocate for residents in nursing homes and licensed assisted living facilities. In 1972, the Older Americans Act established the Ombudsman Program. State and federal laws authorize the ombudsman program, which is administered by the local Area Agency on Aging.

My day begins with a list of several nursing home and assisted living facilities to visit. My territory covers three large counties located along the Alabama Gulf Coast. As an ombudsman, one of my responsibilities is to conduct unannounced visits to nursing homes and assisted living facilities. Nursing home visits are conducted quarterly, and assisted living facilities are visited every six months. Since I have 73 facilities in my area, I spend many days driving throughout the three counties visiting nursing homes and assisted living facilities. I am fortunate to have the opportunity to meet many wonderful residents and staff members through my daily travels. My travels lead me to different parts of the state that I would not otherwise get to see.

Today, I visited a nursing home in a small rural town. During the visit, I spoke with the residents, the administrator, the director of nursing, and the social worker. We discussed concerns and upcoming activities. I spent the rest of my time conducting a mini survey of the facility. I inspected the facility for safety hazards, violations of residents' rights, and the overall quality of care for the residents. The facility I visited today is a positive reflection of nursing home living. The staff has a deep genuine affection for the residents. The neatly groomed residents were out of their rooms. They were participating in a sing-along in the activity room. The kitchen staff was busy preparing lunch. Many of the residents stayed busy by maintaining a vegetable and flower garden. On special days, the residents help prepare fresh vegetables from their garden. This facility also promotes an intergenerational program. Located next door to the facility is a child daycare center. The children from the daycare center visit often and participate in several activities with the residents. Most of the residents I spoke with are pleased with their care and the services they receive from the staff.

The next visit is not so pleasant. This is a small, specialty care, assisted living facility. The residents appear tired and bored. I introduce myself to the residents and staff. They all acknowledge my presence with little effort. The staff pretends to look busy. The staff tells me that the administrator is not available.

The residents gather in a small living room area to watch television. I notice no activities scheduled for the day. The residents speak softly and tell me that they are doing well. I check the kitchen pantry to see if there is adequate food. As I check the kitchen, the staff becomes busy preparing lunch. A few minutes later, a nurse arrives. I immediately ask the nurse for a meeting, explaining to the nurse my role as ombudsman. I report to her my concerns regarding the somber appearance of the residents. During this meeting, I explain the importance of having formal activities and nutritious lunches. The nurse states that she will discuss the concerns with the administrator. I inform the nurse that I will return to see if the changes have been implemented. I also request that the administrator call me when she returns.

This is just one day and outlining two visits offering a quick sample of my daily experiences. The other days and other visits are not always so simple. The work of an ombudsman is much more than an advocate for the nursing home and assisted living residents. The work requires the traits of a diplomat and patience of an educator. Good communication skills are paramount. The bulk of my time is spent working with families, friends, and facility staff to resolve complaints and difficulties. In many cases, there are no solutions, and listening is the only alternative.

Every day there is drama and chaos within families. Some days are very sad. Family members are never "really" prepared to see their parents live their final days in a nursing home. It is heart wrenching to see adult children crying over the death of a parent. Adult orphans have many issues, and complicated grief is inevitable.

Fighting and feuding between ex-wives and ex-husbands creates havoc for everyone involved. Families argue and disagree regarding the care of their family member, but ultimately the focus remains on the resident. What is in the best interest of the resident? It is my responsibility to see that residents' rights are observed. Residents are to be treated with respect and dignity at all times. Residents have the right to be free from all forms of abuse, including verbal, mental, physical, chemical, and financial exploitation.

As an educator, I must be able to explain Medicare and Medicaid regulations, eligibility criteria, advanced directives, and residents' rights to residents, families, and staff. As an ombudsman, I conduct in-services on several topics. The topics range from explaining Medicare Part D to helping staff perform activities of daily living, such as giving baths to combative residents. Every visit to a facility is an opportunity to share information, resources, and guidance.

One of the main duties of an ombudsman is to investigate and resolve complaints on behalf of the residents. At times, I will visit a nursing home that has problems with staffing or family complaints. It is my responsibility to mediate the problem or concern with positive results. If the situation requires additional interventions, I am obligated to report the deficiency or concerns to the State Department of Health, Division of Licensure and Certification or Department of Human Resources (elder abuse). As an ombudsman, I cannot enforce sanctions or fines. My role is to report the deficiencies to the larger state agencies.

In conclusion, I am proud to be an ombudsman. As a social worker, I am able to apply my training and skills to help elderly residents live in a safe environment. If you enjoy a daily challenge and wearing a variety of hats, then this is the job for you. Where else can you work with the "greatest generation"? Take my word— they are the greatest. I know this because I see them every day, doing their very best to live their lives to the fullest!

If you are interested in becoming a volunteer ombudsman, contact your local Area Agency on Aging.

Think About It

1. Should ombudsmen have the authority to enforce fines and sanctions to nursing home or assisted living facilities that are providing below standard care?

2. Discuss your first visit to a nursing home or assisted living facility. Did you feel comfortable? Would you enjoy living there?

3. Who should pay for nursing home care—the private sector or government?

Chapter 23
Long Term Care Ombudsman: Another Perspective
• •

by Laura N. Norman, MSSA

A long-term care ombudsman's daily experiences are never routine. Neither are the issues and concerns that residents encounter and endure in long-term care facilities, whether it is in the typical nursing home, an assisted living facility, or another form of supportive residential environment. In this chapter, I shall endeavor to provide a sampling of the kinds of daily issues and concerns with which I was confronted when working as an ombudsman and emphasize that serving older adults in this capacity constitutes a specialized calling. Many skill sets are required in effectively representing residents' rights, including the ability to perform several tasks at the same time and to negotiate resolutions. The ombudsman career track is not for everyone, but it constitutes one of the rewarding methods through which to serve older adults in our society.

Although I arrived at my office each business day with tasks and a schedule in mind, this would change soon after reviewing my voice messages and e-mail. The situations I describe below actually occurred and range in severity. No matter how complex and/or demanding the situations may have seemed, one constant remained true throughout—that I had to be prepared to contemplate quick and creative solutions to problems faced by residents, be knowledgeable about the legal rights of the residents, and be able to either work toward or advocate on behalf of solutions in a professional, but firm, manner.

I recall how one day I was completing documentation for issues with which I had been tasked earlier in the week, when I received a call from a nursing home resident I had helped in the past. I had known and assisted this resident on a variety of complaints and concerns in the previous few years. I commenced to listen to her concern. She told me that she had been outside on the nursing home's patio where a tree was shedding its leaves and found a caterpillar on the ground. She took the caterpillar back to her shared room and placed it in a jar for safekeeping. The housekeeping staff and management subsequently discovered the jar, which contained the caterpillar. They advised her that she was not allowed to keep the caterpillar. Realizing my day was already full with planned follow-up visits to other clients with complaints, I proceeded to make some suggestions regarding how to handle the situation. The caterpillar did not pose any threat to the residents of the facility, as the staff had indicated to me. Being able to keep the caterpillar seemed important to the resident. I could have taken up her concern and contacted the nursing home administrator, but considering the history with this client and current facility management, I attempted to diffuse the problem. After discussing the resident's concern for a few minutes, it was concluded that the best place for the caterpillar was, in fact, outside.

As I returned to my documentation, one of my co-workers arrived and informed me she had seen on the news that one of the nursing homes I was assigned to had experienced a fire the past evening. Having already received a voice message from a Department of Health surveyor in the building investigating and the social worker at the nursing home, I returned the calls and discussed the situation. Apparently, a male resident had barricaded himself in a corner room and set fire to the curtains. The resident had been reported to suffer from dementia. The fire was quickly extinguished, was contained to the one room, and no one was injured. The surveyor advised that there appeared to be some issues concerning the mental status of the resident just prior to the incident and concern regarding his ability to obtain a lighter, which was used to set the fire. The resident had been sent to the hospital and was currently in the psychiatric ward for an evaluation. The social worker, who I also spoke with that day, indicated the nursing home would not be accepting the resident back once he was released from the hospital. Utilizing my knowledge and experience of the discharge law in my state, I advised the social worker that without a valid discharge notice, even though the circumstances of the fire could be considered an emergency, the resident had a right to appeal and a right to a hearing before he could be denied residence at the nursing home. The social worker was convinced he did not need to issue a discharge letter, despite my continued advisement of the law. Serving as an ombudsman requires representing the wishes and decisions of the resident, as though the resident is speaking for him- or herself. This requires changing a pre-set schedule to visit a resident in a number of settings, including the hospital. I had to consequently adjust my schedule to visit him at the hospital to determine whether he desired to return to the nursing home. Knowing that it was unlikely he would be able to tell me much, I proceeded to the hospital, as I was mandated to make my own assessment regarding the client's ability to direct me and provide informed consent.

I attempted to converse with the resident. He furnished inappropriate responses to my questions. He also appeared not to be in a position to furnish consent to me to further advocate on his behalf. I had to find a legal representative for this resident who could provide me such information and consent. Once I returned to my office, my supervisor advised me that a report had just been made that a male staff member had raped a female resident in one of my assigned facilities the night before. Other staff who had walked into the resident's room witnessed the assault. The nursing home staff contacted the police. The female resident was reported to suffer from dementia. It was reported that she would not be able to recall what had occurred. The resident had been taken to the hospital, examined, and returned to the nursing home. The staff member was arrested.

Under the policies and procedures with which ombudsmen must comply, and because of the grave nature of the reported complaint, this was considered a situation involving harm. These are the most serious type and level of complaints that ombudsmen must investigate and address. Investigations of harm are required to be commenced within one day of receipt, according to my agency's policy. Knowing this facility and its management staff, I thought it would be prudent to immediately visit the resident to determine her capacity to direct me. It was important for me to quickly render observations and interview the staff at the facility regarding the incident.

Established under the Older Americans Act, the ombudsman program's purpose is to investigate and resolve complaints about long-term care facilities and service providers. Ombudsman programs, although mandated federally, vary from state to state in regard to the details of program operation, ombudsman certification and training, and the state-specific regulations associated with resident rights. Each state has a State Long Term Care Ombudsman, which typically includes support staff, but also includes local or regional ombudsman programs. Although the State Ombudsman is responsible for overseeing the operation of the state program and the regional programs, it is the regional programs that are responsible for the day-to-day investigation and resolution of complaints, general advocacy, management of a volunteer program, the monitoring and implementation of laws and rules, and consumer education about ombudsman services within the region. Regional programs are sponsored by local agencies such as nonprofits or Area Agencies on Aging and have additional agency-specific policies. With limited funding for full-time staff ombudsmen, many states rely heavily upon the usage of volunteer ombudsmen to assist with monitoring of facilities and resolving simple or uncomplicated complaints. This critical assistance is furnished under the supervision of the staff ombudsman, who may be responsible for monitoring multiple facilities. Staff and volunteer ombudsmen are typically required to undergo training to be certified. The duties of each are specific and limited based upon certification level, but all work closely together to protect resident's rights.

Since each Regional Ombudsman Program faces its own challenges and variances in the number and types of facilities located within its region, as well as the number of residents residing in those facilities, regional program staff can be very small with only a few staff or much larger with multiple staff. Regional programs in large, metropolitan areas may cover multiple counties, as in Cleveland, Ohio, where the regional program serves five counties with approximately 200 nursing homes, 100 assisted living facilities, and almost 200 adult group homes or board and care homes. Each state varies in the agencies that have jurisdictions over long-term care facilities, and although some states utilize Adult Protective Services (APS) to investigate complaints in long-term care facilities, APS does not have such jurisdiction in Ohio.

In addition to investigating complaints regarding personal care, ombudsmen also engage in representation of clients in administrative hearings. Hearings include discharge issues, such as the appeal of a facility's decision to discharge a resident. There are limited reasons for discharge, and the burden of proof is left to the provider. There are also level of care determination hearings, which include more complex understanding of state rules and regulations to ensure the client was assessed properly and given an accurate determination regarding his or her ability to live in a less restrictive environment. Representing clients in administrative hearings is very similar to preparing for a legal trial. Extensive and adequate preparation is needed to understand a resident's situation, the rules and regulations that are favorable to the resident's reason for appeal, and the provider's adherence, or lack thereof, to the procedural requirements. Ombudsmen may present their position on behalf of the client and object to the lack of procedural adherence or failure to meet substantive requirements that would result in the provider meeting the burden of proof.

As an example, an ombudsman might represent a resident in a discharge hearing when the facility claims it is unable to provide care for the resident because of his weight. In this situation, the facility has a duty to provide adequate care, including appropriate equipment to accommodate the weight of the resident. The price of the equipment, such as a wider wheelchair, a bigger bed, and more staff to assist with transferring the resident to a bed, which the provider claims is cost prohibitive, is not the issue of the resident, but rather the issue for the provider. This type of situation is not uncommon in a nursing home industry that has seen a decline in bed occupancy as a result of the increase in regulations and monitoring of facilities over the last three decades and the increase in long-term care provider choices, such as assisted living and home- and community-based care.

Long-term care facilities frequently contend that changes in regulations that would ensure better service delivery, such as rules requiring increases in staff levels to provide more individual care and monitoring of residents, are so cost prohibitive that the providers would not be able to operate. Because many providers are unable to comply with procedural requirements, I was able to win the majority of my discharge hearings. I also acquired an ability to sense when providers were less than truthful and whether policies and procedures were being followed. Whether via the telephone, or in person, I had to rely on my training, instincts, and experience as a social worker and ombudsman, in addition to my study and knowledge of state laws and regulations, to be able to quickly apply such information to make sure residents received the kind of care they deserved and that was mandated by law.

It takes a dedicated and resourceful person to become an ombudsman. It is not a job for those who cannot multi-task, handle pressure or demands, or think on their feet. Ombudsman work is "dirty," as my director used to say, and requires diligence and perseverance to ensure the rights of older adults are upheld. To be an ombudsman, you must be able to be assertive without being aggressive, stern without being rude, and professional at all times, even in the face of blatant lies, deception, anger, and aggression.

Being passive is not a characteristic of a good ombudsman. Your interaction with the residents and families you serve and the providers you confront are a challenge each and every day, continually requiring reflection and adjustment. It is imperative that your grasp and recall of laws and regulations be extensive and complete, in order to be effective in advocating for residents' rights. More important, however, is the ability to be creative in your approach to problem resolution, employing either practical suggestions or situation specific and sometimes unusual solutions, to resolve problems.

As a social worker acting as an ombudsman, I initially found some conflict between my training as a social worker and the mandates of serving as an ombudsman. Ombudsmen are required to be advocates for their clients, whether the client's request is in his or her best interest or not. I struggled, at first, with knowing that a request was not in the best interest of my client but honoring my client's right to choose. The *NASW Code of Ethics* guides social workers to "respect and promote the right of clients to self-determination," with some limits when there is a risk to self or others. The ombudsman, however, must advocate for the client's wishes, even if the decision could be perceived as harmful to the client. As I became more familiar with my role as an advocate, I realized my job was to ensure that, regardless of the general consensus, my clients had a right to make poor choices, as long as they were fully informed of their decisions and the consequences that could result. An example I encountered early in my ombudsman career was a diabetic older adult's choice not to follow the doctor prescribed restricted diet and eat the chocolate cake she so loved and enjoyed. Mrs. R knew what the cake would do to her blood sugar levels, but it was her choice to make, and I advocated to the nursing home staff that her choice be honored.

The skills I developed as an ombudsman are beneficial in other settings. Such skills include active listening, validation, honesty, silence as a tool, and observation. Pitfalls include interrogation, blaming, over-asking of the question "why," and forgetting what the client really wants. Ombudsman practice is also difficult to measure, since the resolution of a problem is not only a reflection of your work, but also the responsiveness of the provider. Ombudsmen are not frequently recognized at the level they should be for the service they provide, or the daily dedication required to come back to deal with difficult situations arising in long-term care facilities, interpersonal family conflicts, a lack of social supports for residents, and the lack of appropriate medical care and response continuing to plague long-term care service delivery systems. However, the job includes celebration and praise by the residents and families you help. The celebration and thanks, and the satisfaction of serving those who cannot represent themselves against often careless institutions, make the long, stressful hours worthwhile. Despite the occupational stressors and physical demands associated with the position, ombudsmen serve a vital role in ensuring that residents' rights are upheld.

As one of my colleagues stated, "We speak for others when their voice has been devalued." Older adults in long-term care settings are perfect examples of a population group whose voice is frequently devalued and who need assistance from an outside advocate.

Think About It

1. How do social workers incorporate their values and skills into ombudsman practice?

2. What role does the nursing home lobby play in regulation formulation and changes?

3. What are the various ways in which a long-term care ombudsman can advocate on behalf of residents?

4. What are some ethical issues an ombudsman might face?

5. How would you react if you had a client who wanted to make choices that you felt would not be in his or her best interest? Compare and contrast the role of the ombudsman with the client who wanted to eat chocolate cake with that of the social worker in Chapter 19 in a similar situation.

PART 4:
Special
Populations

Chapter 24
Working with Geriatric Inpatients in Acute Mental Health

• •

by Thomas Horn, BA (Hons), MSW, RSW

W
ith close to an hour of highway driving (sometimes longer when the weather is poor or there is construction) from my home to the hospital where I work in a mid-sized city in the province of Ontario, my goal is to arrive on my unit sometime around 8:30 a.m. and work until 4:30 p.m., with a schedule of Monday to Friday shifts. Although I spend quite a bit of time on the road and I put a lot of mileage on my car, I still consider the benefits in terms of job security, pension, and salary well worth the drive. Hospitals in Ontario generally pay their social workers better than most other employers. I am required by the Department of Social Work to work 37.5 hours per week, but I can flex it as needed professionally and personally. The psychiatric unit to which I am assigned expects me to be on time for team meetings twice per week, where we discuss the status and plans for the patients on the two teams for which I am responsible.

I am one of two social workers on my 30-bed acute (read fast-paced) inpatient unit and work closely with two psychiatrists who each have a caseload of approximately eight patients. Sometimes they have medical students or residents working with them, as this is a teaching hospital. Social workers on acute inpatient units, whether medical or psychiatric, are responsible for the smooth discharge of the patients and, therefore, I deal with all issues related to housing, income support, medical insurance, family issues, referrals for psychiatric follow-up and outpatient counselling, transfers, collaboration with outside agencies (including child protective services, known in Ontario as the Children's Aid Society), and basically any issue that is not medical in nature but affects a patient. I have even facilitated the transfer of a pet dog and cat for a patient with acute psychosis from an animal control shelter (which would have put the animal to death if not retrieved within 10 days) to a kennel that was willing to accept a dog identified as a pit bull.

Patients usually enter an acute mental health unit for assessment and stabilization of a serious psychiatric condition, which, according to our "benchmark," should be no more than two weeks. By then, they should ideally be discharged to outpatient psychiatric services or referred to another psychiatric unit with the resources and mission statement for longer term inpatient treatment. On any given day, approximately 20% of our beds are filled with men and women age 65 or older. In spite of the acute nature of my unit, I have a geriatric patient who may be with us for years. "Kaye" will never again be eligible for community care or housing, in large part because of the capacity assessment that I was required to make. She has joined the long wait list for Long Term Care (LTC).

Let's go back in time to the point of my first contact with 70-year-old Kaye. Nine months ago, a dishevelled lady who looked to be in her eighties shuffled unannounced into the office I share with the other social worker on my unit and sat silently in the guest chair closest to me. She wore a hospital gown, sat in a slouched manner, and appeared disoriented. There was a long string of thick drool coming out of her mouth all the way to her chest. I did not recognize her, but it was a Monday morning, and it is common for us to get new patients over the weekend. This is not generally how we meet, however.

"Hi there. May I help you?" I asked. No response and no sign that she even recognized I was talking to her.

"Are you looking for someone?" Still nothing.

I looked over at my colleague, and we both shrugged. She did not know her, either. My co-worker volunteered to escort her back to the nursing station to find her primary nurse for the shift. It turned out that she had been assigned to one of my teams.

I went on with my day of attending team meetings, sitting in on initial psychiatric assessments, meeting with patients to clarify discharge plans, reading charts of new patients and writing social work assessments, and completing referral forms for community follow-up. I could not get my mind off Kaye, however, and even after reading her chart, I had to wonder how this fairly young 70-year-old got to this point. She has a diagnosis of schizophrenia, but that could not explain her level of stupor. She was transported by ambulance to the ER when a passer-by found her sleeping, dehydrated, on someone's front yard on a hot day (90° F). Apparently, she frequently wandered away from her special care home that provides meals, staff supervision 24/7, and some support around activities of daily living (ADLs), such as bathing and dressing, if required. While on the unit, she made it clear that she did not like her former home ("they are evil") and that she wanted to live independently in her own apartment, as she had only a year or two prior to her admission.

Over the next few days, it became apparent that this lady had some significant cognitive and psychiatric problems. Her inpatient psychiatrist determined that Kaye could not make her own treatment decisions and, therefore, according to provincial legislation, a substitute decision maker had to be appointed. Ideally, a marital partner, an offspring, a parent, or another family member would step up and take on the role. Kaye had never been married, had no children, and had burned all the bridges to her siblings, because she had been quite emotionally and verbally abusive to them during her lifetime of illness with paranoid schizophrenia.

Her psychiatrist was forced to obtain consent from a public guardian appointed by the provincial government to treat Kaye with necessary and recommended medication. The psychiatrist also determined that Kaye was incapable of making financial decisions and, therefore, a public trustee was appointed to manage her money. She had the opportunity to appeal the decision regarding her involuntary stay, her incapacity to make treatment decisions, and her financial incapacity. Even with obligatory rights advice from a third party, she did not appeal. It did not take long for the psychiatrist to diagnose Kaye with progressive dementia. She had no insight into her struggles, and there was no treatment possible that would return her to her previous level of functioning. She once was a school bus driver. I saw a bus pass photo of hers from only a few years ago, and it showed a lively woman in her 60s with a sparkle in her eye. We rarely see that sparkle now.

Kaye has problems with incontinence during night time hours, and it falls on me to make sure that she has a regular supply of pull-ups available through the outpatient pharmacy. The hospital provides adult diapers only, which are not very dignified for someone who can toilet herself. With my hospital ID, I receive an employee discount when buying the pull-ups, but anytime the clerk realizes the purchase is for a patient, the price goes up to its regular rate. Kaye is on a fixed income, and her public trustee holds the majority of her pension income, but sends monthly checks to a hospital account set up in her name for personal needs. Sometimes Kaye can be pretty functional (cooperative, responsive to others, able to express thoughts with more than three words, able to dress herself without verbal cues or hand-over-hand help by her nurse). On these "good days," when I have time, I take Kaye off the unit and down to the main floor of the hospital, which has a pharmacy, convenience store, coffee shop, lounge, chapel, and information desk/cashier. At the cashier, she is able to withdraw some of her money from an account kept for her. When Kaye is unwell, however, I have to withdraw money from this account on her behalf to make purchases for her. The change gets locked up in the nursing station. She frequently asks me where her money is and why she cannot have it. Sometimes she accuses me of robbing her of her money. Every couple of weeks, I have to explain yet again how she would undoubtedly lose a $20 bill if I gave it to her. There is nothing that can be purchased on the unit, anyway. On a few occasions, I did give her $1-$3 from her account so she could carry it around and perhaps feel some empowerment, but within a couple of hours she would complain that it was somehow stolen (or more likely put down or dropped by her and then picked up by someone else).

Kaye can be unpredictable, and even on what would seem to be a good day, she can be stubborn and refuse to cooperate. There appears to be an attention-seeking quality to her behavior, like the time she walked into my office and decided to lie down on my floor, and then smiled when we tried to encourage her back to her bed. During one of our trips downstairs, Kaye wanted to stay in the chapel and refused to return to the unit. I tried every trick in my bag for de-escalating, compromising, and managing her uncooperative behavior, but was forced to call up to my unit for nursing support. Two nurses came down with a wheelchair, and even then, Kaye required some physical persuasion by them (gentle help into and later, back into the chair) in order to return to the unit.

At my hospital, social workers have been assigned the task of conducting capacity assessments when it is questionable whether or not a patient is able to appreciate the need for placement in a nursing home/LTC facility. Some event or finding that puts into question a person's ability to make safe decisions must exist as a trigger. We are all allowed to make bad decisions, but most of us understand the necessary information required to make an informed decision, and we are able to foresee and weigh the consequences of our actions. A person who might be found incapable of making shelter decisions probably lacks an understanding of the requirements of independent living in regard to self care and safety of self and others, but also lacks the capacity to realize and put in place appropriate strategies and interventions to manage a problem.

Kaye's psychiatrist determined that she was incapable of making her own treatment or financial decisions, and that even with pharmacological interventions and hospital stabilization, there was only moderate improvement in Kaye's condition, and that there was evidence of a degenerative dementia. Thus, I had a "trigger," which is required to set in motion the process to conduct a capacity assessment for shelter decisions. This is a huge responsibility and one that I was forced to make by my role. Kaye is clearly not well and there is no possibility that she will suddenly develop insight and skills for taking care of herself. I am supposed to remain neutral and as objective as possible as I conduct the assessment. Even with a significant mental illness or cognitive limitation, it is possible that one could improve enough to gain some insight and learn the skills necessary for independent living. If Kaye is allowed to decide on her own where she lives, though, she may put herself at risk by walking into traffic, not accessing medical help in case of emergency, not taking life-saving medication as prescribed, or not eating or sleeping as her body requires. She may also inadvertently put others in danger by not being safe around flames, heat, and electricity, and then not respond appropriately to a fire or other emergency. Would I feel safe with her as a next door neighbor if she decides it is chilly and turns all the stovetop burners on high and keeps open her heated stove to warm up?

During the assessment, I had many guideline questions to ask, but had specific ones I made up, such as, "While living by yourself at home, what would you do if you had severe pains in your chest and arm?" Kaye's response was, "I never get chest pains." I then asked what she would do in the event of a grease fire on her stovetop. She chuckled and replied that it would never happen, but if it did, she would merely blow out the flames with her mouth. The assessment revealed that she did not seem to understand the responsibilities of living on her own and had no appreciation for the consequences of decisions she might make. I found her incapable of making shelter decisions and, therefore, stripped her of a fundamental right that we all share. I had to keep telling myself that the decision was in her best interest and the interest of the public.

Unfortunately, given the lack of LTC beds, even within a 200-mile radius, acute medical and psychiatric inpatients in my community are required to stay where they are, unless a safe alternative can be found with family and community supports, where they can wait for a placement. Since Kaye has no family willing to speak for her, the public guardian decided on which LTC waitlists she was placed, with consideration for what she thought Kaye would like. It is a sad truth that the only way to move up the waitlist of a nursing home is for a resident to die. Kaye could be with us for two years or more, trapped on a unit meant for acute stays of no more than two weeks. Senior management at the hospital and government officials are fully aware of the financial and practical problems of blocking acute beds and are actively seeking a solution.

I have conversations with Kaye every day and try to meet her needs as I can, including helping her find her room when she gets lost, looking for her missing slippers that someone "stole" (they are usually in her room), and reassuring her that her money is safe and that someday she will be moved to a comfortable home.

These are some of the numerous duties, activities, and experiences that I have on a daily basis while caring for geriatric patients in acute mental health.

Think About It

1. You decide to take Kaye out for a walk, off the hospital grounds. She starts to walk quickly toward an intersection and does not listen to you. Kaye is very sturdy and equally stubborn. You have no two-way radio or cell phone, no other hospital staff can be seen, and you have left your hospital ID in your office. What would you do? What could happen?

2. If Kaye had been an involuntary patient and requested a Review Board hearing that subsequently ruled that there was no valid reason to keep her in the hospital against her will, she would have been free to discharge herself against medical advice. Since the social worker found her incapable of making her own shelter decisions, which she did not appeal, what would be the actual and theoretical implications of her decision to leave?

3. What if you were in the middle of doing the capacity assessment for shelter decisions and Kaye suddenly said she no longer wanted to live independently and was willing to accept placement in a retirement home (but not a nursing home with locked doors). Would you end the assessment without a finding, end the assessment with a finding of capacity because she is sounding more reasonable, or complete the assessment and still find her incapable, as the writer did? Why and why not?

Chapter 25
Stella's Orchestra: Social Work in Rural Geriatric Mental Health

• •

by Mary Pat Sullivan, Ph.D., BSW, MSW

I feel like the conductor of an orchestra and I am slowly losing my violin section. And I am invisible here [in hospital].

Stella would never know how powerful those few whispered words were that day. Suddenly, she spoke to me on behalf of all the older patients on my new referrals list handed to me that Monday morning—on behalf of all those people who, instead of being called by name, were usually described by nursing staff as the "placement problem in bed 4-62" or "the hospital is not set up for dealing with this kind of patient (87-year-old man with Alzheimer's disease and severe agitation) and the family is completely uncooperative refusing to take him home." Intellectually, I understood the concept of ageism. I also understood, however, that as we age the issue of needing care, whether temporarily or on an ongoing basis, provokes a need for change in the life of the older person and his or her family, and the community as a whole.

Many social workers have met a "Stella." How many embrace these individual encounters as opportunities for change and development? The obstacles are great and the challenges overwhelming at times. Even so, these are opportunities that, if overlooked, would permit the lives of vulnerable citizens to go unnoticed—in Stella's words, to be invisible. Despite positive developments in health and social care, face-to-face practice encounters highlight that, for some, the struggle for a meaningful life in advanced age is still a reality. For social workers around the globe, aging in an ageist society means an opportunity remains on our doorstep.

So here I was practicing hospital social work. Here I was in a small, culturally diverse community in northeastern Ontario, where health resources were stretched owing to a larger catchment area, and a significant portion of the population dispersed in rural and remote areas. Here I was practicing social work in a community where the responsibility for the care of older people, particularly those with mental health problems, lay primarily with family. And here I was with a demanding opportunity to engage in practice that would challenge my understandings of social work, of interprofessional/interagency working, of community, of policy and service development, of diversity, and of aging.

The committee I established that oversaw the eventual development of a successful proposal to establish an interdisciplinary outreach geriatric mental health team represented various sectors of the community. Despite hospital management's reluctance to support the endeavor in favor of other priorities such as the expansion of emergency services, and despite the mental health community backing the development of an eating disorders program, the arrival of a team of professionals dedicated to working with older people was indeed a celebration. It was a celebration because it marked the first of many celebrations dedicated to the contributions of older people and their family carers, and it represented the beginning for strategically planning new ways of delivering mental health care.

Two years after I met Stella, my new team with its very conservative budget enthusiastically developed its vision statement, and set out to reach its service targets: assessment and care management, consultation and education to the long-term care and acute care sectors, shared care with the primary care sector, and education and development in the outlying areas of the vast region. Team members also decided to strategically involve themselves in other community initiatives to emphasize cross sector development; for example, I became Chair of the regional Alzheimer's Society and was a member of the regional mental health planning committee. Provincially, I became part of a knowledge exchange to share best practice in geriatric mental health, and I worked with the Ministry of Health on newer policy directives in relation to rural and remote service delivery issues.

After a snowstorm cleared one Tuesday morning, I drove for about 60 kilometers until I finally reached the farm "with the two red barns." The snow was sparkling in the mid-morning sun as I approached the house—a huge German Shepherd barking at the far corner of the garden. Jack, 73 years old, was caring for his wife, who was chronically ill and expected to die before spring. A visiting nursing team had referred Jack for assessment, as he appeared to be depressed and was becoming aggressive with his wife. Jack spoke broken English, having immigrated from Poland many years ago. His wife, who was confined to a wheelchair, spoke little English at all. Jack and I spent a couple of hours talking, even though I was late for another visit. He told me of his isolation and loneliness, his fear of losing his wife, his sorrow that she was sometimes physically uncomfortable despite his constant efforts, and his guilt that he could have been a better husband.

With Jack's permission, I contacted his family physician the following morning to let him know of my involvement, and I asked a Polish-speaking social work colleague to accompany me on a second visit. With the support of my Polish colleague, Jack and his wife were eventually reconnected with the Polish church community, who agreed to make outreach visits, provide respite for Jack so he could attend social functions, and ensure his wife had regular visits from the priest. I maintained periodic telephone contact, and Jack called me ten months later to tell me his wife had died. He also told me that, over time, the Polish community had rallied together and was extremely supportive. They had even helped him find a young woman from a neighboring farm who sat with his wife when he needed rest.

Jack and his wife helped me recognize the value of natural networks helping older people to cope with the multiple losses that can be so common in old age. As I reflected on my practice further, I recognized the amount of time I had spent working with the formal care sectors to respond to the needs of an aging population. I had sometimes overlooked opportunities to promote and support the contributions of family, friends, and community.

Over time, the team was able to more formally engage with local community groups (e.g., church-based, veterans, culturally affiliated organizations, and senior centers) to raise awareness regarding mental health in later life. A partnership with an older people's nursing team from the regional public health office led to a strategy to address social isolation among older people in light of their emphasis on health promotion.

Working with the public health nurses in early spring also resulted in the formation of a committee that organized community-wide and hospital-based activities in June to celebrate the lives of older people—June was designated *Seniors' Month* by the province. An excerpt from the internal hospital newsletter read:

> *This celebration should not involve more running around, doing more, or trying to be more efficient, but rather allowing ourselves as professional caregivers to express our own personhood in order to*

celebrate the meaning of the older person to us all...let us partner in an interdisciplinary and interdepartmental way to celebrate the meaning of the lives of older people....

The general premise was to transform the older patient from being a "problem." The impact throughout my hospital was quite extraordinary. Almost daily, I received word that nursing, dietary, ER, surgical, or even maintenance staff were celebrating in their own ways. Social workers worked with a group of local artists who, after interviewing an older patient, depicted the patient's story in a painting. The paintings hang in the hospital today.

It was during Seniors' Month, in my mind Stella's Month, that Maria was referred to the team. Her letter carrier contacted us as he had growing concerns about her weight loss, memory difficulties, and her house, which desperately needed repair. Referrals from members of the community were not uncommon. He and his wife were doing Maria's grocery shopping, and despite several attempts, she was refusing to arrange builders to repair a damaged roof. He was also concerned because his daily delivery often contained letters from electric and water companies marked "final notice." The next day I visited with the nurse on my team.

Maria was a 79-year-old widow with no children. Her small home had a porch with a lone wicker chair, and the front steps were falling apart. It was isolated in a quiet wooded area—row upon row of pine trees lined up like little soldiers. The closest neighbor was about a kilometer away. She lived with her three dogs and interacted with them like they were her children. Although very pleasant, Maria was very suspicious of her visitors that day.

After almost two weeks of daily visits, sometimes with the letter carrier, Maria agreed to accept my offers of help. She did, however, continually express her fear of having to leave her home and abandon her dogs. She was also concerned that any offers of help were indirect attempts to place her in care. I was able to arrange a carpenter to temporarily repair Maria's roof. Unfortunately, the house had other extensive structural problems, which meant she could eventually be forced to leave. Maria did not have a family doctor (they come and go in rural communities), so I arranged for her to visit one nearby. The doctor reported Maria to be in relatively good physical health, but cognitive impairment was also noted. The urban-based geriatric psychiatrist who sometimes worked with the team agreed to visit Maria to further assess her mental health and her capacity to make decisions. The psychiatrist diagnosed Maria with dementia and felt that, although she was still capable of making decisions regarding her social situation, she needed assistance with her financial matters. My referral to the public guardian resulted in Maria's outstanding bills and other pension issues being organized.

Maria was monitored by the outreach nurse and me. The goal at the time was to encourage Maria to move to a seniors' apartment complex in a neighboring community and occupy a ground level unit, in order to keep her dogs. Maria finally agreed to relocate, and the following summer was settled into her new small apartment. The move was not kind to Maria, and despite having her beloved dogs with her, she was unable to fully adjust to the new surroundings. I introduced a homemaker, but Maria often refused her entry. Neighbors were welcoming, but Maria was reluctant to accept their offers of support.

Maria suddenly fell ill that autumn and was admitted to the hospital. As the likelihood of discharge home became more concerning, recommendations for nursing home care were debated among those professionals involved in her care. Was she capable of making the decision to remain at home? What did "home" mean to Maria? What did "home" mean to the people who worked with her? What was an acceptable level of living at risk? Maria's health continued to deteriorate, but before she died, I was able to arrange for one of her dogs to visit her.

"You want me to permit a dog to visit the ward?" questioned the head nurse with a look of disbelief.

"Yes," I responded, "But it will be during visiting hours, of course." Maria knew her dog instantly. Her smile that day left an impression on many of the inpatient staff, and I thought to myself, "Ahh, now they have met a Stella, too." Although I had managed to ensure her dogs were cared for while she was in the hospital, following Maria's death her dogs were sent to a kennel, where they were eventually destroyed.

It was a very emotional ending for those who had worked with Maria. I had eventually discovered Maria was from London, England and had been a war bride—promised a paradise by her young lover only to end up in a rural mining community. Leaving her family, she never had a family of her own, and her young lover eventually became an angry alcoholic.

A gentle winter had set in, and two days before Christmas, I received a call from the ER. Sam, age 79, had come to the hospital with a chest infection and had gone home following treatment. Sam was a bachelor who lived alone with almost crippling arthritis. "What is your immediate concern?" I asked the referring physician.

"Well," he said. "Our only concern is that Sam is alone. The ER staff would like to put a Christmas parcel together for him, and we just wanted to know if you could deliver it when you're out on your home visits."

"Yes, sure," I said with a smile, and I ran out to my car to go meet my next client at the local nursing home.

Think About It

1. Consider social work's core values in relation to practice with older people who have mental health problems, in relation to practice in rural settings, and in relation to diverse communities. How do social workers blend these values with relevant social work knowledge and best practice?

2. What are some of the social work practice and personal challenges of working with vulnerable older people in rural communities?

3. How can social workers respond to the issue of ageism in their daily practice?

4. How do we engage older people with mental health problems in service development and evaluation?

Chapter 26
Social Work at the Alzheimer's Association
• • • • • • • • • • • • • • • • • • • •

by C. Michelle Niedens, BSW, MSW, LSCSW, LCSW

I reckon the ingredients are a little frustration, the sorting of changing priorities, lots of listening, a good measure of clarifying and reducing both problems and emotions into manageable and honest pieces, the offering of information, a bit of sadness, some laughter mixed in, a few hugs, and a constant reorientation to meaning. That, in a nutshell, is my day.

I came to the Alzheimer's Association to be the Education and Program Director much as I have come to other roles throughout my social work career—in a moment of awakening. The possibilities of jobs within the social work field are so broad, the right place almost has to find you. I have come to know that the only viable reaction for me is to be open to the possibilities as they emerge. That's what has worked for me. If someone had told me while I was in college that I would be spending a long career working with older adults, I would have dismissed them as quickly as chocolate disappears around my beloved sister. But I have. And if someone told me there would be a day when I would choose to work with individuals with Alzheimer's disease and their families, well, let's just say I would have been wondering how extensive a role delusions might have played in their life. But that has been my choice. And how lucky I have been that I didn't goof it all up and run from choices I had not contemplated.

My responsibilities at the Alzheimer's Association, Heart of America Chapter, include elements of individual work, group work, community work, administrative duties, and advocacy. On any given typical day, I perform various pieces of all of those practice arenas. There are times when some, or perhaps even just one, of those arenas might take the main stage. One of the many gifts of working at the Alzheimer's Association, as is the situation in a number of social work roles, is that the duties are broad and many. The job brings with it a need for creativity and ability to include ideas and planning into the process of reaching people and their families with the disease. I have much freedom to put ideas in place, as long as funding can be secured. I also support my colleagues by encouraging that same freedom, all within the parameters of the goals we have agreed upon to be the most important for the year. In an environment that functions with such individual staff autonomy, it is important that the agreed upon goals direct our efforts. I review the goals monthly and document month-to-month status, so all the staff in the program and education department can see where we are in our pursuit of accomplishing our desired outcome for the year. Those goals are important even when I look at my day-to-day schedule, as I refuse to get too much off track and diminish the value of our team effort. In some ways, it is very much like a basketball team, all having to work together if the game is to be won. And like the basketball team, each knows the strengths of the other players and utilizes those strengths for the good of the team—in our case, for the good of those we serve.

A primary and constant goal for us is to be there for individuals with questions, issues, and concerns about the illness. A day usually begins with phone calls, either getting some returned or having new ones coming in, often from family members of loved ones with the disease. Their questions might be around a new diagnosis, expressing grief issues, or resource questions about nursing home options, elder law, or support groups. Embedded in all those questions is a set of feelings that, except in highly unusual instances, gets exposed and discussed. That is important, as we want those individuals calling to understand that coping is possible, that there can be and will be brighter moments, and that life and relationship is not over. Things change, yes, but losing sight of connections with individuals and missing a deeper understanding of love and caring is far worse than any disease process, including Alzheimer's disease. So I have these conversations with people about pain, about love, and about capturing moments. Sometimes, advocacy is what is needed. Sometimes they have doctors who dismiss their concerns. Sometimes we recognize signs and symptoms of additional processes or a co-existing process like depression that calls for both education and encouragement to seek additional assessments. Sometimes they are facing discriminatory practices, such as illegal discharge and transfer from long-term care facilities, and they need information about rights and next steps. Sometimes the calls are from people we have seen in consultation or in support groups, or those who were in audiences where we gave a talk about Alzheimer's disease. Sometimes they have found us through the Internet, the phone book, or a referral by a physician. There are no external boundaries governing how long we stay involved with a family. It is completely based on the needs. Therefore, we may be involved in a case for years, as the disease progresses and questions and concerns change.

A day, likely, includes listening and sharing information with people who come in to the office with many of the same concerns that we receive from individuals using the helpline. It is common to see families in the office who have different perspectives of the needs of the person with Alzheimer's disease, and mediation becomes a part of those conversations, supporting an understanding of the feelings and issues underlying the differences and the absence of perfect choices in many of the situations faced.

One of my favorite parts of my job is facilitating a support group for individuals in the early stages of the disease. They talk about their losses with honesty, but talk about how they are living and seeing life with this disease. One member described his being part of the group as being in a place where he feels whole. Powerful description. Those folks have to be some of the most courageous, positive people I know. Each has transformed from the devastation of the diagnosis to advocates for the cause. An important part of my role in that group is to recognize the many ways they contribute to others and the larger world. Despite conversations, I don't think they really know the profound impact they have on me. When one faces such a life changing disease, it is impossible for the world to look the same. It becomes impossible, for those who successfully continue their lives, to hold on to the silly stuff that so often clouds our lives like fog in the low country, impairing our view to see what is important and beautiful.

Most days, writing is a part. I write grants, reports for current funders, monthly department reports, articles for newspapers/ newsletters, curricula for educational talks, documents necessary for various projects and partnerships, and the list goes on. There are days when writing is a major part of my day, primarily around the end of quarter and end of year. I may even work from home on those writing intensive days, so that I maintain focus and complete the project in a more timely fashion. One thing about working in such a close knit, gregarious office is that the day can come with many interruptions. While the door to my office is always open, and I believe in being available, there are times when that might translate into long hours completing necessary reports. A day at home to complete the necessary writing when on deadline seems to be an efficient way of dealing with those challenges.

There seems to be an increasing demand for various statistics. That, perhaps, is my most significant challenge. At times, it seems that numbers are constantly being figured and refigured to meet the needs and desires of a variety of partners. This can be required without a clear purpose as to how the information translates into client care. That, quite honestly, drives me a bit crazy. On days highly concentrated with reports involving statistics, I make sure I'm wearing comfortable clothes, have plenty of chai tea available, play Enya, and have a candle burning. My colleagues often recognize the signs and know they may hear gruff conversations emerging from my office as I talk to myself and all the non-specific participants that are moving us toward an increasingly complicated world.

I spend a piece of most days on the education front. That might take the form of facilitating a training session at a nursing home on the care of individuals with Alzheimer's disease. It might take the form of talking with community groups about Alzheimer's disease, or it might involve leading a class that we have initiated on some aspect of the disease. We facilitate family classes, classes for professional caregivers, and classes for individuals in the early stages of the disease. Recalling our goals, a priority is to reach out to individuals in the early stages and support not only early diagnosis, but also participation in interventions that may contribute to coping with this disease in a way that empowers rather than a private, reactive, despairing manner. Advocacy is often mistakenly thought of as being confined to the legislative process. Advocacy is far more than that, and it certainly includes education. Most talks I give include a discussion of recognizing early symptoms and the importance of addressing them. Alzheimer's, I have been told, is not the most exciting of topics. Therefore, part of providing education is figuring out how to share important information in a way that is understandable, usable, and captures the attention of the audience. At times, I have wished I hadn't given up tap dancing.

Intermixed in all of that, a day for me would also include arranging speakers for specific talks (such as coordinating individuals in the early stages of the disease to talk to audiences in classrooms, attorneys speaking on legal issues, and pharmacists speaking on medications), coordinating and facilitating advisory groups, talking to legislative members, sharing information about public policy issues with our public policy e-mail/phone tree, working on new programs, attending to budget monitoring, supporting staff in our regional offices, and keeping abreast of the needs and successes of all the department staff. My job, like the run-on nature of the above sentence, can be an intimidating list of responsibilities.

But what I see is lots of diversity and interesting experiences. I am not hard on myself. I know my limitations, and I am committed to doing the best I can. That's enough for me. I figure I subscribe to E. B. White's philosophy conveyed is his famed quote, "I get up every morning determined to both change the world and have one hell of a good time. Sometimes this makes planning my day difficult." If we are practicing strength-based social work, we must be able to translate that to our own lives as well.

While this narrative does not convey a full picture of the wonderful work I get to be involved in at the Alzheimer's Association, Heart of America Chapter, it does extend a picture of the most typical day. Yes, I appreciate the opportunity to be there every day. Yes, I enjoy working with elders. Yes, I feel we are making a difference. Yes, there is more to do.

No, I won't ever give up.

Think About It

1. Have you known anyone who had Alzheimer's Disease? What were they like before they had the disease? What were they like after?

2. Which social work skills do you think would be most important for the type of work described in this chapter?

Chapter 27
Parkinson's Disease and Social Work Practice

• •

by Christina L. Erickson, Ph.D., MSW, LISW

B
ob and Wendy were the first visitors to the clinic that Monday morning. Wendy was 59 years old, newly diagnosed, and deciding whether she should tell her family, friends, and employer that she has Parkinson's disease. Bob, her husband of the past four years, always joined her on these clinic visits. They were friendly and pleasant people and drove nearly two hours to get to our specialty clinic. Bob and Wendy chatted with other patients in the private waiting room as they drank coffee and read some of our literature.

I am the coordinator of a National Parkinson Foundation Center of Excellence at the University of Illinois at Chicago. Bob and Wendy have been coming to our clinic for the past five months. In that time, I have gotten to know them well: about their work, the ages of their grandchildren, and the symptoms of unexplainable falling and difficulty getting out of bed in the morning that brought them to our clinic.

Once we were in the privacy of a clinic room, I probed Wendy about her perceptions of telling others about her Parkinson's. It's not easy to tell someone about your own chronic illness, and Wendy felt nervous. I could empathize. I had relatives with Parkinson's and had dealt with my own health issues. I could understand her desire for personal privacy while simultaneously needing support from loved ones. Wendy decided she would tell a few close friends and two of her neighbors. She wasn't ready to tell her colleagues at work. Since her Parkinson's symptoms were mild and very manageable, she didn't have to tell anyone before she was ready. I supported her decision, and Bob affirmed that this was a good plan for now. We'd reassess in the future.

Parkinson's disease affects about one million people in the United States. Most people are diagnosed around the age of 58. The illness has physical symptoms that continue to worsen over time, and mental health issues sometimes develop. I knew none of this when I accepted this job in a state I was moving to for the first time. My boss, a neurologist who is a Movement Disorder Specialist, told me she could teach me about Parkinson's disease, but she couldn't teach me about working with communities, helping individuals, or developing programs. That's why she wanted a social worker. She needed someone with the micro, mezzo, and macro skills to work with all of these groups.

I had spent the previous five years working with refugee youth in a community center. I was now switching gears to gerontology work in a health care setting. I was intimidated and wondered how much I would like the work. But I also felt some confidence. My social work training had been broad, and I thought I would like working with older adults. At least I hoped so.

On this particular Monday morning, I had scuttled into the office early and put the coffee on. I made sure we had enough educational material for 15-20 patients, grabbed a few exercise bands, and quickly checked my messages. Our clinic was funded through state dollars, and our state administrator left a message asking for information on the number of clients we served, the programs we offered, and outcomes for our program's objectives. The state budget was tightening its belt, and we had to advocate for the continuation of the grant. I left a detailed message for our administrator and called our state representative, who was supportive of our program and was working to help us maintain our funding. Our outreach services to underserved populations, especially the Hispanic community, required the funding from this grant. We were working hard to build our Spanish-speaking Parkinson's clinic and outreach activities. A cut to our funding could jeopardize the continuation of the program.

As I walked across the University of Illinois at Chicago campus and over to the clinic, I realized I had never imagined I would be a social worker on a large metropolitan university campus. I was met by the nurse and a pharmaceutical representative, who brought in fruit, bagels, and cream cheese. We readied a special waiting room set aside for patients with Parkinson's, where they could visit with each other, read educational material, drink coffee, and be comfortable during their clinic visit. We also made sure the medication samples cabinet was stocked. Samples from us can help patients who have limited or no prescription drug coverage to have medication for the entire month. I finally poured my own cup of coffee just as the clinic began getting busy.

As patients came into the clinic, I collaborated on patient care with the neurologist, pharmacist, nurse, and exercise physiologist. I visited with patients, discussed social and emotional adjustment, and made sure each patient got his or her needs met by the group of interdisciplinary professionals. This team approach is important to the way we offer services. Our efforts aim at helping the entire patient, physically, mentally, and socially. The neurologist and nurse provide the foundation of this care. The exercise physiologist provides exercises and equipment for all patients to use at home to expand their movement or improve their balance. The pharmacist reviews all the medications to be sure of no drug interactions, and I provide information on local social services, patient information, and guidance.

On this particular morning, Franklin came in for an early appointment. He is 69 years old and has been living with Parkinson's for a number of years. He was quite dissatisfied and even frustrated with the quality of his symptom management. The neurologist spoke with Franklin and, upon her return from visiting with him, expressed concern that he was not taking his medications as prescribed. Not doing so could exacerbate, or even cause, his limited symptom management. Franklin's first language was Spanish, and luckily, many of the clinic staff, including our pharmacist, spoke Spanish. I called on the pharmacist to help Franklin with a prescription medication plan that could work for him. I also verified his participation in the prescription drug coverage program offered in our state and found the nurse to get him some free samples. I didn't want a lack of medications to keep him from successful symptom management. If these efforts didn't work, we would refer him to the neurosurgeon on our multidisciplinary team.

Clinic ended at noon, and I headed back to my office for lunch. I had more messages waiting for me on my phone. A national speaker on "Living with Parkinson's Disease" agreed to provide the keynote at the annual conference we were providing for our clients and their families. I had already secured several break-out workshops as we built our integrative health portion of the conference. Free massages, a speaker on Chinese medicine, Latin dance as exercise, and a speaker on spirituality were just some of the holistic programs we wanted to offer at our conference. Our first conference had been a success, and we hoped the addition of the integrative health series would capture a lot of interest from clients and professionals alike.

After attending to the phone calls, I headed to the neurology department for a research meeting. Our research projects were often interdisciplinary and included speech and language clinicians, kinesiologists, psychiatrists, and clinical trials for new medications. At this meeting, we began developing a survey to learn more about perceptions of Parkinson's disease among ethnic minority communities.

Within an hour, I was traveling on the elevated train in Chicago to give a presentation to a large group of in-home nursing assistants. I provided information on our program, education on Parkinson's, and tips for helping people living at home. I enjoyed the public speaking, mainly because it made me aware of how little people know about the signs and symptoms of Parkinson's disease. People, even health care workers, often assume that slow movements or falling are simply attributable to being old. Normalizing aging as a time of health rather than disability is a large part of my work educating others. We all hold myths of aging, and these affect the expectations we have for our clients and their quality of life. I hoped I could raise the bar for these expectations and help people recognize that growing old without disability is a norm. Symptoms such as slow movements should be addressed by a physician.

It was my last event of the day. I was tired. I mentally created the next day's to-do list: finishing up the conference brochure details for the printer, addressing our outcomes more thoroughly in hopes of retaining our funding, facilitating the monthly team meeting of our interdisciplinary partners to work out the bumps in the program, building our relationships to one another, and addressing specific client concerns. I mentally added Franklin's name to the list.

I was grateful to have a master's degree in social work; it was my ticket into this job. Helping older adults like Wendy, Bob, and Franklin is deeply satisfying, and advocacy and planning create programs that help many more people. My boss had been right. My generalist social work skills had been transferable. Counseling individuals, coordinating programs, building relationships across disciplines, and educating communities were all important social work skills that crossed boundaries of age and issue.

Think About It

1. Identify social work micro, mezzo, and macro skills in the story. Which of these practice areas are appealing to you? Which make you feel intimidated?

2. Identify two points about social work practice from the story. Can you apply them to work, volunteer, or internship experiences in your life? How is the writer's experience similar to or different from your experience?

3. In what ways does the story integrate with the "strengths perspective"? With "person-in-environment practice"?

Chapter 28
A Social Work Perspective on Geriatric Addictions

• •

by Nicole Sarette MacFarland, LCSW-R, DCSW, CASAC

On a cold winter day in January, the doors of Senior Hope swing open at 9:00 a.m., and I enter the small outpatient clinic located in Albany, New York. As I enter the inviting waiting room, I reflect upon how today will be another memorable day in my life of serving seniors. As clinical director of the only geriatric addictions outpatient facility in the state of New York, I find my role varied and always exciting. I often remind myself that social work is a field for those who possess an innate ability and desire to help others and that the work we do can be very rewarding, once we find the right career path. Long ago, a family member once shared with me a statement I have never forgotten. He said, "When you find a career that you love, the dividing line between work and play will no longer be evident." I have replayed those words in my mind over the years as my career path has progressed in various directions.

As I enter the clinic, I am greeted by our office manager, who smiles and welcomes me the way he greets all our senior clients. He reviews with me the appointments for the day and then proceeds to offer me a cup of coffee. At Senior Hope, clients are greeted and made to feel valued, welcomed, and respected. The waiting room begins to fill as our older population filters in from the cold weather outside. Shortly after 9:00 a.m., the founder of Senior Hope enters the clinic with a smile on his face. He is the visionary of the clinic, who realized years ago that a generation of people was being forgotten and untreated. As "Dr. Bill," age 76, removes his hat and coat, I am again reminded that his calming disposition and nurturing presence help to make Senior Hope a clinic unlike any I have ever worked for thus far in my career. As I enter my office to begin the day, I think to myself how much I admire Dr. Bill, a retired academic, and his wife, a seasoned therapist and administrator. They are a couple with strong morals and principles who have given of themselves, their time, and resources to create a clinic that has helped hundreds of older adults cope with the ravages of addiction.

My office is filled with paperwork and messages as I make my way behind the big wooden desk. The role of clinical director is so diverse that I often find myself amazed at all the hats I wear on any given day. It is 10:00 a.m. and my first client enters the office. She is a beautiful 68-year-old woman who has raised five children and maintained the role of homemaker, wife, and mother for more than three decades. She is a widow now, and her children have all grown up. She had lost meaning and purpose in her life, and the bottle seemed to ease the pain. She came to Senior Hope after she was found on the floor in a drunken stupor by her eldest adult daughter. She is stronger now and ready to face the world sober. She realizes now she is not alone and that her adult children will be there for her during her road to recovery. As she leaves my office, I think to myself how courageous this woman is and how fortunate she is to have a family that loves her.

The phone rings, and I am reminded that it is time for me to start my 11:00 a.m. group. The clients who comprise the "Mental Health and Recovery Group" struggle with dual diagnoses. As the men and women filter into our group room, I look around and realize how much I have learned from their stories of hardship. The struggles that these clients have shared at times can move a facilitator to tears, as she realizes the pain and suffering addiction and mental illness can inflict upon the human spirit. As I begin the topic of forgiveness, I realize that for some of these clients, family will never be able to forgive them for their past behaviors. They are a generation of people with certain values and beliefs that often are very different from those of the younger generations. Most of the members who frequent our rooms remark that they have always felt they were "mom or dad" when they attended other outpatient addictions agencies with mixed age groups. They tell me with such relief in their voices that this is the first time they can relax and feel they are among their own peers. Our clients share so many similar life stages together. As the members begin talking about forgiveness, one member begins to cry. He states that he has searched for years for a clinic where people understood his disease and where he was free to talk about how his mental illness often influences his use of alcohol. He talks about retirement and how once he retired and the kids were out of the house, he became depressed. He lost meaning and purpose in his life and alcohol seemed to numb his pain. The group continues with these mothers and fathers, grandmas and grandpas, all reflecting on life's accomplishments, life's losses, those they have hurt, and those from whom they wish to receive forgiveness in the future. As we near the end of the group session, I am moved by their honesty and realize that it is never too late to begin to heal and move toward mental wellness and recovery.

At noon, my staff begins to leave for lunch. I often eat lunch while completing some administrative task in my office. Today the monthly report must be sent electronically to our licensing agency—the Office of Alcoholism and Substance Abuse Services (OASAS). OASAS requires that I analyze the units for the prior month and report the number of individual and group sessions per full-time clinician. It is an important part of my role as clinical director, because I need to let Dr. Bill and OASAS know the client flow that enters and exits our clinic. The report is complete and my lunch is finished.

It's now 1:00 p.m., and "Ellen" enters my office with a crisis. She has just begun her evaluation with "John," a retired executive who drove himself to the clinic. My senior clinician has a panicked look on her face as she asks me for an emergency clinical supervision. I welcome her into my office and close the door. She tells me that John has a positive blood alcohol level and is demanding to drive himself home. I look at Ellen and realize this is her first time encountering this situation. My administrative role includes supervision of all staff and clinical operations. I realize what I must do to help with the situation. I calmly let her know we cannot let him drive home, as he is clearly impaired. I accompany her into her office, which smells strongly of alcohol, and look John in the eyes. Dr. Bill enters the room, and we work as a team to help John understand that he is impaired and that he must let us drive him home. After some time, he finally nods and we chauffeur him to his home. As I leave the clinic, I turn around and make eye contact with my senior clinician. She mouths the words "thank you," and I smile, knowing the next time will be easier for her to handle. During the ride to John's home, he shares his story with me. He speaks softly as he mentions his role as executive for a company and how retirement changed his life forever. He looks over at me with tears in his eyes as he shares how lonely he is and how meaningless his life has become. This is a story I have become all too familiar with over the years, as I realize why we are seeing more clients like John at our clinic. With the youngest age of 50 to our eldest of 85, we have heard the following story time and time again. Retirement, loss of social supports, loss of one's career role, loss of physical vitality, loss of loved ones, and loss of a spouse lead to increased use of alcohol and/or other drug use. After dropping John off, I head back to Senior Hope knowing that what we offer at our clinic is so special, so unique, and so appreciated by all we serve. John will be back when he is ready and able, because he knows at Senior Hope we offer a custom tailored approach to helping meet the unique needs of the geriatric addicted population.

It is time for our 2 p.m. case conference. The staff and administration value these times of interdisciplinary collaboration. We review cases, share crises, and discuss treatment plans. Laughter is always present. I learned a long time ago that the team you create can make such a difference in the services you provide. As I look around the table, I tell myself how fortunate I am to have such a seasoned, dedicated team of professionals. I look over at "Cindy," our student intern from SUNY Albany, and smile as I watch her share a case with confidence. One of the rewards of being a field placement supervisor is that you get to help train the next generation of social workers. Cindy has blossomed over the past year, and I have truly enjoyed working with her and helping her gain knowledge and skills with geriatric addictions. At SUNY, by training the next generation of social workers to acquire the skills they need in the field of geriatric addictions, I feel that I am helping to make a difference now and in the future.

After the case conference, I run out of the clinic on my way to provide a presentation to social welfare students at SUNY Albany on the subject of geriatric addictions to help inspire them to enter the field. As I sit there on the panel looking into the eyes of these men and women, I recall my earlier years at University of Pennsylvania School of Social Welfare. It was there that I knew at the age of 26 that I would specialize in both mental health and addictions. I knew I would pursue a CASAC (certified alcoholism and substance abuse certificate), because without this dual specialization, my heart told me I would not be able to do justice to the clients I served. After the presentation, the questions begin and I try to help this new generation of graduating practitioners understand the importance of geriatric social work with the mentally ill/chemically addicted client. They are a smart group and realize even at this early stage of their careers that life is hard and the workplace is competitive. They know that they must empower themselves to develop a wide range of skills to be hired after graduation.

At 4:00 p.m., I arrive back at the clinic to be greeted by Dr. Bill. He has been meeting with several local legislators concerning the lack of reimbursement of Medicare for our elderly population. I think to myself how unfortunate it is that we are the only clinic in New York state catering to people 50 and older who struggle with addictions. I then reflect on the fact that today 4.2 million New Yorkers are 55 and older—22% of the state's population. By 2025, it is estimated that 5.5 million will be age 55 or older—about 27%, according to the Office of Alcohol and Substance Abuse Services. According to the National Council on Aging, nearly 17% of all seniors 55 and older are at risk of—or already suffer from—alcoholism, medication misuse, and substance abuse problems. The obvious needs of our aging population are growing in unprecedented numbers. Yet, with baby boomers entering the senior ranks, we continue to be the only free standing nonprofit clinic in the state helping this population. Dr. Bill and I know that there are obstacles agencies will face based on the ages of the clients they serve. Medicare offers a set reimbursement rate for outpatient addictions services, and this rate is less than the average hourly wage of any MSW practitioner newly entering practice. Because of this financial limitation, it is very hard for outpatient facilities to succeed fiscally in this competitive time. As a social worker in administration, I am aware that part of my role is to let government at the local, state, and federal levels know this societal concern is not going to disappear and that the need to re-examine how our aging population is served by their health insurance remains a significant policy issue.

It's 5:00 p.m. The day is over, and 25 clients have received support, education, and nurturing here at Senior Hope before the office is closed for the night. I pack up my things and get ready to head over to SUNY Albany again, as I am taking classes toward my Ph.D. in Social Welfare. As I walk out to my car, I look back at the clinic and smile as I think to myself, "The line between work and play is no longer evident in my life now that I have found Senior Hope."

Think About It

1. How do the needs of older addicted adults differ from the needs of younger addicted adults?

2. What are some of the roles an administrative social worker engages in when working with the geriatric addicted population?

3. What are some barriers to identifying and treating older adults with substance abuse problems?

Chapter 29
Working With Homeless Older Adults

• •

by Kelly Mills-Dick, BSW, MSW, LMSW

The only "typical" aspect of a day in the life of a social worker is that it is influenced and inspired by each day that came before it. Currently, my days are spent completing my Ph.D. in social work and teaching full-time in a BSW program. Juggling a variety of roles and responsibilities is challenging and demands that I remain focused on my goals and purpose. A large part of my focus and motivation comes from recalling my prior work with homeless older adult clients. Indeed, my past experience with older adults is the impetus for my current teaching and research.

A unique setting, the community health center where I was employed provides health care to adults over age 60, regardless of insurance status. In response to the health care needs and insurance status of many homeless older adults, the agency established a special program to meet the needs of this population, as part of Health Care for the Homeless. As a result, my primary role was to provide clinical and case management services to those patients/clients who were homeless. The following description illustrates some of the many facets and challenges of this work.

I get to the office at 8:30, so I have just enough time to check e-mail and phone messages before our team meeting. There are a few e-mails regarding meetings and upcoming events that I will have to reply to later. There are several phone messages from Charles, wondering if I have heard from Section 8 about his application and if I have any new leads. He doesn't leave a number or location where I might find him. Shelly from the homeless service center downtown has called to let me know that a client I have been asking about showed up last night for a bed and looks like he has gangrene on his left leg. The day is already starting to look full.

The team meeting starts at 9:00. The social workers arrive first, socialize with "hellos" and "how was your weekend" and relay important information to each other. The nurses arrive and make sure important details regarding specific clients are translated to the specific social worker involved. When the doctors arrive, the meeting begins. The interdisciplinary team meeting occurs once each week and is intended as an opportunity to discuss special and/or urgent situations requiring team involvement. The day-to-day communication regarding patient/client status is conducted via progress notes included in the patient chart. Team meetings are utilized instead to problem-solve and develop care plans for the more complex cases. Although there are several important cases to discuss today, none involve housing issues or a homeless client, so I leave the meeting with no new work added to my day's schedule, which is rare.

I get back to my office and call the housing authority office to follow up on Charles's status. He has been on the list for almost three years, and his name is finally at the top. Years of sleeping in shelters, on the street, and with friends have been hard on Charles, but he is one of the few who have held out hope. There is a low-income senior housing building that recently opened up, and we have been informed that it is likely he will get a room soon. I call and talk to Julie, who knows me well by now, and hear the good news that the room is open. Charles needs to come down to fill out some paperwork, and the place is his. This is the best news I've heard all month. Now, if I can just track down Charles!

It's 11:00, and I decide to head to the homeless service agency to check in on the client Shelly called about and see if Charles is there. Shelly tells me she hasn't seen Charles in a few days and the other client took off first thing in the morning, but is on the list for a bed again tonight. I ask her to call me on my cell if/when she sees either one of them. I hang around for a half hour or so, talking with some of the clients and doing outreach, making sure to introduce myself to anyone who looks like they might be over 60. I call to check my voicemail at work, and Charles has left another message telling me he is headed to the health center to see me.

I race back to the office hoping I don't miss him. He is in the waiting area and jumps up when he sees me. To avoid a huge commotion in the waiting area, I take him up to my office and tell him the good news. He is overwhelmed and in disbelief. He can't believe that after all this time, he will finally have a home. I drive him over to the housing authority office to complete the paperwork and then take him and his sole bag of belongings to his new place. I've been to the building with other clients before, but each time, I am struck by the difference between how the clients and I view the rooms. Charles immediately lies down on the bare mattress and declares thanks for having his own room—with a window! We talk about how and where he might be able to get some household items such as sheets, towels, and silverware. I agree to contact a few local agencies on his behalf, and he makes a plan to get his phone hooked up. He thanks me, and I congratulate him on maintaining his sense of hope and for finding a home. I leave happy for Charles but processing my own concerns. This building is far from downtown and in a high crime neighborhood. How will Charles get to his appointments? Will he be safe? It has been a while since he has lived on his own. Will he be able to pay his bills? Take care of the cooking and cleaning? I remind myself that Charles has been resourceful during his three years of homelessness, and will likely continue to take care of himself.

I have a 1:00 p.m. appointment scheduled with Virginia, who is enrolled in a substance use/abuse study being conducted by a local university in conjunction with our agency. The study involves a substance use/abuse assessment and brief alcohol intervention for those eligible. Virginia used to be homeless, but now lives alone in a one-bedroom apartment downtown. She has no cognitive impairment but is physically frail, using a walker to get around her apartment and requiring assistance to go anywhere. She has used the health center for primary care for several years, and since she values the care she has received, she agreed to participate in the study. Virginia drinks two shots of whisky in her morning coffee and keeps a flask by her recliner, which she sips on throughout the day. Although she does not identify as having a "problem," Virginia has agreed to participate in the brief intervention, and I am here for our third visit. After hearing what constitutes a standard drink and the risks of alcohol use/abuse for older adults, Virginia has decided to cut out the shots from her morning coffee. At our meeting today, she reveals that she has reduced her morning drink to one shot and has also noticed more alcohol left in her flask daily. I acknowledge her progress and she discusses positive physical and emotional changes resulting from the decrease. The revised plan is for Virginia to further reduce her morning drink by a half an ounce and keep track of how often she is refilling her flask. We schedule a meeting for next week and say goodbye.

It's a little after 2:00, and since I am downtown, I take advantage of the opportunity to do some outreach. The park nearby is a frequent stop for many of the city's homeless, so I walk around looking for clients I haven't seen recently and other older adults potentially in need of assistance. It is a nice day, so the park is crowded, but there are few older adults in sight. I see James, actively engaged in a sidewalk soliloquy on the coming of the devil, but he looks physically well, is wearing clean clothes and shoes, and I remember from his chart that he made it in for his appointment last week.

A woman I attempted to engage a few days ago is here again. I think she may be new to the area, since I haven't seen her before and she doesn't seem familiar with the city. I decide to walk over. It is about 75 degrees and she is wearing several layers of clothes, including a winter jacket. She has a wheeled cart full of bags and discarded food. Her shoes are worn through on the sides and heels, and she looks as though she hasn't slept or washed in days. When I attempt to introduce myself, she looks away and does not respond, but I sit down. I sit silent for about 20 minutes before she looks at me and asks, "What do you want?" I tell her who I am, where I'm from, and what my job is. I tell her about the free health care available through our agency, as well as the many services that I connect people to, including shelter and meal programs. She doesn't respond, but doesn't turn away either. I continue by acknowledging the hesitance that many people have in using services they haven't used before, and by telling her that I have worked with many of the other people in the park to help connect them to the things they need. I say that my job is to help connect her to what she thinks she might need and desire, not what I think she needs—and that my priority is to make sure that she knows what is available to her in the community. She smiles and I smile back, internally acknowledging the importance of respect, authenticity, and engagement.

As she begins to speak, I am attentive. She hasn't seen a doctor in "a long time" and has been having "a lot of trouble with my feet." She slides one foot out of her ripped shoe to reveal her extremely red, swollen extremity. I inform her that one of our specialties is taking care of feet and ask if she would like me to make her an appointment. She agrees, so I immediately take out my cell phone and call the office. They are able to get her in today because another patient cancelled, so I schedule the appointment and tell them I'll be bringing her in. She can't believe someone can actually see her today, and it seems to bring a smile to her face. While my car is right there, I decide to take the bus there with her since she reveals she doesn't know her way around. I use the opportunity to show her how to use the bus system, while I conduct an informal assessment. While we wait for the bus and ride to the office, I learn that

Mary used to live in Southern California with her sister, but when the sister passed away six months ago, Mary was evicted and has been homeless since. She has no other living family and no place to go.

While she is in her appointment with the doctor, I call around and find Mary a bed in the older adult shelter. Fortunately, this happens quickly, so I have enough time to enter case notes for the day. When her appointment is finished, we take the bus back to my car and I drive her to the shelter. I introduce her to the shelter staff, and she is assigned to a case manager there. We are fortunate to be one of the few cities with a seniors-only shelter, since older adults are often hesitant to utilize shelters and have different needs than many shelter users. Our agency works in collaboration with the shelter in many cases by referring to each other and working in conjunction to meet client needs. In this case, they agree to take the lead and I agree to come by tomorrow morning for a treatment plan meeting and to maintain some continuity for Mary. As I say goodbye, Mary shakes my hand, looks into my eyes, and says "Thank you. I can finally get some rest tonight." I am thankful she won't have to sleep on the street tonight.

It is well after 5 p.m. when I get home, but I don't complain, because this work makes me realize on a daily basis just how fortunate I am. Each day feels like a quest for balance. There is the organization of the day's priorities and consideration of each client's needs, as well as reflection of whether, how, and in what ways I can make a difference in clients' lives. Homelessness is a complex issue, with many intersecting individual and societal factors. Addressing the myriad potential causes and solutions can feel like an overwhelming challenge. It is helpful to maintain focus on my primary role of direct practice and working with individual clients and their families, while simultaneously addressing larger policy issues whenever I can. I find myself educating others about the realities of homelessness for clients and writing letters to legislators about the dire need for more affordable and accessible housing and health care, both actions I view as policy practice.

As I look back at my experience working with homeless older adults, I am inspired to continue blending direct practice with teaching and research as I move forward in my social work career. The clients I was privileged to work with are both a source of hope and a force for change.

Think About It

1. What is your initial reaction to the idea of working with homeless older adults?

2. What skills does a social worker need to establish rapport with homeless older adult clients?

3. What safety issues or concerns might arise when working with homeless clients?

4. What types of ethical issues might arise when collaborating with multiple agencies?

5. How are older homeless adults' needs different from those of younger homeless people?

PART 5:
Nontraditional
Methods
and Settings

Chapter 30

Tapping Into the Creative Parts: Art Therapy With Older Adults

• •

by Jennifer Clements, Ph.D., MSW, LCSW

I remember very clearly when I was in my social work master's program taking an elective in art therapy. I was so excited about this type of work and at the same time had a sinking feeling that I was in the wrong field. I was quickly reassured by my instructor that clinical social workers are more than qualified to use the techniques and interventions of an art therapist. As the semester rolled on, I knew that I would want to use art therapy in my career. I just was not sure how.

My typical day includes working a full-time job in a large child welfare agency. I work part-time at a nursing home facility on the weekends. The agency contracts with me to provide art therapy services as a licensed clinical social worker. Since I do not work with older adults on a full-time basis, this part-time work is usually a refreshing change from the day-to-day struggles of child welfare. The agency has asked me to provide services to a small group of clients referred to as "end stage" residents. These residents are in the final stages of various diseases, and their doctors have given them less than six months to live. When I agreed to take this job, I had no idea how powerful and life changing my experiences would be working with these older adults.

I am responsible for facilitation of two groups, as well as individual sessions with the residents. The group members were chosen based on their interest in participating. All of the group members are engaged in a 12-week mutual aid group that centers on the use of art therapy to develop memory books as part of a life review process. Many of the residents were initially very resistant to the art work, but as the sessions continue, their confidence builds.

It is Saturday morning as I begin to pack up my supplies for the day. These include the usual items you would expect, like paper, markers, and pastels, but I do have some very special supplies that help me to aid the residents through their sessions—patience and positive encouragement! As I arrive at the home, one of the nurses tells me that John, a resident in the group I facilitate, passed away just last night. This is an expected loss, as John was dealing with end stage cancer of the stomach and lungs, but no less painful. Death is something that I do not have to deal with on a regular basis at my other job, so I am not sure how to handle this as I head over to my group.

I have about a half hour to prepare for group. I am gathering everyone's lifebooks, additional supplies, and my composure. Ideas run through my head about how we can process the loss of John. Should I bring it up, should I wait for one of the group members to do it, or should I just not mention his death? I rationalize in my head that the nursing staff will be dealing with this and that there are other social workers there to help them. Right at that moment, I find John's lifebook—full of his art work, memories, and not yet completed. This feels very sad. I decide to head over to the activity room to get set up.

Several residents are already there and begin to ask me what they will be drawing today. I tell them that we will be working on the page in their books about their fondest memory. As the staff help several residents get situated, I begin to hand out everyone's lifebooks. As I get to John's book, I carefully place it back in the box when Aggie, another resident, asks me if that is John's book. I answer her truthfully, with a knot in my stomach. She asks me what will happen to his book, and I share with her and the group that I am not sure. The group then begins a discussion about John, as they remember their times with him at the home.

The group is bursting with mutual aid, as they support each other through the process of losing John. Some of the residents are tearful, but most of them enjoy the stories of John. Then the subject of his lifebook comes back to me. The group asks me if it is possible to get his book to his family. Ellen, one of the residents, says that John has a son who visited him pretty regularly. I agree with the group's idea of getting his book to his son and decide to make a phone call to him after the group is over. Another suggestion by the group is to help complete his book with artwork of the stories they have of him. I am amazed by the great ideas and agree to help them add to John's book.

Each of them begins to draw—some of them with my help, some independently—their memories of John. Fran, a group member, yells out that John was the youngest of them in the group. Statements like "It just seems unfair," "It will be one of us tomorrow," and "I feel like I need more time" come out of members' mouths as they draw and process. The process is cathartic. Many of them cry, laugh, and yell out to the point that staff checks in on us a few times to see if we are okay. I check my watch, and we have gone well over our two-hour time frame. I ask the members to begin to wrap up what they are drawing.

As the artwork nears completion, I carefully add their pages to John's book. Many of them have used pastels, so I need to apply a fixative (basic hairspray) so the pages won't smear. This has to be done away from the residents, since many of them are on oxygen. The group wraps up and the residents head back to their rooms. Once the room is clear, I get to my work of preserving John's book. I am moved by the content and the submissions of his peers.

I check in with the nursing staff first to see if they have made contact with John's son. It turns out that the son will be arriving at the home later today to retrieve a few important belongings of his dad's. I ask them to inform me when he arrives, so I can pass on the lifebook. I have several individual sessions scheduled today, which I am now very late for, but all of the residents understand.

I hear my name being paged over the intercom. I am sure that this is about John's son. As I arrive at the front desk, John's son is standing there with a box of personal items. I introduce myself to him and ask him if he has a few minutes to chat. We walk over to the family room, and I begin to explain the lifebook and how John was working on this in group. I also explain the final pages and how they were contributions from the group based on memories they had of John. The son looks over the book and turns to the page we developed weeks ago about "a day I knew I was important." It is a picture of John, holding his infant son in his arms. I had written out at the bottom what John had asked me to write. "I knew the day my son was born that I was important—not because I had a child, but because I was holding a gift from God. A gift that was on loan to me and that I better take good care of him." John's son cried as he read that page, and I sat there with him in his grief. I do not remember how we wrapped up that moment, other than the fact that he thanked me and the staff as he walked out the door.

I walked back to the activity room and gathered up my supplies. I would need to go back to my office and write out some case notes of the session. As I finished up the paperwork and filed it away, I decided that I should thank John. I learned a lot about social work today and especially about myself.

Think About It

1. In what ways did the artwork facilitate the social work helping relationship?

2. Are there challenges to using art therapy with older adults that need to be considered?

3. Check out the Web site for the American Art Therapy Association and print out a resource you could use in your own practice.

Chapter 31
Integrative Touch and the 15-Minute StressOut

● ●

by Gerald W. Vest, MSW, BSW, ACSW, LISW

I am very happy to introduce my social work experience as an integrative health practitioner and teacher. I am officially retired, having served as a professor and field director for more than 25 years at New Mexico State University School of Social Work. However, I continue to teach a course in "Social Work Practice with Elders" every Spring semester, offer stress management classes for the U.S. Army and other human service programs, and serve as team leader for the newly-formed Las Cruces Health Promotion Team with Elders.

Integrative health practice includes applying methods that incorporate the whole being—physically, mentally, emotionally, and spiritually. We integrate the conceptual and theoretical bases of lifestyle approaches to health promotion, health fitness, and various holistic approaches to well-being for individuals, couples, groups, and communities.

Integrative Health Practices with Elders—Nourishing Touch

I fell in love with gerontological social work in 1995 while participating in and introducing our nourishing touch program at the Second Global Conference on Aging, Jerusalem, Israel. As author and developer of the *15-Minute StressOut Program,* a chair type massage program (stressouts), I had the good fortune to introduce our safe and nourishing touch program for this international conference and for the Center of Gerontological Research, also in Jerusalem, with Haya Daskal, Director of International Programs and MSW intern.

With this *15-Minute StressOut Program,* both the giver and receiver serve as partners to connect the vitality of breath with the power of touch. With my health promotion teams, this skillful touch program has been introduced to thousands of participants throughout New Mexico and the Southwest during the past 25 years. In 1984-85, I designed, developed, and introduced holistic health practices, including touch, which were offered in a state-wide project to prepare 300 senior health promotion advocates to introduce holistic practices with our elders throughout New Mexico.

From this experience, I learned that our multicultural elders are generally very enthusiastic and receptive to touch. After completing this project, I designed and taught holistic health courses for students at New Mexico State University (NMSU) to prepare them to incorporate integrative practices, including safe, non-erotic touch into nursing homes, with families, in senior centers, work sites, public schools, military installations, private industry, and employee assistance programs such as NASA—White Sands Test Facility.

A Day in My Life as a Social Work Practitioner and Teacher

Wednesday, 8:00-9:00 a.m., November 14, 2006—Professor Linda Schaberg, RN, and I met this morning to review and discuss the placement for her advanced nursing students for the Spring semester. Nine of her NMSU senior students, enrolled during this Fall term in her Community Nursing class, completed a nine-week session, giving our stressout program on Wednesdays (9:00-11:00 a.m.) in the Las Cruces, Munson Senior Center.

In addition to giving the stressout to several hundred elders, as part of their internship, the students are also required to organize and administer a research project and deliver a major team presentation to the senior community and others at the conclusion of their field experience. Linda reported that she and the students were so pleased with this project that the nursing department will send us two classes during our Spring term. Thus, we discussed dividing her students and our social work students into four teams, so they could give stressouts with elders in all four diabetic clinics, located in each of the senior centers throughout our city.

In the Spring semester, our social work students will join in-home care workers and introduce our stressout program with staff and residents in nursing homes.

9:00-11:00 a.m.—Ms. Elizabeth Frost, one of our most experienced volunteers, and I set up our meeting room, started the music and prepared ourselves to give stressouts with our walk-in clients and our participants in the diabetic clinic. Individually, we generally give five (5) stressouts and receive one; however, we are prepared to give more interventions or fewer interventions, depending on the number of volunteer workers and participants. With our students, we can give 40-50 stressouts each session.

11:00-12:00 noon—Met with the recreation director, the activity specialist, and the volunteer coordinator to discuss organizing regularly scheduled training sessions after the holidays, so we can expand our base of senior workers. I have designed a certification process for all of our students and workers, so everyone clearly understands our ethical guidelines for the safe use of touch and also agrees to observe our standards and follow our protocol or step-by-step procedures.

1:00-3:00 p.m.—Met with Francesca Smith, BSW, Director, In-Home Care Services and her staff to introduce my presentation outline for the annual, county-wide Caregivers Training Workshop to be held on Thursday, November 15, in the conference center in the local Methodist church. More than 90 participants have enrolled, and I am responsible for the afternoon workshop and closing session from 1:30 to 3:30 p.m.

Caregivers Workshop Agenda

My workshop design includes the following:

Exercise #1—Practicing Awareness Breathing—Through relaxation breathing, our mind becomes more open, accepting, and allowing. Learning to be in the moment while observing our breath relieves stress and allows us to interact and relate with others and our environment more effectively.

Exercise #2—Introducing healthy breathing exercises and movements from tai chi and Master Level Exercises-Psychocalisthenics—Being aware and mindful of our breathing and our center of equilibrium during meditation, relaxation, and moving exercises, the body, mind, emotions, and spirit find a balance. By maintaining our body's vitality with strength, coordination, balance, and flexibility, our caregivers and our workers can sustain a healthy outlook and support their family members and patients more effectively.

Exercise #3—Introducing approaches to maintain our spiritual well-being using safe, skillful, and nourishing touch—This exercise includes aspects of our *15-Minute StressOut Program* as described on our Web site's home page.

Using acupressure, coordinated with the breath to balance our body, mind, emotions, and spirit, is a heartfelt or empathic experience for both the giver and receiver of this partner massage.

While systematically applying pressure points and introducing the "laying-on-of-hands," we ask that givers and receivers maintain an awareness of their breath throughout the activity. While we refer to our stressout program as a chair-like massage, it may be more accurate to describe the experience as a partner meditation—relaxing and energetic.

3:00-5:00 p.m.—I return home feeling very enthusiastic, relaxed, energized, and ready to check my e-mail and visit my forum and Web page. I also maintain a blog titled: *Learning to Learn and Play with Children,* so I update my articles and respond to colleagues and others. Additionally, I prepare materials for my redeployment workshop to be held on Friday evening for children and their mothers at Army Community Services, Ft. Bliss, Texas.

Relationship with Community Services

Our team relates to all of the community senior programs, and many of their workers attend our training workshops. The team leaders and directors for senior programs in our community are primarily BSW professionals, and all have been students in my health and social work classes during my tenure at NMSU.

Summary

While respectfully following our guidelines, our progressive social workers, nurses, senior volunteers, and other professionals in our community have challenged the zero tolerance of touch policies established by many institutions and have learned to use safe, skillful, and nourishing touch to help promote health and well-being for our elders and for self-care. We know that many elders may live out their lives in isolation, loneliness, and despair in nursing homes, hospitals, and other institutions without being supported with loving, skillful touch—a basic human need for survival.

By observing our breathing and using skillful touch, we know that interested social work professionals can directly experience an empathic connection and healthy relationship with elders, while participating in our *15-Minute StressOut Program.*

Think About It

1. What are some benefits of touch for elderly clients?

2. What are some ethical concerns when using touch with clients?

Chapter 32
A Win-Win Partnership: Intergenerational Social Work
• • • • • • • • • • • • • • • • • • • •

by Joann T. Jarolmen, Ph.D., MSW, ACSW, LCSW

For many years, I worked in a high school environment as a school social worker. I chose school social work because I wanted to work with children, particularly adolescents. It was a great profession earning a very nice salary, since I was paid on the teachers' scale. There is a certain omnipotence that adolescents experience, and it is uplifting at the very least. Their highs are the highest, but their lows are also the lowest. In my last year at the high school, I was given the task of case management for a class of upperclasspersons who were recalcitrant in their school failure and unbelievably resilient in their ability to imaginatively "act out" in an effort to sabotage their education. The philosophy used for creating this class was to give these students probably their first successful school experience and, oh yes, to have them graduate from high school.

Having set the stage for you in describing the group that I was dealing with, I will proceed to tell you my tale of intergenerational social work with these students. Providing these children or young adults with motivational activities and getting them to acquire self-esteem for socially acceptable activities required quite a bit of ingenuity and imagination.

On one particular day after meeting with this group as I often did to discuss concerns, both emotional and academic, I realized that community involvement might help them to use some of their positive communication skills in working with others. I recall racking my brain to engage these young people. Alas, I came up with the idea of having them contact and hopefully develop a relationship with individuals in a nearby senior citizen complex. My idea was that if they could help others in some small way, they might begin to see the worth in themselves and additionally to see how satisfying it is to reach out and help others who are in need. In addition, the wisdom and common sense that these elders could contribute to these students was the creation of a perfect partnership.

I reviewed the idea with our school principal, who gave me the "green light." I went to the class during the afternoon community period to present the idea. The response was oddly positive. I honestly did not expect them to want to speak to old people with whom they felt they had very little in common. I was very mistaken. These students, many of whom had lost a loving grandparent and had difficult family situations, embraced the idea with enthusiasm—well, at least, enthusiasm that I had never before seen in them. They had some questions, of course. "What will we say to them? Do you really think they want to speak to us? Won't they want to talk to more successful kids like the honor students?" I reassured them that the conversations would be easy to start and that they could include everyday events. The students needed to do something else that they were not used to. That was to listen. Many times just listening is helpful to both parties.

I then called the social worker at the local senior facility, who told me that, ironically, there was a meeting that afternoon. If I could get there, I'd be able to present the idea to the community and maybe even have some of the residents sign up for our "phone contacts."

I prepared myself for the encounter, not knowing what kind of reception my idea would receive. Having never worked firsthand with that population, I feared they would reject the offer or not be at all interested in student phone contacts. The stereotype that many older people have about adolescents is negative, and they oftentimes are fearful of them. *"Kids today" are not very respectful and sometimes are downright mean to us (the elderly). "Kids today" are not what they used to be. They use drugs and profanity.* These were comments that I fully expected to hear.

When I arrived at the facility, it was a very comfortable, relaxed atmosphere. I was directed to the community room where the meeting was being held. The agenda was long, and my presentation was the last item on it. With trepidation, I spoke to the 50 or so residents who were present. I told them that I was a school social worker for adolescents in the high school down the block. I worked with a special population who had many needs. I explained that many of them had come from a disruptive family background as do so many youngsters in our society today. I explained to them that some had lost grandparents and had fond memories of their days together. The adolescents missed having the contact with their grandparents and it would be so helpful to these students to be in contact with older adults who had the ability to give sage advice based on a lifetime of experiences.

After I finished my presentation, there were many questions about the children (young adults). *Were they troublemakers? Were they good students? Did they take drugs? Were they respectful to their teachers? What exactly would they talk about to these youngsters?* Without revealing the specifics of any of the students, I answered the questions as honestly as I could. My hope was to get some of the more isolated residents interested in the contacts, as it would be most helpful to them.

Now it was time for the group to sign up for the "phone contacts." I held my breath in anticipation that a few of them would sign up. To my delight and surprise, about ten people signed up and gave their phone numbers. The particulars of when the calls would be expected and who would be calling them were to be discussed at a later time. Many of those who signed up told me that they were alone and did not live near their children or grandchildren. This presented them with an opportunity to have someone to give some "grandparently" advice and to help the youngsters.

It certainly was a day for me to remember. I had created a program that would turn out to be a win-win partnership. Students would be able to get a sense of self-efficacy and motivation to reach out and relieve the loneliness of the elder person, and the elders would feel a sense of usefulness and feel as though they were able to do some good for these students who may need some guidance or just simple advice. In retrospect, I believe that these two groups (adolescents and elders) have a great deal in common. Both groups are surrounded by peers and greatly influenced by them. It is a mutual age of independence, yet both groups need to feel connected with family and the influence of the others in the group. Both groups live with their peers and sometimes these peers are in constant change. As the program progressed, I saw that each was helping the other reach the goals that I tacitly set for them. For the students, it provided contact with an adult who was happy to hear from them. For the elders, they felt that they were positively influencing the lives of young people who may need direction and expertise based on experience.

I witnessed some other programs in the high school that partnered the elderly and the adolescents. The "Sweetheart Dance" was a yearly event where the elderly individuals came to the high school and danced with the adolescents. "Senior Citizens' Day" occurred each year, and a bus brought the elderly residents to the school for a day to follow students through classes and through lunch. Each of these events was validating and exhilarating but only occurred once a year. The program that I set up with the phone contacts continued through the year on a weekly basis, which helped the participants know each other personally and see each other as unique individuals, not just as a high school student or a senior citizen.

I believe that consistent contact intergenerationally is essential in our society, where extended families are becoming extinct and isolation of generations is the norm. The elderly are made to feel useless and live out their final years in institutions without the contact and stimulation of the young. Young people muddle through life experiences without the help or consultation of the older generation.

There are some who chose to change this inevitability. In a rural New Jersey county, the elderly have developed an online volunteer service to give advice to others who need it. The Web site *http://www.elderwisdomcircle.org* has given the elderly the potential to feel useful and contribute their many years of insight and experience to others. They provide advice for everything from wayward children and relationship commitment to unruly rose bushes (*Bergen Record,* March 9, 2006).

This topic also brings to mind the need for educating the elderly on the computer and Internet activities to keep them connected both locally and globally. A local nursing home in my area is advertising for "play groups" between its residents and early childhood groups.

I believe both sides of the spectrum benefit from this interaction, as well as the "phone contact" that was set up at my high school. In our turbulent times when people seem so rushed and overwhelmed, it is refreshing to see intergenerational communication and acceptance.

Think About It

1. How did this project benefit the seniors? How did it benefit the high school students?

2. What are some other ways social workers can work intergenerationally?

Chapter 33
Social Work in a Law Firm

• • • • • • • • • • • • • • • • • •

by Roseanne Tzitzouris, LMSW

When I tell people what I do—that I'm a social worker, at a public interest law firm, working with the elderly poor— the response usually follows something along the lines of "oh, what a 'noble profession;' you must feel so good about what you do; that's so great, we need more people like you." And that's usually the extent of the conversation. Unfortunately, poverty and aging are not sexy topics—no one wants to think about getting old (something we are all inevitably doing on a daily basis, like it or not) or not being able to afford the comforts of life, never mind life's basic human needs. The focus usually quickly moves on to the next person, unless I'm coaxed into telling the story of one eccentric client in particular, who pretty much kept to herself—and her eight cats.

Because of declining mental and physical health, Ms. P had inadvertently allowed her federal housing subsidy to lapse. Although she continued to pay her monthly portion of the rent, the lion's share had not been paid by the government for over a year. The landlord sued her for nonpayment of rent, but she put the court papers in a drawer, rather than answer them, and did not start to deal with the problem until a City Marshal showed up at her door with a 72-hour Notice of Eviction. Ironically, this form of denial is not uncommon among my clients. It's part of their magical thinking—out of sight, tucked away in a pile in the drawer, out of mind—no more problem. They also think that they cannot be evicted simply because they are elderly. This is obviously untrue, and it usually takes a lot of patience and counseling to change this stubborn and detrimental mind set.

It took more than nine months of legal and social work intervention to get Ms. P back onto public benefits, get repairs made in her apartment, and ultimately resolve her housing court case. But, when all that was left to do to close her case was dot a final "I," she was nowhere to be found. Assumed by neighbors to be in Argentina visiting family for the holidays, no one gave her absence a second thought—until my unreturned calls and unanswered letters became too many for my liking. Two consecutive days of home visits and careful investigation led to my decision to call in the police, who climbed through a window and discovered her body—which I had to identify for the medical examiner and police to help rule out any foul play. Not only was I the person who found her, but it was determined that I was probably one of the last people to meet with her, as I was clearly the only person to have had much contact with her during the final weeks of her life. Had she not been a client of our office and had I not been following up with her, who knows how much longer she would have been dead in that apartment before someone finally noticed. Three and a half months was clearly already too long—not only for her decomposing body, but even more so for her eight starving feline companions, who unfortunately turned on her for their own ultimately unsuccessful survival.

So what's the point of telling this story? It's not to gross you out—although that's the reason why you'll ultimately remember it. It's to demonstrate how so many of our elderly clients, through life and circumstance, are truly in it alone. Your involvement in their lives in your role as their social worker, be it long-term or short-term, is critical. Whether functioning as their direct service provider or linking them to other services such as senior centers, Meals On Wheels, or home care, just to name a few, it is you that will keep them linked to the outside world.

I have to admit, I got into gerontological social work pretty much by accident. I say this because I always thought that my client population would be children. However, after graduating from college with a bachelor's degree in social work, I accepted a job in a nursing home figuring I'd get some solid experience in a medical setting with an unfamiliar population. Little did I realize the challenges I would face as one of two social workers managing admissions, discharges, care plan meetings, family dynamics, staff dynamics, and a plethora of anything and everything else that happened on a daily basis that seemed to inexplicably fall under the title of "social work" in a 180-bed short-term rehabilitation and long-term residential facility. My mother couldn't understand how I had "an office job" yet worked into the evening hours and occasionally on weekends. I was forced to face many of my own fears and misconceptions about the elderly and the infirm and became all the more grounded in the field for having done so.

Next came graduate school. Since I had my BSW and some practical social work experience in the working world, I decided to apply only to those graduate schools of social work that offered "advanced standing." A full academic year and one summer semester later, I received my Master of Science in Social Work (MSSW) degree from Columbia University's School of Social Work. New York City itself was a massive learning lab—and I wasn't ready to leave it quite yet—so I applied for positions both in New York City and in my home state of Rhode Island, deciding that I would allow the position to choose my home.

I've been the social worker (the one and only) at the Legal Aid Society's Brooklyn Office for the Aging for almost 11 years now. Unlike the traditional social services setting, the venue is a law office, and the interdisciplinary team is comprised of attorneys and case handling paralegals. My work product is considered part of the attorney-client privilege, and I am not subject to mandatory reporting rules. All of the above makes for an interesting social work practice. I suppose that's why I'm still here 11 years later—that and the truly awesome team of case handlers I work with, who themselves deserve honorary social work degrees.

My commute to the office, via subway, is not bad compared to that of most others who work in the greater New York City area. However, it's rarely uneventful, so I've taken to knitting for those 15-20 minutes and even bought myself an iPod to insulate myself and create my own much needed morning "quiet" time—which I consider to be the quiet before the storm. My only stop is at the corner coffee stand, where I'm greeted by Bobby, with a smile, a great tasting cup of coffee at an unbeatable price ($.50), and usually a flirtatious compliment to start my day.

Once I get into the office, the battle begins: what to do first—return phone calls? Read and respond to e-mails? Start drafting that letter to Medicaid for Mrs. Jones? Any of these will do, unless there's a client scheduled for an appointment, an attorney hovering at my door, or an emergency, unscheduled visit from a distraught new applicant for our services. Coalitions, task forces, every kind of work related e-mail group imaginable—my in-box always seems to be overflowing and my capacity at 96%! If I have to ask the guys in MIS to increase my storage space one more time.... I usually spend the first 15-20 minutes of the morning skimming through them and reading only those e-mails from co-workers within my immediate office and point people, those I know who'll have answered the most important questions and correct/summarize the points made in the previous five e-mails.

I usually make a good faith effort at a "to-do list" at the end of the day, so that the next morning I remember exactly where I left off and have set a priority list. Unfortunately, that list is often ignored or, rather, re-prioritized. While our office has an official intake system (a specific schedule by which we accept new cases), we also screen for emergencies and respond to previous clients' and community based organizations' requests on an ongoing basis. The attorney-in-charge is the point person for these emergency walk-ins/call-ins, but I am her backup.

This day in particular starts off with a home visit. Since our clients are elderly and many of them physically as well as mentally disabled and thereby homebound, home visits are occasionally necessary. It's fall and it gets dark early, so for safety's sake, I intentionally schedule a morning home visit. It takes me forty-five minutes, two subways, and a ten-block walk to get to this client's home, where I'm greeted by her two very old and diminutive yet vicious-sounding mutts who, she believes, help keep the drug dealers from squatting in the burnt out vacant apartment upstairs. I am here today to notarize a couple of documents and complete the Federal Section 8 Housing Subsidy application that is vital to the resolution of her housing court case. While I am careful not to put my pocketbook down anywhere that would allow easy access for the many cockroaches scuttling throughout her apartment, I am also conscientious about reacting inappropriately or disrespectfully in my client's home. I sit in an open back chair at, yet sufficiently away from, her table, with my pocketbook inconspicuously placed upon my lap. Today's visit is brief in comparison to our initial interview several weeks ago, which lasted approximately three hours. Once I'm back in the office, I meet briefly with the attorney who's representing this client in housing court to review the case, give her the file, and move on to follow up with Ms. G., a client from this week's intake.

Ms. G has a shut-off notice from the electric company, which references a previously unpaid balance (from 16 years ago—she has been current ever since). Public Assistance was the guarantor on record until she recently moved to her new apartment in a senior housing complex. After conference calling the utility company with her, explaining the situation to three different representatives, and faxing over her income verification information, we were finally able to get the shutoff date postponed, giving us more time to get to the bottom of the situation. Like most of my clients, Ms. G was unable to maneuver through a large bureaucracy on her own and needed someone to advocate on her behalf.

I then return two consecutive voice mail messages. The first is to Ms. B and the next is to her granddaughter who lives in Florida. Our office is not only representing her in an eviction case, but we are also assisting her with numerous public benefits issues. While Ms. B looks like she couldn't be a day over 65, she is actually 83 years old. She masks her impairments well. She is clearly concerned and anxious about her general situation, yet unwittingly withholds information critical to her case. Her mental frailties coupled with her cognitive impairments tend to make her a poor and unproductive interviewee. Therefore, the collaboration between lawyer and social worker is vital in piecing her case together. While the attorney gets the court file, does the legal research, and works more directly on the legal case, I work more closely one-on-one with the client and her collaterals building rapport and addressing her psychosocial needs, which will ultimately help move the case forward.

Right now I'm working on getting Ms. B's SSI benefits reinstated, and advocating for the SSI overpayment she's been charged with waived, preferably, but otherwise recouped at a reduced rate. Also, I am working to have her two life insurance policies (the ultimate cause of her overpayment and discontinuance) cashed in and turned into an Irrevocable Pre-Need Funeral Agreement, since her sole purpose for those policies was to pay for her burial. I am trying, for the third time, to explain all of this to her granddaughter, who is now the owner of Ms. B's life insurance policies and has the sole rights to them. It is imperative that we get Ms. B's SSI benefits reinstated as soon as possible, because her Social Security retirement income is not enough to cover her rent and utility bills. She is already in housing court for nonpayment of rent, and she is falling into arrears on her utility bills. All of our discussions today are in preparation for her upcoming conference at the Social Security Administration, to which I will accompany her and at which I will serve as her representative.

Unfortunately, most of my clients don't have support systems that are intact or reliable. In fact, for those clients who do have family and/or friends, often those adult children or others are actually a major contributor to the client's presenting problem. These cases require the most social work intervention, and the successful resolution of the client's legal problem often depends upon it.

Next I return Ms. S's call. She begins to balance out the day with good news that reflects the fruits of our labors. She just received notice that her Medicare Savings Program (MSP) application was finally approved, which means that she'll be receiving a retro payment of $700 and that her ongoing Social Security retirement check will now be $596 instead of $507. By virtue of her participation in an MSP, she will now also be automatically eligible for "extra help" with her Medicare Part D prescription drug plan. I already counseled her on her Medicare Part D plan, and she hasn't had any issues since then. She is yet another example of how important it is that we take the time to learn about as many different government benefit options as are available. It's a requirement of being a good case manager.

I believe that this law office's approach is in sync with that of the social work profession itself—it's a holistic approach. We look at the whole person, at all of his or her issues, because to simply compartmentalize the housing court problem, the result of non-payment of rent, for example, and turn a blind eye to the financial problems, would be a disservice and simply result in recidivism. Most of our clients' legal problems are actually rooted in their social problems, and it's my role as the social worker to help identify and address those problems. Brooklyn has the highest concentration of seniors (individuals 60 years old and older) in the country. Yet, given our limited resources, we have to turn away many potential clients, because we simply do not have sufficient staff to address the tremendous demand for our services. As social workers especially, the above is an important thing to do—to acknowledge and accept not only our clients' limitations, but our own limitations. We cannot help everyone, and that's okay.

And finally, I would be remiss if I didn't briefly mention some of the other tasks I perform in conjunction with our legal cases, as well as independent of them. They include providing formal psychosocial assessments and affidavits in support of motions for guardians, providing financial management and budgeting counseling, serving as a community liaison, and arranging and performing community outreach and education. And last but not least, inherent in my role as the social worker for the office is the task of being a compassionate listener for the staff itself, for whom I will also try to find the time to close the door, let them vent, and listen to their problems.

Think About It

1. Would you be interested in practicing in a non-traditional social work setting, such as a law office, where it is likely you would be the sole social work practitioner? What are some of the challenges you think you'd face, and how would you deal with those challenges?

2. A social worker, regardless of his or her practice setting, takes on many roles. Define what you think your role as an advocate would be for your elderly clients. List some characteristics and qualities that would make you an effective advocate.

Chapter 34
Geriatric Care Management in Private Practice
• •

by Andrea Shankman Eisenstein, MSW, LCSW

Frustration had been following me for many years during my career as a social worker with seniors—first in a community center, learning of the difficulties accessing services, in a mental health clinic, with the same issues, to a nursing home to a rehabilitation hospital (especially at discharge time) to an adult day center. The parameters of the jobs left my involvement at the discharge door. Enough years went by and I could practically predict what would happen next without the follow-up and support needed to ensure improvement. Why wasn't there any continuity to assist older adults to follow through with the services they needed?

Finally, my opportunity came when I discovered the name for what I wanted to do: Geriatric Care Management, private practice. The timing turned out to be good, as I had connections in the geriatric field who could be potential referral sources, and I could, finally, be independent and follow my clients as far as needed.

So, here I am, five years into geriatric care management and not one bit sorry. I have referral sources, I have satisfied clients, and I am satisfied that I have done my best on behalf of my older adults and their families. Of course, there are those few times when I felt I could not assist after being hired, and I discharged these clients with that explanation.

A day in my life is sometimes predictable, or sometimes gives rise to many surprises, as probably most social workers experience. My services are 24/7, and since I am a sole practitioner, I work with one or two nurses, as needed, for assessment and assistance when there are significant medical issues to monitor.

It's Monday morning, and I receive a call from a private caregiver who assists one of my clients. She informs me that Mrs. J. fell over the weekend, the daughter took her to the emergency room, and she has a fractured hip. Since she is not a candidate for surgery, she was returned to her home and the staff will need to provide increased physical assistance for her. I call my nurse to plan a visit within the next 48 hours to be sure the caregivers are instructed in maintaining good skin condition, that they elevate her properly so her lungs remain clear, as she is susceptible to pneumonia, and that her pain medications are appropriate for someone her age and weight. It's not uncommon for doctors who treat older adults not to account for metabolic differences from younger adults. I also confirm that home health therapies will be initiated by the doctor.

As I am typing up my notes on this situation, the phone rings. It is the out-of-state daughter of an older couple in town. She has been referred to me to discuss what services I can offer for evaluating her parents. She has received a call from a neighbor who says that her parents seem to be very forgetful, their apartment is pretty messy, and she has been helping them pay their bills. We work out a strategy for her to introduce me to them by phone, and I offer to call them later to set up an appointment to meet them at their home for an interview, which will really be an assessment.

Over the phone, I explain care management and get as much information on her parents as possible. I already anticipate that they can benefit from some in-home care a few hours a week for housekeeping, meal preparation, and medication monitoring. I also see that I will have to have one of my nurses visit to set up medications. I tell her I will need to e-mail or fax my contract for services to her and receive it back before I can visit her parents. When one is self-employed and being hired for assistance, it is important to be sure the terms of payment and expectations are fully outlined before initiating services. (Fees and contracts are not often dealt with in graduate school.)

This is much of my morning, and I haven't even left my home office yet!

I meet a home health agency representative for lunch to discuss the services the agency offers people at home, and then I am off to visit Mrs. K., who has dementia and lives in an assisted living community. I visit her once a week to be sure her skin problems are being treated, take her to the bank to cash her bi-weekly spending checks, and, when necessary, follow up to be sure her blood thinning medication lab work is not forgotten. Even then, sometimes the lab forgets to send the results to the cardiologist, and I must be diligent on her behalf.

Mrs. K has multiple medical issues, and I am frequently in touch with her primary care physician, her psychiatrist, and the nurse at the assisted living community to be sure her medical and physical needs are being met. I even assist her with her monthly pacemaker phone checks. Sometimes I will take her to her doctor's appointments, or to purchase clothing. My greatest pleasure is to take her to lunch after a doctor's appointment, and she enjoys that time with me, also. Her children live in another state and cannot visit often, but I do keep them informed regularly through phone calls and e-mails.

Additionally, my biggest challenge in working with Mrs. K was arranging for care and monitoring prior to surgery. She had to be without food or water from midnight before the surgery, and she also needed post-surgery care to prevent her from pulling out stitches and tubes. I do not believe in tying the hands of anyone with dementia, but it takes a special caregiver to manage someone who is confused, fearful, and might be flailing about.

After visiting her, I have planned to visit a personal care home (small group home) to see if it might be one I would recommend to clients.

By the time I arrive back at my home office, it is nearly 4:30 p.m. and I have notes to do and telephone calls waiting for me. I see that another client might be discharged from the hospital in a couple of days and the in-home care must be set up immediately. I will need to interview caregivers to screen them for compatibility with Mr. B. I prefer to use an agency, but his family also wants me to narrow down the choices they will have to make. Sometimes, they want to leave it up to me, but I make sure they at least do a phone interview with the candidates. We discuss their impressions after the phone interview, and although most of the caregivers available for hire are honest and hardworking, I will not make the final decision. I do have to inform the family that there are taxes to be paid for the caregiver if they do not choose to go through an agency.

I know tomorrow I will have to deal with the family dynamics of one of my clients whose children are not comfortable making decisions about their parent, despite my recommendations. The children disagree with each other on every recommendation made by their parent's physician or me. Increasingly, I am uncomfortable working with this family, as I feel they may be allowing their parent to be living at risk despite my pleas for assistance for their parent. This compromises my personal and professional code of ethics, and I am constantly reconsidering whether to remain involved or call the state adult protective services to intervene. Well, I think, one more day of trying to be there for the elder client might make a difference—hope springs eternal.

By 11 p.m., I have finished my notes, returned phone calls, and tried to do a little billing toward my end-of-the-month invoices. My day has been filled with advocating on behalf of my older clients, following up on continuity of care, and working with family members to empower them in the maze of community services. I love my work.

Think About It

1. How does the social worker help clients find meaning in their lives as they become more fragile?

2. How does the social worker educate and discuss end-of-life options with the family?

3. How can a social worker help clients change doctors if they feel they are experiencing age discrimination by their physicians?

4. Regarding business practices, how much information should the social worker provide on the phone before obtaining a contract to provide services?

5. How comfortable are you with the idea of running a business, in addition to providing social work services?

Chapter 35

Caregiver Psychoeducational Support Groups: Gerontological Social Work in Business and Industry

•••••••••••••••••••••••••

by Emma Giordano Quartaro, DSW, ACSW, LCSW

More than the huge parking lots, the security at the gates, and the preponderance of jackets and ties, it was the ladies' room attendant in her crisply starched uniform with her identification badge on the collar stating, "I do not speak English," that reminded me I was not in a social work agency. In my best professional suit and new silk blouse putting finishing touches on the make-up I rarely wear, I was about to begin my morning doing social work in a corporation.

Having been in the field of gerontology for some time, it occurs to me how different, and yet how much the same, this sub-field of gerontology in business and industry is to the more typical settings in the age-service system, such as senior centers, hospitals, and nursing homes. Here in business and industry, the setting both facilitates and constrains what most social workers think of as good practice. But let me tell you what I do in this specific corporation, which I will call Northeast Communications, Inc., otherwise known as "Norecom."

In addition to conceptualizing, demonstrating, and training a cadre of social workers and nurses to implement the Caregiver Psychoeducational Support Group Program, I facilitate/instruct some of the psychoeducational support groups of Norecom employees to help them improve their capacity to care for their elderly and disabled family members, most of them in their own homes. Rosters for the workshops, as the psychoeducational support groups are referred to in the corporation, the room set-up, the materials distributed, and the media utilized are supplied by the human resources officers on the basis of recommendations made by the workshop facilitators/instructors. Each workshop group meets two mornings within the same week, usually Tuesdays and Thursdays, in a corporate site of which there are several in two states. For a total of six hours per workshop group, I sit at a conference table with the 12-15 workshop participants summarizing pre-developed lesson plans created for that purpose.

The lesson plans are a flexible structure that is modified if and when the group participants bring unanticipated but important concerns to the table, which they are encouraged to do. Although every group is different, as is every group participant, today the group and its participants are particularly memorable. As the participants introduce themselves to each other and to me, each volunteers a short statement of what brings each one to the workshop.

"My mother's Alzheimer's is driving me crazy. She's beginning to see and hear things that aren't there. Yesterday, she called the police because she was sure burglars were in the house. I don't know how long I can keep her with us without quitting my job."

"My brothers and sisters refuse to help me with Grandpa. They offer but then do not follow through when their turns come to take him in."

"I'm tired of taking care of my teenage kids and my elderly parents at the same time. The kids are tired of them, too. Lately, I have been going home at lunchtime to be sure Mom and Dad are okay. I don't know how much longer I can do this."

One employee sheepishly admits to coming to the workshop to learn how to deal with his own aging in his own future.

A most moving introductory comment comes from an African American woman who says in a soft, faltering voice, "I'm here because after 30 years, my mother showed up at my door. Now I have to take care of a sick old woman I do not really know who never took care of me."

As some group members stifle tears and others nod their heads in recognition, she explains her mother had abandoned her as an infant but needs her now as she is her only surviving relative. She does not question her biblical duty, as she puts it, to honor her mother. "I don't know how to do it," she says.

Later in the same session, a group member announces she knows her mother is dying and that it is "just a matter of time." She explains she knows what to do, as she is Jewish and the rituals are clear and mandated by tradition, to which the other group members respond, "You're so lucky."

"Lucky," they tell her, "because you do know what to do. We aren't sure what our parents want. Nor do we know what the rest of the family wants for them."

Another member tells the group how horrible and expensive it was when her father died, because no one knew what to do. The family was devastated by the unexpected and unprepared-for death.

Another workshop member expresses concern about his wife, whose self-care abilities are rapidly deteriorating as a result of progressive multiple sclerosis. The new medication taken intravenously slows the downward trajectory of the disease, but not enough, and not for long. He insists his wife is not old enough for this, and her disease is intolerable. To this outpouring, the group is uncharacteristically quiet and vaguely ill-at-ease. I discover later he is a young executive being nurtured for top-level management, literally on the way "up," who has not previously acknowledged his wife's condition to his employer or co-workers. Immediately after the meeting, during his regular lunch hour, we meet individually to work out a referral to a full-time case manager who might be able to give him the "second opinion" he thinks he needs. And any other resource he may be able to put in place for himself through Norecom or privately.

During the next workshop session, our group continues to work through the agenda, some items directly with hand-outs, some through computer-based presentation, some from the lesson plans, and some indirectly, and often more effectively, through the group members' real life experiences in this role they are eager to fulfill more effectively. A few members will consider, and should, giving up the primary caregiver role in the interest of the better care of their dependent family member and their own good health. Other than mentioning this option, which is always there, it is not directly nor fully pursued during the workshop. Such is for other times and bigger spaces.

After exploring a wide range of topics, the clock tells us it is time to wind up, which our group does by discussing the effectiveness of the workshop and by responding to evaluation forms provided for the task. We end this last session by viewing a short and old but great video portraying the importance of human contact to persons at every stage of development. It provides a stunning intellectual and emotional prelude to our exit and goodbyes. We take our leave knowing we have all been changed by our having been together.

Two weeks after this wind-up session, the Jewish group member's mother passes away. I am invited to sit shiva with the family at home, which I do. I report my post-workshop activity to my corporation contact person—in this instance, the visionary human resources leader at Norecom. I do not ask permission. After the condolence visit, the group member says she will call me. She does not. I do not contact her, which I might have done in other professional contexts.

So, what were the facilitators and constraints to good social work, to good helping, in this setting and sub-field? In case you need some suggestions:

- how to avoid putting something in motion that cannot be adequately followed up and how to follow up directly and appropriately when and if necessary within the built-in limits to social worker autonomy in business settings and the resources of the in-place Telephone Information and Referral Service and the Employee Assistance Program (Pace, 2006);

- how to manage the formalities of the business context, including instructional style, crisp, very focused, technologically sophisticated;

- dress, business conservative, in this corporation, only computer technicians "dress down;"

- language, including assessing and encouraging the most useful level of emotional investment and expression, technically known in the people-helping professions as "optimum cathexis" always cognizant of the short-term nature of the intervention and the expectation that workshop members return to their business tasks immediately after workshop sessions;

- record-keeping, what is committed to paper and why;

- how to make sure the risks of care are identified and protected against through clear procedures and protocols and through formal insurance coverage, including both risk management and safety assessment;

- and perhaps the most difficult, how to guarantee the group members' confidentiality and job security; that is, that omnipresent ethically perplexing imperative: Who is the client? Executive management who pay the workshop facilitators/instructors' fees or the employee workshop members?

Indeed, working with groups in business and industry presents several challenges not usual in most social work with groups in social work service delivery systems and other age-service systems. First, there are obvious differences of caregiver group members' younger age, younger than the elders to whom they provide care, but often not too much younger. Second, the members have greater functional capacity. The major differences of groups in business and industry are largely consequences of the context—the larger social system in which the groups function, the corporation, business, or the for-profit facility.

As indicated, the most critical challenge is the potential for conflict between the employee's job interests and help-seeking for self and family. Balancing confidentiality and self-disclosure, always sensitive elements in groups, is even more daunting when job status may be at stake, real or imagined. Most workplaces are very competitive, and many employees, especially older workers, feel threatened by what they fear may be perceived as weakness or inability to cope at home. Legislation such as the Age Discrimination in Employment Act (ADEA), the Americans with Disabilities Act (ADA), the Family and Medical Leave Act (FMLA), and the National Family Caregiver Support Program (NFCSP) were intended to relieve that pressure.

Another difference between groups in corporate settings and groups in other social service systems is reflected in the influence of the degree of client choice (Germain & Gitterman, 1980), the extent to which the service is sought, mandated, or proffered; with consequences singly or in combination for group process and the role of the group worker and group members. Conceding that under certain circumstances mandated services can be therapeutic, there seemed to be no compulsion for employees to attend the workshops, but the group facilitators did not develop the rosters. Workshop members rarely dropped out, but it did happen. Perhaps contributing to employee apprehension, inadvertently or otherwise, may be the more common practice of requiring individual, case by case, intervention when problems arise in workplace productivity. Also the bulk of social work direct service-delivery in business and industry is contracted out, with few institutionalized full-time social work roles in the workplace, limiting employee familiarity with what social workers can or will do. Large and mid-size workplaces employ a nurse, sometimes several, on-site, year-round, full-time. Furthermore, social workers in business and industry frequently function outside the scope of social work practice as traditionally defined. For example, social workers are directors of on-site child care centers, public relations agents for assisted living facilities, and admissions officers for residential care settings. (Zastrow, 2004)

On the plus side for social workers contemplating careers in corporate life, salary levels per diem and per hour do tend to be higher in corporate settings as contrasted with other more traditional age-service settings, but most per diem arrangements cannot replace a full-time job with benefits. The context and the model of service delivery will differ in each corporate/business/industry site. However, in both corporate and in social service agencies, when face-to-face with other people with the pressures of serious problems needing solutions, people in groups can and do leave what could become the negative influences of context outside the door. However, it isn't easy for them or the social worker.

Overall, social work with groups in business and industry tends to be more short-term, more subject to the influence of larger system factors, and more limited to group programming not dependent on continuity, with less discretion and professional autonomy for the social worker. Within the group qua group, universal small group processes pertain, including variables of belongingness/affiliation and avoidance; sentiment/morale and feeling-tone; activity/purpose; interaction/stratification, sub-group formation and role taking; norms/persistence and change; and worker definition and influence, all of which is familiar territory to social workers who know, value, and are skillful in and with groups. Social work assessment sorts out the similarities and differences of contexts (external social system factors) and of groups (internal social system factors) but the epistemological dilemma (Germain & Gitterman, 1980) of how to know how much you need to know before you can begin/intervene will always be in play, as will be the humbling realization that no one ever knows "enough." Rapidly changing families; rapidly changing professional ideologies, funding auspices, and sponsorship patterns; and rapidly changing workplaces nationally and globally add to the dazzling complexity that can be comprehended, if not fully understood, and managed through professional know-how, creativity, and readiness to take reasonable risks. New settings, new organizational arrangements, and service models will continue to emerge and will likely be even more complex and more challenging. In that largely uncertain and depersonalized future context, in any context, help giving and help taking will never be easy. But you will know it when you see it, can do it, and can give it a name, even when it's not in English.

Think About It

1. For-profit service delivery systems are proliferating. What current or future for-profit settings in the age-service system are likely to employ social workers or might be improved with social work input? How? Consider banks, real estate agencies, travel agencies, and so forth.

2. Several synonyms for social work in business and industry have emerged, including "Occupational Social Work," "Social Work in the Workplace," and "Industrial Social Work." Identify the qualities of these settings differentiating them from the more traditional settings in the practice of gerontological social work.

3. Although there are elements of group process universal to all human groups, there are many different kinds of groups that are relevant to social work practice. Differentiate: membership groups, reference groups, activity groups, counseling groups, therapy groups, support groups, psychoeducational groups, task groups, focus groups, social groups, self-help groups. Can you think of others?

4. Why is there so much emphasis on family caregiving and services for elders "in place"? For years, professionals have focused on "caregiver demand" or "caregiver strain." Today, "caregiver gain" is recognized. What is it, and why is it an important concept?

5. How has the ever-growing application of information technology affected social work with groups, especially in the workplace? Include both positive and negative implications.

PART 6:
Policy
and Macro
Practice

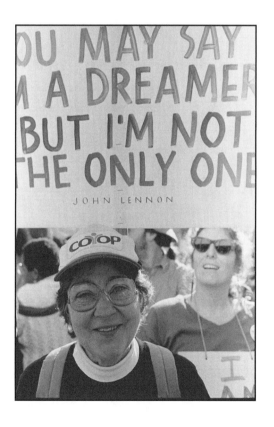

Chapter 36
Community Organizing in State Government

●●●●●●●●●●●●●●●●●●●●●

by Dale K. Laninga, MSW, ACSW

What a difference one year and one gubernatorial election can make. At the beginning of the year, I was the executive director of the Intra-Governmental Council on Long Term Care, a Council established by the state legislature made up of secretaries of Cabinet level departments; legislators; consumers; advocates; and representatives of state organizations like nursing homes, personal care homes, home health agencies, insurance, and housing. The purpose of the Council is to advise the governor and legislators about issues in long-term care. We did studies, issued reports, and made recommendations on issues such as the need to balance the long-term care system by putting more public funds into home- and community-based services rather than nursing homes to respond to what consumers have asked for, assisted living, recruitment and retention of direct care workers, removing barriers to consumers wanting to receive home and community based services, increasing the amount of affordable and accessible housing, and how to help people understand and plan for their long-term care needs.

At the end of the year, an election had occurred, a new governor was elected, and many of the recommendations the Council had made in its transition report to the new governor were being taken seriously and starting to happen. The first order of the new governor was the creation of a new Governor's Office of Health Care Reform. I was asked to be the Co-Director of Long Term Care Reform. Long-term care became a key component of health care reform in the state. Studying, recommending, and advocating is one thing;

implementing and making statewide system change is another. As the saying goes, "Be careful what you wish for; you may get it."

My social work education was in community organization, and I practice in state government. My days include lots of meetings. I meet with stakeholders to hear what they think is important and what they think needs to be changed. Sometimes I call the meetings, and sometimes they call the meetings. I may invite them to come to our offices, or I may go to where they are. There is some added value of going to where they are. It provides me the opportunity to not only hear but see how policy is being implemented and what needs to be improved, but also the opportunity to talk to front line staff and consumers. Frequently, I am asked to attend annual meetings or training conferences to make formal presentations.

Many meetings are with professional staff from the different departments of state government that have a role in long-term care—the Department of Aging, the Department of Public Welfare (which includes the Medicaid Office), the Office of Income Maintenance, and an office representing younger persons with physical disabilities. The primary purpose of many of these meetings is to get the various offices to work together to improve services for consumers. The topic may be how to make it easier for a person to apply for and receive services. What are the barriers? How could they be changed? Who needs to do what to make the change happen? Will regulations need to be changed? Will new policy need to be written? How will this affect the local agencies that are in direct contact with the consumers? What kind of training needs to occur before the change can occur? Will we need to change the procedures and forms that workers use? How long will it take to make the changes, have them reviewed by local workers, approved by the head of the department, printed, and out to the agencies around the state?

In all of the meetings, there is always the 800-pound gorilla in the room—the budget. Although many meetings are held to specifi- cally address budget issues, in all of our planning and designing, budget issues are always a consideration. There are initiatives to reduce costs, efforts to do more work with less money, and initiatives to start new programs to meet unmet needs. Medicaid budgets are a large, if not the largest, part of state budgets. There are always greater needs than resources, so every meeting, if not specific to cost, includes considerations about cost. Frequently, I am the advocate for the consumers and the funding needed to meet their needs. There is a perception that social workers only know how to ask for more funding and are not good managers of funds. It's encouraging to see social workers in management positions administering large budgets and doing so within the budget constraints they have. In my position, it is essential to understand the funding sources, know what the constraints and opportunities are, and be creative in working with others to maximize the use of public funds.

Another part of my day is spent meeting and talking with legislators and legislative staff to explain what we are doing, why we want to do it, and answering their questions. Some of the most valuable time spent is with the legislative staff. They are the people who write up positions and explain issues to the legislators. Their understanding and support is critical to making change legislatively. Legislative committees have both majority and minority staff. Although it is the majority who are in power today, that can and does change, so time and effort spent with minority staff often pays off when legislators change and the minority staff become the majority.

Development of grant proposals in response to requests from federal agencies or private foundations may be a part of the day. These grants often are the only new money I can find to try out a new idea or improve something we are already doing. Not every grant opportunity is worth pursuing. The time and support needed to make it happen if we were to receive the grant may not be there. There may be extensive reporting and process requirements that make the grant undesirable. While there is often pressure to bring in more funding, it always comes with strings attached. Explaining to consumers and agencies why you want to (or don't want to) apply for the grant, getting their support including letters of support, projecting budgets, and securing all the official signatures can be very time consuming.

Another aspect of my day is communicating or meeting with people from other states. Because we have developed some innovative projects, I am frequently asked to spend time explaining to staff in other states what we are doing. Sometimes they come to see and meet people; often it is done through conference calls or in person in meetings convened by federal officials or national organizations. Each of these requires time to plan and carry out. The flip side of this is contacting other states to find out what they are doing, whether it worked, what it cost, and what are the pitfalls to watch out for. I do a significant amount of sharing and receiving information from staff in other states. This may involve being part of a national study or reviewing proposals for funding sources that are planning to give out funds.

So what is a community organizer doing in state government? That's a question I have often been asked. My response is "organizing." Ever since I started work in state government, I have been using my organizing skills to get things accomplished and bring about change that will benefit the consumer. In our state, responsibilities for long-term care are located in many different departments and agencies. To start a new program or make changes requires getting many people with vested self interests to come together around a new idea or new way of doing things. It's what organizers do best. My community happens to be consumers, advocates, state agencies, state and local organizations, legislators, and other interested persons. The skills I use today are the same that I used when I was organizing tenants in a neighborhood. The social work values remain the same and serve as a foundation for practice and decision making. Learning about the power structure and figuring out how to influence it are the same. The difference is the venue. My community is the entire state.

There are many skills needed in this kind of position. Probably first and foremost are facilitation skills. Collaboration is essential, so I need to convince people why they should be involved and what's in it for them and the people they serve. In almost every situation I work with, there are competing interests. For example, the effort to balance our long-term care system by making it possible for people to receive care at home rather than going to a nursing home has potential negative implications for nursing homes. For example, a vibrant in-home long-term care program might mean that nursing homes will lose funding or at least not continue to be the only option in town to provide long-term care services. This can create conflicts between advocates for nursing homes and advocates for organizations that provide home- and community-based services. It's not unusual to have younger persons with physical disabilities, some of whom refer to nursing homes as prisons and engage in civil disobedience, sitting across the table from nursing home administrators who are promoting their interests. Budget officials are sitting across from advocates who want more funds. Legislative staff may have ideologically polar positions on a subject. State agencies may have a different point of view from local agencies or from each other. My job is to facilitate the collaboration needed to get the task accomplished.

Trust, respect, and fairness are critical. If the people I work with don't trust me or don't think I will be fair to their point of view, they will not stay involved. How issues are framed and the words that are used to describe something have to be carefully thought through. This applies to both oral and written communication. I believe that some practical experience in an agency or organization that interacts directly with consumers is essential before someone takes a position at the state level working on policy or system change.

Patience, perseverance, and being ready to seize the day are helpful in this job. There are times when the subject area of long-term care is hot and on people's agendas, and there are times when it is not. In government, that can change very quickly. A major fire with lives lost immediately makes personal care homes a top agenda item for legislators and administrators. A new legislator elected to a key committee post who has had practical experience, either good or bad, in getting care for his or her mother can quickly change the committee's interest in the issue. When opportunities arise, it is important to be prepared and ready to present recommendations and solutions to the issue of concern.

A major issue in long-term care (or long-term living, as some people say) is balancing the system, which means making home- and community-based services as real a choice for people as nursing homes. Under Medicaid, the primary funding for long-term care, nursing home care is an entitlement, and home- and community-based services are not. Yet consumers consistently say they would rather receive their care at home rather than in a nursing home, and the cost is generally less in the community than in a nursing home. Growing Medicaid cost is a significant issue and it is exacerbated by the demographics, which include the upcoming baby boomers. Increasingly, people want a choice in where they receive their care and services and how they receive them. They also want to make the decisions instead of being told what to do by a care manager or agency. Related to this are workforce issues. Direct care workers—those persons who provide the hands-on care—are paid low wages and often can make more money and get better benefits in other industries like fast food and retail. Recruitment and retention of direct care workers is an issue that needs to be addressed. Already, projections show that there will not be an adequate number of workers to meet the upcoming demand. Wages, working conditions, and training are all part of this issue. An additional issue is how much of the cost of long-term care should be paid by the person with private funds and how much should be paid by public funds.

There is little time left in a day to respond to e-mail, answer phone calls, and take care of the normal administrative tasks. Increasingly, meetings are being called earlier and later in the work day to accomplish what needs to be done. But that's something that social workers who do community organization have known for some time. That's why this is being written on the weekend!

Think About It

1. How is this social worker's role similar to organizing tenants in a neighborhood? How is it different?

2. The writer says, "A major issue in long-term care is balancing the system." What does he mean by this?

Chapter 37

Gray and Gay: Lesbian, Gay, Bisexual, and Transgender Aging

● ●

by Lisa Krinsky, MSW, LICSW

I am the Director of the LGBT Aging Project in Boston, an organization whose mission is to ensure that lesbian, gay, bisexual, and transgender elders have equal access to the life-prolonging benefits, protections, services, and institutions that their heterosexual neighbors take for granted. Until our formation, there was no organized effort in Massachusetts to understand and address the needs of this invisible, isolated, understudied, and unquestionably disenfranchised population. Typically, LGBT elder activists replicate mainstream services and provide them directly to elders. While this is important work, the LGBT Aging Project has a different approach: we are a catalyst for conversation, consensus building, and change within the vast aging services infrastructure that already exists. We offer education and technical assistance to fair minded mainstream providers who are willing to serve all clients competently, equally, and sensitively—but in this case, simply don't know how. We offer a framework for elders, their families, and caregivers who are willing to advocate for themselves.

Like many small nonprofit organizations, we are an overwhelmingly volunteer-based organization. I am the only full-time staff person, and we have recently hired a part-time outreach/education coordinator through a grant we received. I also have a great social work intern who has experience in elder care and is focusing on macro practice in gerontology. I report to our Steering Committee, which oversees the LGBT Aging Project.

So what do I do? Much of my time, I am conducting educational trainings for elder care providers, consulting with mainstream elder

239

care organizations, giving presentations to community groups, advocating with state legislators on behalf of LGBT elders, planning events and programs, writing grants, and working with a caregiver support program. I spend a lot of time multitasking and working independently. This is really exciting, innovative work. There is no one else in the state of Massachusetts doing this kind of work, and very few others across the country.

So, a typical day in a job that has no typical days....

8 a.m.-9:30 a.m.: I get to the office about 8 a.m. The LGBT Aging Project rents office space from a mainstream elder care agency, so I have the benefit of being with other people (rather than working from home, or in an office all alone). It's nice to have this sense of connection, rather than complete isolation. I also spend a lot of time out of the office, consulting with a variety of mainstream elder care agencies throughout the state that are working on becoming inclusive of the issues around LGBT aging. This means I also spend a lot of time in my car.

As with many jobs, a lot of my communication with our 250 members and constituents is through e-mail, so that can be time consuming. But there are two very exciting e-mails awaiting me this morning.

First, our Public Policy Committee is working with local legislators to refile the MassHealth Equality bill, and 42 of 200 state representatives and senators have signed on as sponsors. This bill proposes that Massachusetts' Medicaid program will grant to all married same-sex couples the same responsibilities, rights, benefits, and protections guaranteed to opposite sex married couples recognized by federal law. This is particularly important here in Massachusetts, because we are currently the only state with same sex marriage. Federal law does not recognize these marriages, and Medicaid is funded through state and federal matching funds. For elders, this is a crucial matter, as they face long-term care issues and consider how to pay for a spouse's long-term care without impoverishing the community spouse. Medicaid has regulations regarding income and home ownership in place to prevent the community spouse from impoverishment and homelessness. We believe that Massachusetts has an obligation to extend these benefits and obligations to all married couples, regardless of the state and federal split.

We have refiled this bill, since it didn't make it through the legislative system in the last session. This has been a great way for me to learn about the legislative process.

I e-mail the Public Policy Committee that we'll have to schedule time to visit legislators at the State House to talk with them further about our bill. I also contact an LGBT senior couple to join us. Real people help legislators "see" real issues. These two women, in their late 60s, have been together for almost 20 years and married for three years. These issues are a very worrisome reality for them.

The second exciting e-mail is from the National Gay and Lesbian Task Force. The task force is hosting the second meeting of its National Roundtable on LGBT Aging in DC in a few weeks. About 30 of us have been invited to participate in this work group to craft a national agenda on LGBT aging. I attended the first Roundtable meeting last June and RSVP that I'll be there again. It's great to work with other professionals who are dedicated to the issues around LGBT aging. The downside of being a leader in an innovative field is that I have few colleagues who actually do the same kind of work I do, so it's encouraging to build a network with people in Chicago, California, DC, Wisconsin, and elsewhere throughout the country. Many of these people are also members of the American Society on Aging (ASA) and its affiliate group LGAIN (Lesbian and Gay Aging Issues Network), which issues newsletters on a regular basis and keeps us up to date on what our peers are doing.

9:30 a.m.-12:00 p.m.: I spend the next two and a half hours working on a new grant proposal. Most of our funding comes from grants. We have a very small budget (less than $150,000/year), and each grant is extremely important to maintaining and hopefully expanding our efforts. This grant proposal is for general operating expenses, so I will focus on a broad overview of our mission and our efforts. Some grants have been more program specific—we have a caregiver grant that supports our LGBT Caregiver Support Group and the LGBT Bereavement Group we hope to start soon. I am a good writer, and the only daunting parts of writing a grant proposal are finding quiet time without distractions (phone calls, e-mails, piles of other work) to concentrate on writing. Sometimes I'll do that at home, or take my laptop to the library.

Part of preparing a grant proposal includes the financial budget information, so I am on the phone with our accountant to prepare the details of our budget for this grant proposal. She e-mails me a draft of the budget, and we review it before including it in the grant proposal.

As a small nonprofit, we don't handle the "business" end of our work. We work with an organization whose mission is to support small nonprofits by acting as their fiscal sponsor. We operate under the fiscal sponsor's 501(c)(3), which certifies federal tax-exempt, nonprofit status, and our organization is provided with the accounting, financial management, legal, and contract writing and signatures, human resources services, and benefits. I am officially an employee of the fiscal sponsor and receive salary and benefits through that organization. We pay the fiscal sponsor a small percentage of our operating budget for its services. This has been a great resource for the LGBT Aging Project, as my background is in clinical social work, and I don't have the skills for that kind of accounting and financial management.

12:15 p.m.: I jump into my car and head off to a local hospital for a presentation. I leave myself enough time to find parking and the location of my presentation. My social work intern is joining me to observe this presentation, and we chat about her project on our way there. Official supervision is at the end of the week.

1 p.m.-2:30 p.m.: I am presenting "LGBT Aging 101: What You Need To Know About Lesbian, Gay, Bisexual, and Transgender Elders" for the geriatric medical team at this large teaching hospital in Boston. There are about 30 people present—staff physicians, nurses, social workers, and the interns working with them. This team provides hospital- and community-based care for the elders of Boston. I use my standard PowerPoint presentation and have distributed handouts so they can follow along. I give them an overview of our mission, and then educate them about general LGBT information before focusing on elder-specific issues—legal, financial, social, historical. One of the participants tells me, "I treat everyone the same," and this leads to a terrific conversation about what has been unique in LGBT elders' experiences. Having experienced institutional homophobia by medical, educational, faith, legal, housing, and employment providers, many LGBT elders learned to be invisible to avoid discrimination. That lack of trust in systems whose intentions are to be helpful means that how providers approach their clients can have a powerful impact. We focus on interviewing techniques, how to ask questions, and ways to talk about LGBT issues with elders. Some participants share their experiences working with LGBT elders and their families and learn from each other as well as from me. Evaluation forms indicate they found the presentation interesting and valuable to their work. That feels good.

2:30 p.m.-3:30 p.m.: I have left the hospital after the training and checked my office voice mails (because if I'm out of the office, then the office is closed!). Nothing urgent. I can follow up tomorrow. I head off to an eldercare agency about 20 miles away for a meeting with the staff.

3:30 p.m.–5:00 p.m.: I am at a mainstream elder care agency outside of Boston. They are one of a dozen agencies participating in a program I developed called "Open Door Task Force," which provides technical assistance and consulting to agencies who want to become inclusive of LGBT elders. These meetings occur every other month, and the Task Force consists of a cross section of their staff that reflect the communities they serve. At each meeting, I find a way to reiterate my training mantra: "This is cultural competency work to enhance your professional skills." We agree that all elders should be treated with respect and dignity and that regardless of anyone's personal feelings about LGBT issues, they have a professional obligation to their clients. Although no one in the work group disagrees with this message, I still repeat it frequently.

This Task Force has reviewed its own internal policies on hiring, benefits, and training for staff, and it has looked at how it works with its clients and their families. We looked at the Task Force's outreach materials, its intake forms, practice skills, and work with community partners. This agency has made a commitment to being inclusive of LGBTs, and our next step will be an outreach effort to LGBT elders and family caregivers in its service area. The LGBT Aging Project will use our connections in the LGBT community to support these efforts and give this mainstream group credibility.

5:00 p.m.-6:00 p.m.: I am driving home and call the outreach/ education coordinator to talk about the plans he is developing for our participation in Boston's Gay Pride week in June. He really enjoys event planning and I don't, so it's a great relief to have him on board juggling details with a smile on his face. This year, we will host our fourth annual Tea Dance for LGBT elders and their friends. It is the only official Pride Event that caters to older people. We are proud of this event and usually have a few hundred LGBT elders dancing, eating, socializing, and having fun!

So how did I become the director of the LGBT Aging Project? I have an MSW and have done both clinical work in community mental health and about 15 years in mainstream community-based elder care, from case management (my own caseload of about 65 elders) to grants manager to the director of home care (overseeing a staff of 20 case managers with about 100 clients each). I had been an active member of the LGBT Aging Project since its inception in 2001, and I pursued this position because working with the LGBT Aging Project was an opportunity to meld personal and professional interests. So many of us in this field also ask—what will happen to me when I get older? What do I want for myself? Most of us share the basic desire to live our later years with respect and dignity.

The LGBT Aging Project is an opportunity to do new, exciting, and innovative work. I am thrilled to be part of a culture change that is creating visibility for a previously invisible population.

Think About It

1. How would you advocate for inclusion of LGBT elders in a conservative agency or community? How would you draw out or engage LGBT elders themselves?

2. Consider that "tolerance" includes a balance of giving voice to disagreeing parties. How do you create space for those who do and don't support LGBT rights? How do staff members reconcile personal biases and a professional obligation?

3. How well do you know your own work style? How much structure do you need to be successful in your work—managing tasks, creating schedules, networking, and marketing your services? How well do you work alone? With a team? With a colleague? With a supervisor? As a supervisor?

PART 7:
Student, Educator, and Researcher Perspectives

Chapter 38
Field Placement in Geriatric Case Management
• •

by Trevor Gates, MSW, ACSW, LMSW

W hat led you to the social work profession?" asked the field coordinator at Norfolk State University, upon my interview for my first field placement in my Master of Social Work program.

"I believe in the human potential, and that I can make a difference in people's lives," I said, the idealistic social work student.

After completing my bachelor's degree, I explained, I realized that my path would change. Attending law school no longer seemed so appealing. I had completed internships in social service agencies, such as the Older Adults Program at Episcopal Charities and in Adult Case Management at Probation and Parole. I had worked with children and families at a local nonprofit agency serving at-risk families. My work in the community had nurtured my love for people and helped me realize that a career as a social worker could be an option.

"I would like to work with older adults," I responded, as my field coordinator helped me explore my social work practice interests.

Several months prior, a professor who specialized in gerontology and taught Human Behavior in the Social Environment encouraged me to consider a social work placement working with older adults. Gerontological social work is a growing practice area, with lots of opportunities. Even if I eventually decided that gerontological social work was not my calling, she said, a field placement working with older adults would be excellent training ground for a new social worker.

The field coordinator had a place in mind for such an experience. Although the site would be a bit of a drive for me, Our Lady of Peace Independent Living Center (OLP) would be an excellent place to gain social work case management experience.

Off I was to OLP, to develop my practice skills as a budding new social worker!

My Typical Day

Fast forward several weeks, and I have interviewed and been accepted as the new MSW intern at Our Lady of Peace Independent Living Center in Portsmouth, Virginia. OLP is a nonprofit independent living center, funded by Section 8, primarily for older adults. All of the clients, or "residents," as we call them, live in separate apartments, on unlocked units, and are able to come and go as they please. OLP has several full-time staff, including an executive director, registered nurse, and bachelor's level social worker. Although the agency offers an array of social service and supportive activities, each resident must be able to function independently. This typically includes being able to complete activities of daily living, including bathing, keeping their apartments clean, and preparing their own meals (or arranging for meals to be otherwise delivered, such as by Meals on Wheels).

Days at OLP can range from laid back and casual to hectic and fast-paced, which is excellent training ground for geriatric case management. Below reflects a "typical" day during my placement at OLP:

7:00 a.m.: My day begins about an hour earlier than my scheduled time at my field placement site, as the traffic tends to be unpredictable. The full-time workers at Our Lady of Peace (OLP) Independent Living Center tend to have some flexibility on their arrival time, as the executive director understands that travel time is difficult to estimate. As I leave my studio apartment in Norfolk, VA, I see that the traffic at the Hampton Roads Bridge Tunnel is at a standstill. It looks like today will be another day of listening to several chapters of my books on compact disc on the way to work.

8:00 a.m.: I arrive to Our Lady of Peace five minutes before our scheduled morning meeting, so I head straight to the conference room. OLP executive director, Kenyetta Harrison, is already seated at the table. Judy Jones, the nurse case manager, "called to say she would be a few minutes late," says Kenyetta, and Domingo Rodriguez, the agency BSW-level social worker, "is filling the coffee carafe." One of my first lessons at OLP, when I began my placement several months ago, was that no staff member was too proud to make coffee. In fact, Kenyetta joked during the field placement interview that the ability to make coffee was one of the prerequisites for all of the agency positions, the executive director position included.

8:20 a.m.: Several minutes lapse, and Judy, the nurse case manager, has called again to let us know to begin the meeting, as she is delayed in traffic. Domingo has returned with the coffee carafe and empty cups for all. Kenyetta begins the daily meeting by reviewing several of the high-risk clients. Although the center does not provide full nursing care, the agency has a policy and appropriate staff to address the psychosocial needs of the residents. "I received word from one of the residents that Cloris Wilson, in 303, has not been seen out of her apartment in about a week. I'd like for someone to assess her before noon today," says Kenyetta. Domingo will be out in the community doing marketing and outreach today, so the task of assessing the client is assigned to me, the social work student. "Please come and see me after you've seen Ms. Wilson, even if it means interrupting a meeting," says Kenyetta.

9:30 a.m.: Our daily meeting ends, and I am proceeding to the chart room, to review Cloris Wilson's chart. Ms. Wilson's chart has a very limited history, as she has consistently refused case management contacts by the agency staff. Since the agency is an independent living center, the residents are not required to participate in social work services, including activities and case management. The chart does reflect, however, that the client is a 65-year-old woman with a history of bipolar disorder with psychotic features. She was sexually assaulted while in the Armed Forces, 20 years ago, and has an intensive case manager who follows her at the Veterans Affairs Hospital. A release is on file for the VA, as she receives all of her ongoing medical services there. As I approach the room, I notice that the door is open. I knock on the door and hear a grunt from Ms. Wilson. She comes to the door, has a disheveled appearance, and appears to have soiled herself. Ms. Wilson invites me inside her apartment, and I immediately notice what appears to be feces spread on the walls. I determine after several minutes with Ms. Wilson that she has "lost" her medication and has not showered in several days. I determine from our initial meeting that she may require services beyond what is available at the independent living center. I consult with my executive director, and we determine together to call for an ambulance from the VA hospital. Additionally, we page the client's hospital case manager, who will meet Ms.Wilson in the emergency room.

11:00 a.m.: I return to my office to gather my supplies for one of my weekly activity groups. Among the activity groups that I lead at the facility, my crocheting group is one of my favorite. Eight women and one man, with ages ranging from 55 to 75, participate in my weekly crocheting group. The group offers them an opportunity to socialize with one another and to participate in an activity that they enjoy. In this setting, there seems to be a great deal of stigma that accompanies participating in a therapy group. However, many of the clients are more than willing to participate in activity groups. At first, the residents seemed quite amused that a young male social worker, in his mid-twenties, was adept at crocheting. Now, the young crocheting social worker hardly phases them. As I enter the group room, I see that Bernadine Gokhale, from 417, is preparing the group's coffee. I place my yarn and crochet hook on the table and make small talk with the residents before group begins. We begin the group with "check-in," or an opportunity for the group members to discuss their activities this week. If my field placement at OLP has taught me one thing, it is that the social worker must meet the clients where they are, and that the social worker must be willing to "think out of the box." My crocheting activity group certainly might qualify as a less than ordinary social work activity!

12:00 noon: Mornings at OLP can be very busy, indeed. After a productive morning, I realize that today is Wednesday, the day that I meet several other MSW students for lunch. When I began the MSW program, I soon learned that making time to have lunch with other students was an excellent opportunity to collaborate and to offer one another ideas. Even more, our lunch meetings allow us some additional time to vent our frustrations and to share with one another our struggles in field placement. (In fact, spending lunch with other colleagues in the community would become a practice that I followed after completing my MSW.) I arrive at the local Korean buffet, finding my fellow students and colleagues Ebony Jackson and Derrick Wilson waiting. Ebony and Derrick are completing their field placements at a local child welfare agency. I approach the table as Derrick is recounting an incident during which he was spit upon by a client, as well as called racial and homophobic slurs. Ebony offers Derrick reassurance that field placement is very time-limited, but says that he should not accept abusive language. It sounds as if my colleagues have had an exciting week, as well.

1:00 p.m.: I return to OLP after lunch, feeling refreshed after spending some time with my social work colleagues. I have a regularly scheduled case management session with Roderick Nelson, who lives in 514, at 1:30. Roderick has recently lost his partner, Jose, after a long battle with AIDS, and is looking for ways to reconnect with the local gay and lesbian community. I arrive at my office to find several clients waiting. Judy Jones, the nurse case manager, has since arrived and is taking a resident's blood pressure. Judy motions to several people waiting in the lobby and asks me if I have a few minutes to see a client or two before my afternoon case management sessions. I scan the list of clients who are waiting and see that Diana Lamberson, in 219, just needs help completing her re-certification paperwork for Section 8 assistance. I call Diana back to my office and discover that she has completed the majority of her paperwork herself. Diana just needs help with making photocopies of her supplementary documents, which is a task that takes well under the time I need to prepare for my 1:30 session.

1:30 p.m.: I head to the common area to look for my scheduled client, Roderick. One of the other gay men living at OLP, who is friends with Roderick, spots me looking around the lobby. "If you're looking for Roderick," he says, "he had to leave to go to the Divine Hope Metropolitan Community Church Food Bank." The man continues, "They came by without calling, to take him to go shopping, and he has to go whenever they come to get him." I've come to learn that missed appointments in this setting are not terribly unusual. I make a mental note to look for Roderick later in the day. There's always other work to be done.

2:00 p.m.: I return to my office area to find that Judy, the nurse case manager, has seen all of the drop-in clients who were waiting. Since all of the clients have been seen, I decide to spend a few minutes working on documentation. I typically use the time both to work on agency-related documentation and to write my process recordings, as required by the university as part of my field placement. As I begin working on my documentation, the telephone rings. The caller is Joseph Jenkins, Ph.D., LCSW. Dr. Jenkins has been serving as both my field liaison and my field instructor, since the agency does not have an MSW-level social worker on staff. Dr. Jenkins asks whether we can reschedule group supervision from Thursday to Friday, as one of the other group members has a sick child. OLP has offered its conference rooms for the supervision groups, so Dr. Jenkins asks that I make sure the rescheduled time is okay with the executive director. I briefly glance at the conference room meeting schedule calendar, and I see that the conference room is free on Friday. I end the call and return to my documentation work.

4:00 p.m.: My afternoon and documentation work is complete, interrupted only once by resident Georgia Nelson, a high functioning 88-year-old woman who was a veterinarian assistant prior to retiring. She drops by the office most days just "to talk." I shut down my computer for the day and head to the parking lot. In the parking lot, I see Roderick, my earlier client, just returning from his visit to the food bank. Roderick apologizes for missing his appointment, but says that he will call tomorrow to schedule another time. As I end my day, I reflect upon my day's work at OLP. I'll have plenty of time to reflect on the day's work, as I have about an hour of traffic to endure. I'll drop by a fast-food restaurant on the way to school, just in time for my 5:30 class, "Social Work with Individuals." Life as a social work student is always on the run, and always busy—which undoubtedly will be good preparation for my daily work after graduate school.

Gerontological social work is a growing practice area with many opportunities available. Although my field placement at OLP ultimately may lead me to other practice areas, I found that the generalist case management experience I obtained at OLP was both useful and timely. Not only did my experience at OLP teach me about the broad field of gerontological social work, but the experience also taught me about the diversity of the older adult experience. The field of gerontological social work represents people of varying ages, ethnicities, cultures, and sexual orientations. My field education at OLP was, indeed, great preparation for my career as a social worker!

Think About It

1. What are the differences between geriatric case managers trained in social work and those from other allied disciplines, such as nursing and counseling?

2. How can you develop your cultural competency in working with older adults who identify as lesbian, gay, bisexual, or transgender?

3. What generic skills in gerontological social work are transferable to other settings?

Chapter 39
A Graduate Student's Experience in the Hartford Practicum Partnership Program

● ●

by Kathryn C. MacLean, BA

My classmates thought I was having a financial crisis. Why else would a person choose to work with older adults? I had only worked with youth in the past. A year with AmeriCorps in a community school and more than a year teaching in a self-contained classroom for at-risk youth made me want to try something new. Older adults faced different challenges from the youth I had worked with in the past. I wanted to explore a career path where I could make a difference not just in someone's life, but also in their day. The Hartford Foundation's Practicum Partnership Program (PPP) seemed like a great opportunity to explore something new.

When I applied for the program in December 2005, I wasn't sure what to expect. The program called for an intensive practicum rotation model. I would work at three practica sites for 10 weeks each. The goal was to discover if short, intensive exposure at numerous sites increased a student's competency in each of several aging competencies for working with older adults. (Since I started the program, the model has been changed to include longer rotations and a leadership seminar.) To give you a sense of the unique nature of my practicum experience, I will provide a snapshot of a day during each of my rotations.

I began my field experience at an assisted living facility run by the Catholic Church in Saint Louis. It was small, sad, and had that odor that makes people avoid visits to their grandparents. My first thought was: *how fast can I complete my hours and move on to someplace less depressing?* Day after day working in this facility would surely end my interest in aging. I was interested in macro-level practice, so the idea of creating a care plan for a resident didn't appeal to me.

I held on to these thoughts for the first few days. Then, something amazing took place. One of the residents' daughters brought her dog to the assisted living facility. I had never seen such a dramatic response. Molly, the pup, brought joy and excitement into the usually depressing facility. Everyone wanted a turn to pet her and give her a doggie biscuit. She had never eaten so well! A visit from a dog spurred what had been only a marginal interest into a career. How rewarding, to make someone's entire day, if not week, with one furry guest. My previous ideas about aging were slowly fading into new ones. I realized that I might actually be able to do the "good works" that made me choose social work as a profession.

My days at the facility were spent working in direct care services. On some days, I helped one of the residents, who had terrible tremors, write letters to her son. The two hours that we spent together were so meaningful to her. She found something that she could look forward to each week, and it also helped me greatly to know that my simple actions could affect someone in such a positive way.

While there, I also spent time with the community social worker, visiting caregivers and their loved ones in their homes. The objective for most of these visits was to help support the caregiver and work on finding resources.

At the conclusion of my first 10 weeks, I moved to the St. Louis Area Agency on Aging. There I applied my macro skills by organizing the local chapter of the Silver Haired Legislature, a group of seniors over age 65 who advocate for state support of senior services. They were active, articulate older adults who participated in meetings as mock senators and representatives of their constituencies. I learned much about the political process from them. For my final task, I helped them plan a trip to Jefferson City to advocate for themselves on behalf of senior issues. I made friends among the group with whom I remain in contact to this day.

On a daily basis at SLAAA, I worked in the Information and Assistance Department, connecting area seniors with home-delivered meals, tax help, and any other services that they may have needed. This was an especially interesting agency to work at during the summer, because St. Louis suffered a storm-related blackout. For a significant part of my practicum experience, I helped triage phone calls as SLAAA, city government, and other local agencies provided water, food, and ice to seniors who were without power for more than a week. Because this meant that many were left without air conditioning in the sweltering St. Louis summer, I got to be a part of an evacuation of residents to local cooling sites. It was a crash course in collaboration.

From the AAA, I moved on to my third and final rotation at the St. Louis Chapter of the Alzheimer's Association. At this practicum site, I recognized all of my macro-level interest and talents. I worked in the Outreach Department and, through this placement, worked on several community projects and initiatives. My first major project was the Faith Leaders Conference. Its main objective was to educate interfaith leaders about the signs and symptoms of Alzheimer's disease and how to support both the people with this diagnosis and their caregivers. My other tasks included law enforcement outreach and education, as well as fundraising events. I lectured extensively throughout the area on all facets of dementia support, from research to resources. In a burst of good fortune, my practicum at the Alzheimer's Association led to a temporary position at one of its major annual fundraisers, the Memory Walk in St. Charles County, Missouri.

Every day that I went to one of my sites, my view of older adults and their needs changed. I learned new ways of thinking about aging and the venues in which services are provided. There exist as many ways to age as there are people. The aging field is not only skilled nursing facilities with lonely residents languishing in smelly corridors waiting for their time to die. Working with older adults can be a dynamic experience. My practica experience widened my perceptions of aging.

Through my work at the Alzheimer's Association, I found my macro-level niche at an organization that works for practice and policy change, the best of both worlds. Through outreach and education, I served older adults, and simultaneously engaged the community.

Through my experiences in direct service, local government (the AAA), and a national nonprofit, I realized that there are many ways to work with older adults, challenging current perceptions of aging and the aging process. As the aging population increases, so will the opportunity to work with the aging in new ways. My thanks go to the Hartford Foundation for recognizing a need for gerontologically competent social workers and offering support to bring people into the field.

Think About It

1. Do you think the idea of practicum rotations, in aging or other specialties, is a good idea? Why or why not?

2. Look up the Hartford Practicum Partnership Program online and find out more about what it offers. Is this a program you would be interested in pursuing as a student? How would you go about being a part of this or a similar experience?

3. What are some benefits of bringing a dog into an assisted living facility? Do some research to find information about pet assisted therapy or animal assisted therapy.

Chapter 40
Learning the Ropes as a BSW Intern

• •

by Karen L. Sheriff

It is my first day at my internship at the Agency on Aging. I am both excited and nervous. Although I have a solid education in the generalist approach to social work from an accredited college that has prepared me for this moment, I still question whether I am ready. It is reassuring to know that the other BSW interns are experiencing similar feelings. Before I enter, I begin the process of reviewing what I would consider important for the first day—simple things like knowing who my supervisor is and feeling comfortable in an agency setting. I chose the Area Agency on Aging because I have a minor in gerontology. I consider the aged community a rewarding segment of our population, and I am anxious to be part of the process that will provide them with services they may need.

Initially, it is imperative to learn the procedures for providing services, the agency forms, the roles of the units within the agency, and the computer process. Sometimes patience is not my strongest point, and I most definitely have to practice it at this point. As with any new job or situation, it is essential to understand the operating of the system. My supervisor hands me a manual and instructs me to take the time to read it and complete any quizzes and paperwork inside. This takes longer than I anticipated, and during the process, it is necessary to watch a video. There is an awful lot of information in this manual, and I wonder to myself how it is possible to remember it all. I work really hard at concentrating and staying on task. This is an important part in ensuring that I can be an effective worker and an asset to the consumer. Once I read through some of it, though, there is some repetition, which adds to my overall learning process.

Now it is time to meet with the supervisors of the different units within the agency. First I meet with the ombudsman. The ombudsman has the primary responsibility of investigating and resolving complaints made by or for the aged population who are in long-term care facilities. She relies heavily on her network of volunteers who are trained by the state to work in conjunction with the ombudsman to ensure the safety of all long-term care residents. After meeting with her, I have the opportunity to meet with the volunteer coordinator. He networks to find volunteers within the community who are able to provide assistance in a variety of ways. The primary emphasis is on maintaining independence and, if at all possible, allowing the consumer to stay in his or her home. Sometimes something as simple as having someone to stop by to check in on the consumer or to provide an hour of respite relief for the caregiver can be all that is needed to assure the consumer is able to remain in his or her home. Another unit within the agency is the Family Caregiver Support Program. Its primary function is to assess families who are providing care for an aged consumer who is either residing with the caregiver or receiving the caregiver's services in the consumer's home. I continue to make my way through the different units within the agency, making a mental note on how focused the process is in maintaining consumers in their own homes, if at all possible.

On the second week of my internship, I start to consider research essential to the agency. Research is part of the intern program. By meeting the different supervisors within the agency and also by talking with the executive director, I am able to arrive at a research topic. Currently, this county is one of the few in Pennsylvania that has an Elder Abuse Task Force. The research I will focus on is an outcome evaluation measurement of the effectiveness of the Elder Abuse Task Force since its inception two years ago. This is an area of particular interest to me. The statistics support a staggering gap in the number of cases reported versus the actual incidence of elder abuse. It is estimated in some research that as many as 14 out of 15 cases go unreported. I believe this area needs to be recognized as a growing concern, and my hope is that by providing statistical data, I can arrive at a reportable conclusion. I start to gather data and discover that the Area Agency on Aging is not the only agency within the state that investigates crimes against elders. This adds another layer to my research. Since Pennsylvania does not have a central reporting agency, I will need to call the other agencies to get a copy of their annual reports. Even though this will take longer than I originally anticipated, I am still excited to be able to report this data. It is my hope that this research could possibly be used to advocate to provide additional services for the victims of elder abuse.

One of the care managers stops by my desk to see if I would like to ride along with her to complete an assessment on a new consumer. I agree anxiously. I have only completed paperwork in the manual, so to see an actual assessment will be great. First, we gather all the necessary paperwork to prepare for our visit. There is quite a bit to take with us. In addition, we need to create a file for this consumer on the computer system. The system used by the agency is the SAMS system. Information from the Intake and Referral Unit needs to be entered into the consumer's file, and then this information needs to be imported to the laptop. Laptops are used at the consumers' homes. Once everything is ready, we proceed to our appointment. On our way, we have an opportunity to talk about how the interview may go and what to expect. We are greeted warmly at the door. As we start the information gathering process, I am surprised that there are a total of 189 questions on the SAMS assessment questionnaire. I understand now why two hours are typically given for each assessment. The care manager explains to the consumer prior to his appointment that he needs to have his medications, income verification, insurance information, and any other information he may consider pertinent available for us when we get there. Although it would be easy to deviate from the questions with some personal stories, it is equally important to process the questions and return to the office to create a care plan. The consumer and his wife are very happy with the interview and options offered to meet their needs. During the interview process, the care manager inquires as to whether the consumer is a veteran. She discovers he is. At this point, she can offer an additional resource to possibly provide some assistance to him. He is very pleased with this information. When we leave, the care manager explains she will have a care plan available for him within the week. She will call and explain the process and start services if that is what he wants.

During the third week of my internship, I am able to work in the Intake and Referral Unit. This is the point of origin of all calls coming into the agency. The intake workers need to know enough about all the services within the agency to provide guidance to the consumers calling in. On the second day in the unit, I am trained on entering obituaries from the newspaper into the SAMS system. Even if the person who has died is under age 60, I still need to search for him or her in the system, because there is one service in the agency that is provided to people of all ages. It can be an emotional task to read obituaries, particularly when a child has died. Once the date of death is entered into the computer system, the care manager in the agency who is working or has worked with the consumer has to be informed. This is typically done through an agency form. Next, it is time to listen to the incoming calls. I listen while trying to determine the questions that would need to be asked for these individual circumstances. Sometimes the calls are simply requests about how to obtain services such as home delivered meals. There are guidelines for each service offered in the agency, but the basic eligibility questions that must be asked are: *Are you age 60+? What is your county of residence? What is your monthly income?* Home delivered meals are not related to income, but are related to whether the consumer is homebound and does not have anyone to prepare a hot meal. During this day, eight calls were received that were referred to the Adult Protective Service unit within the agency. Typically, incoming calls are answered in the order they are received, which sometimes means letting the calls go to voice mail, so that other calls can be returned. The exception to this is that the Adult Protective Service calls need to be answered and cannot be put into voice mail. The urgency of these calls supports this procedure. I realize I still have a lot to learn about all the procedures relating to the Area Agency on Aging.

As I get ready to leave, I make sure I am prepared for the next day. I run through the events of the day and try to apply my social work knowledge. I also review the social work values and ethics to each call and see how they applied. One area of emphasis in providing care for the aged population is self determination. Each consumer has the right to decide whether he or she wants the services or not. It is not up to the family, unless the consumer is not able to decide for himself or herself. I leave feeling good about my day and excited about what tomorrow will bring.

Think About It

1. What do you think your biggest challenge would be in working in a new agency?

2. Keeping focused and on task is important when conducting a needs assessment. How would you establish a relationship with the consumer while still completing the assessment in a timely manner? What social work skills could you use?

3. Self determination may be the biggest challenge in providing services to the aged consumer. What social work values and ethics guide social workers in this practice? When might the issue of self determination present an ethical dilemma?

Chapter 41
Teaching Aging by Concept and Example

• •

by Cynthia Garthwait, MSW, LCSW, ACSW

Heading to campus today to teach about the aging experience and about gerontological social work, I find myself mentally crafting what I hope will be effective learning experiences to prepare my students for the growing and fascinating field of gerontology. Fifteen years ago, this would not have been the case, not because I did not want to teach about aging, but because student interest was not at its current level. This encouraging and inspiring trend within the profession motivates me this morning to teach about the aging process, the social context of aging, practice approaches, and social policies that have a direct bearing on the quality of the aging experience. Mentally attributing this burgeoning interest in aging to striking demographic shifts, a growing body of social work knowledge about aging, interdisciplinary development of research about aging, and private foundation support for gerontological social work, I know that the years I spent encouraging students to pursue careers in aging have paid off. Today is one of the days I have been waiting for, a day when students are hungry to learn about aging.

As a social worker and social work educator who has worked in numerous settings with older adults, was the recipient of a federal training grant in aging in graduate school, has continued to expose herself to aging issues, and is involved in a myriad of interdisciplinary aging initiatives in academic settings, I find myself selecting from the assortment of interconnected pieces of knowledge, skill sets, value bases, and personal experiences that have shaped me as a gerontological social worker. This rich array of practice experiences and teaching techniques accumulated over time, polished and adapted to the changing needs of students and the evolving social context of practice, has developed into a resource-rich inventory of potential learning experiences I can customize depending on student needs. Today is my Social Gerontology course, and it is Week 4 of the semester. We have already covered the social context of aging, an overview of the demographics of aging, and the biology of aging. I find myself looking forward to the challenge of the rest of the semester—helping students begin to see the connections between social policy and practice, between research and practice, and between their personal and professional views of aging. Today's class will provide a foundation for those potential connections to be made.

As I prepare learning experiences for this afternoon, I count myself fortunate to be teaching about what I love. Teaching allows me to continue learning; to witness student growth; and to keep abreast of research, practice, and social policy developments in the field. I hope that the lecture I gave in the last class about the sociohistorical context of aging, combined with the service learning project I will describe to them today that involves matching each student with an elder to learn how to facilitate the life review process, will culminate in student reflection papers that detail the joys of connecting with someone more than 50 years older than themselves. I know from experience, however, that most students will be nervous about being able to bridge the generation gap. If they can come to see me as a mentor who understands their wish to connect and communicate with someone who grew up in a very different time than they, today I will be able to help them view this experience as an adventure of learning and growing.

As I assemble two hours of information and classroom experiences, I am simultaneously thinking ahead about how to package the myriad of potential experiences into chewable portions for the remainder of the semester. I cannot separate today from the coming weeks, and it is my job to weave ideas and skills together for my students. Soon I will also need to help them learn how the 2005 White House Conference on Aging social policy recommendations will be implemented nationwide, why current research on dementia holds promise, how issues of poverty affect the process of aging through cumulative disadvantage, and how spirituality over the lifespan influences the aging process. Not only that, I must figure out how to help students see the linkages between policy, research, social conditions, and individual clients' perspectives on their own aging. This is no small task, I tell myself, but a truly exciting teaching challenge.

I chuckle to myself when I recall a question my mother asked me when I began my career in social work. Proud of me because of my commitment to a helping profession, but unfamiliar with what social workers really do, she wondered how I knew how to structure each work day. I have thought about her honest question many times. Because she was a teacher herself and because now I am one, also, I can relate to it even more. How DO I know what to do today and every other day that will be useful to my students in a planful, organized, yet spontaneous (when needed) manner?

What I told her about social work and what I will do today as a professor, is to assess needs, consider alternatives, prioritize possibilities, ask clients (and now my students) what their goals are, select and implement approaches, and evaluate our success together. This process, known to both students and social workers as the helping process at all levels of practice, allows me to determine what students need, make plans to teach and expose them to experiences that will open their eyes and build their skills, offer them the best of what I have to offer, and evaluate my effectiveness in terms of their learning, their continuing questions, and their commitment to the field of gerontology.

To varying degrees, and in ever-changing combinations, I have found that students need both basic information and very stimulating classroom and field experiences to prepare them for this challenging and inspiring field of practice. They need skills at the micro level, such as counseling of elders, case management geared toward maintaining independence, advocacy for elders at risk or those who are underserved, and family support techniques. At the mezzo level of practice, they will need to facilitate groups of elders, design and implement effective programs that involve clients in the design and implementation phase, and secure funding for innovations in practice. At the macro level, my students will need to understand the sociohistorical context of practice and to analyze and effect social change through social policy development. Today, I will mention all levels and show my students that they are not really separate.

I will ask my students to consider how working with elders is unique and different from working with other age groups, because none of us has been as old as they are. None of us yet understands from personal experience the biological and age-related changes in physical functioning. None of us has been on the receiving end of stereotypes about being old. None of us has experienced the series of losses that many elders have lived through. None of us has had to make the psychosocial adjustments required of anyone living to be 70, 80, or 90 years old.

Because I know that my students will hear the elders with whom they are matched reflect on whether their lives have had meaning, I will challenge my students to make certain that they balance the concepts of positive aging, exemplified by elders who enter marathons, travel the world, volunteer in their communities, and enjoy new learning experiences as they age, with the significant challenges of aging, including compromised health, low lifetime earnings, cognitive impairments related to a variety of disease states, and a society that does not fully value the contributions of its oldest citizens. Not wanting to discourage or bias my students by focusing only on the problems of aging, I also will not ignore these challenges in my teaching this afternoon. Not wanting to give them the false idea that successful aging is only a matter of acquiring a positive attitude, I will nonetheless introduce them to real elders for whom retirement is the best time of their lives.

As I plan for today, I know that next week I will need to expose students to emerging research and evidence-based practice, which tells them, for example, that the most frail elderly can benefit the most from physical exercise programs, that elders involved in decisions about where they will live have better adjustments to relocation, and that psychosocial interventions for depression can be as effective as antidepressant medications. I will need to show them the Best Practices in Intergenerational Social Work Practice I developed that were recognized by the Cambridge Scientific Abstract competition for best practices. They already believe that we as social workers must hold ourselves to a very high standard and be the ones who have the vision and will to create new programs. I also will need to help them identify the barriers to providing such high quality services, so they are not surprised by some of the challenges they will face.

Because I always involve students in my ongoing research on a topic related to aging, such as interviewing older persons about spirituality over the lifespan, I will introduce them next class period to the ethical underpinnings of the research in which they will soon be engaged when they interview an elder about spirituality and religious practices. I must remember to reserve the movie called *Surfing for Life* about individuals in their 70s, 80s and 90s who continue to surf, and another called *Still Doing It* about sexuality among older women. By now, students will have read about half of the best selling book *Tuesdays With Morrie,* and will hopefully have begun to re-examine dependency and death as potential growing processes, rather than solely processes of decline. I need to call my gerontological social worker colleagues and invite them to class soon to describe the pros and cons of social policies such as Medicare, Medicaid, Social Security, advance directives, elder abuse reporting laws, guardianship statutes, and social policies supporting grandparents raising their grandchildren.

Having developed a teaching tool called Century in Review, today I will use it to teach my students how to place their older clients "in time" by understanding and exploring the sociohistorical context of everyone's lives. When my students and their assigned elders meet together to discuss the main historical, cultural, and social policy developments of their lifetimes, reflecting on how the varying contexts have shaped their respective world views, coping styles, life opportunities or barriers, and ability to deal with life, they will have this tool to guide their discussions. I remind myself that when I talk in class today about what it was like for people who were born in the 1920s or 1930s, most of my students consider the Vietnam War—which is fresh in my mind—to be in the distant past for them. I will have to find a way to bring history to life by anchoring it in their conversations with their assigned elder.

I am pretty sure that when we talk about life review today, students will begin to examine their attitudes toward their own aging, start to clarify their values about whose responsibility it is to care for elders in need, think about the legacy they want to leave themselves, project themselves ahead in time to age 80, and see the connections between choices they make today and their potential experiences at age 80. Inside, I hope that some spark will be ignited between each student/elder pair, and that something shared in confidence by each elder will inspire my students to live their lives so they do not have regrets when they are old themselves. I will ask them to project into the future, develop a vision of how the aging process can be enhanced for their clients and themselves, and identify their own professional role in creating such a future.

Class begins in fifteen minutes. Armed with what I hope will be exciting, engaging, and effective teaching approaches, I head to class. Smiling to myself, I am hopeful that my students will leave class today with knowledge they did not have earlier, with more questions than answers, and with a desire to understand the very individual process of aging. I know that when class is over, I will have provided my students with opportunities for personal and professional growth, and that I will then evaluate what I saw in their responses, their questions, and their motivation to learn. Hoping that I will see success in terms of learning, growing sophistication in skills and knowledge, and a deepening awareness of their calling to gerontological social work, I have developed several benchmarks by which I measure my teaching and mentoring.

If today I see students making connections between their personal experiences and their professional development, I will be satisfied. If I see them operating just beyond the edge of their comfort level, I will be inspired by their courage in moving into the professional arena. If I see them learning to identify their values, resolve ethical dilemmas, and be open to varying points of view, I will feel successful in helping them think. Should I see them taking an interdisciplinary and increasingly broad view of aging, I will be happy. If I see them committing to a career in aging, I will know that they have a satisfying and inspiring experience ahead of them as I have had. And if, when the course and the semester are over, I see evidence of a thirst for ongoing knowledge and a commitment to making the aging experience more positive for others, I will have done my job.

Finally, if I leave them wanting more, I will know that the many individual days of learning I have provided have been woven together (more by them than by me) in such a way that they can now find their own way through social work practice with elders. As I enter the classroom, all my experience and course preparation blend in my mind as I greet the students and tell them how glad I am that they want to learn about aging. Because I have experienced what I am about to teach, I know that this is my calling. By semester's end, perhaps they will not need me anymore, and that is what I hope.

Think About It

1. How could understanding the sociohistorical context of a client's life help a social worker understand the client's values, world view, sense of self, and attitudes?

2. How can a social worker relate to a client who is much older if the social worker has not experienced being old?

3. How can social work students prepare themselves to be visionaries and creators of innovative services to address the changing needs of elders and their families?

4. How much influence do older adults have over their aging experience? How does the political and economic context shape the aging experience? How does health affect positive aging? How do societal attitudes toward aging influence the experience of aging?

Chapter 42
One Day in the Life of a Qualitative Researcher

● ● ● ● ● ● ● ● ● ● ● ● ● ● ● ● ● ● ● ●

by Dorothy C. Stratton, MSW, ACSW, LISW

I had followed the clinical practice concentration when I studied for my MSW and worked in direct practice for a while. But early in my career, I got the opportunity to teach undergraduate social work courses, so most of my career has been spent teaching. My activities as a professor have been varied and always interesting, but for this essay I want to focus on the most engaging and rewarding experience of being a qualitative researcher.

I understand and appreciate the value of quantitative research, those surveys or testing scales that can be administered to hundreds or thousands of people, which can be used to count or quantify feelings, relationships, and behaviors. But I knew I wanted to be a qualitative researcher–doing what I like to do as a service provider–listening to what an individual has to say about his or her own life and trying to understand that individual's experience as well as I possibly can. As a researcher, I have been able to add to the knowledge base for social work practice and have worked collaboratively with other researchers to disseminate findings and develop theories. But best of all for me personally, I have met and interviewed some wonderful people.

My father's death (and my mother's survival) brought me suddenly to awareness of widowhood. I attended bereavement support groups and was surprised to find men there. After all, wasn't it always the woman who was left behind? There was very little scholarly work about widowed men, I discovered. So, that became my research topic. A psychology colleague and I decided to explore the experience of widowhood for older men and, using the "grounded theory" approach of Glaser and Strauss (1967), to learn about their lives by listening to them tell their own stories. What we heard from men interviewed early in the study helped us formulate questions for later interviews. Themes and theory-building developed out of what the men said about their lives. My colleague and I had designed our research methodology and had it approved through the university's Human Subjects Review Committee before we began our interviews.

One winter morning, I woke to a shaft of sunlight streaming through the gap in my bedroom curtains. The breeze softly pushing on the curtains felt late-spring warm. Was it really winter? A blink of the eyes and I was oriented to time and place. I was not up north any longer; I had come to the very sunny Sunbelt to conduct interviews of elderly widowed men. I had one interview on my schedule: a man in his late 70s whose wife had died about 18 months earlier. The manager in his retirement community had recommended him to be interviewed, because she was worried that he was not coping well with the death of his wife and thought it would be good if he had someone with whom to talk. I had been wondering how I would make the transition from clinical interviewing to research interviewing. I had naively and conveniently decided that all the widowers I would interview would be "adjusted" and happy just to tell me about their lives. Now, on this day of actual interviewing, I knew I would have to tussle with that blurring of roles: could I just listen to a person's unhappy story without trying to help him have a happier outcome?

I had another complication to think about. Three interviews had been arranged for my trip (by a friend who lived in the area), but two of the men cancelled. There I was for several days, having paid for a round-trip plane ticket. What was I to do? I knew there had to be more widowed men in the area and decided to hustle a little to find them. I looked up nursing homes in the local phone directory and made a few calls. One staff person said none of the widowers in her facility would be capable of participating in an extended interview, but she referred me to an assisted living facility owned by the same company. It was about an hour's drive away, but I called and got a staff member on the line who was instantly interested in my research. Half an hour later, she called back and said if I could come that day, I could meet with a 94-year-old gentleman over lunch. After I explained that I already had a morning appointment set, I was invited to dine with him at an early supper. Okay, my day was set!

My first participant's name had conjured up in me an image of a short, trim, fairly formal fellow wearing a sport coat and dress trousers for our interview. I knocked on his condo door and waited for this dapper man to open it. I knocked again, and again. I knew he knew I was coming, because I had confirmed with him by phone the evening before and I was right on time. I was about to walk away to find the community manager when the door flew open and a very tall, thin man with a shock of wild hair looked down at me. His eyes darted over me. I said (probably incredulously), "Mr. A—?" and he said, with his eyes still darting sometimes at me and sometimes away, "I think I didn't hear you knocking, Dorothy. Are you going to come in?"

The apartment's expensive decor and his very casual clothing were monochromatic–white to palest gray. He said the condo was more than he really could afford, but he and his wife had gotten a good deal on it. We sat down and he said, "Well, I guess I should tell you that I am depressed and am seeing a psychiatrist. And I feel a lot of guilt. My psychiatrist said that if I didn't have a sense of humor, I would not be in as good shape as I am in." I had to stop him long enough to get the permission form signed and the tape recorder set up.

The next hour and a half I spent learning about his life, the intensity of his feelings about a great many things, and his hopes for the future. He had been alienated from a son and daughter-in-law for many years and felt bitter about that. He felt guilty about having benefitted from a large insurance benefit when his wife, also his business partner, had died. I said, "But would she not have benefitted similarly if you had died first?" And then I realized I was crossing that line from researcher to clinician. But what are the ethics of hearing something that could be ameliorated, but not responding in a helpful way? At one point he said, "I know I can tell you these things, because you are a professional; this is your business and you know it well." Fortunately, this man did not try to engage me as his clinician, probably because he was seeing a psychiatrist for talk therapy as well as for medication.

I learned that he felt he had to find a new companion and that he was desperately seeking one. From the stories he told, I felt he was probably frightening off any woman who might have gotten to know him. He said he felt he could be very happy with a new woman in his life, but also felt he could never be okay on his own. He was sad, agitated, bitter, and lonely.

We both were growing tired, so we set the date and time for the second interview, which was standard in the study's interviewing protocol. We would meet for another hour or so two days later. I drove away thinking of the contradictions and the complexities of his life. I stopped for lunch and wrote my field notes so I wouldn't have to trust my memory later.

On the way north, I passed a senior center where a dozen or so older men were playing shuffleboard. On an impulse, I drove around the block and went into the senior center office. I told the receptionist that I was a social work researcher looking for widowed men to interview—could she help me? She said she knew of one very nice man and she would call him and ask if he would be interested. "Yes!" I thought. "If he agrees, I have my three interviews, after all!"

Now I was off to interview the man in the assisted living facility. I had to negotiate some big-city freeways and an unfamiliar local driving style; arriving there was like finding an oasis. The building stretched clean and white several stories into the bluest of skies. It was accented with graceful palms, brilliant flowers, and a carpet of green. In the grand white-marble lobby area, I found my helpful contact person, and she introduced me to the man I would interview. My dinner companion was gnarled and wizened with great age, but his blue eyes sparkled through the sagging skin over his lids. He handed me a book of tributes to his wife that were gathered at her funeral and pronounced that the book would tell me all I needed to know—no further questions would be needed. He refused to sign my permission form and said instead that I should sign something for him. I wrote something on a piece of paper and gave it to him, asking if I could write on my permission form that he agreed I could ask him some questions. He said "okay," and I silently breathed a sigh of relief. We started to talk. He quizzed me, he challenged me, but his gruffness turned to the warmth I had suspected was there all along. He told me about his courtship and his long marriage and about the decline of his wife. One day he could not help her out of the bath, and so he called his son and said, "I cannot take care of Mom alone anymore." And so they had moved in with his son. He told me about the close family relationships that he still treasured. When it was time for me to leave, I said that I wanted to come back for another visit. He said, "I have told you everything. There is nothing left for you to ask." I said, "I will think of some things." He said, "Well, if you think of something, you can come back, but I don't expect to see you again." He did expect to see me again, I am sure, and I could tell you how I know that, but that would take me to another day, and I cannot do that in this one-day essay!

On the long drive home, I thought about these two men, so different in personality, but both dealing with a sense of loss, a lifetime of memories, and a need to go on. What would they make of their lives now that their life partners were gone? I thought of my tape-recorded interviews that would be transcribed word-for-word and coded for content. I thought of the richness of the data that I had collected and how my colleague and I would pore over the data discerning themes and compiling illustrative examples. I also thought of the richness added to my own life by knowing these men and all the others I had interviewed or would interview. Later, I would write for my university's alumni magazine that there were times when I didn't know if my heart could hold all the feelings that arose in me during these interviews. Tonight was such a time.

When I got back to my lodging, there was a message from the receptionist at the senior center. She left the name and phone number of the man to whom she had referred. He would be waiting for my call in the morning. I had my three interviews!

Think About It

1. What is the ethical responsibility of a social work researcher to a study participant who needs services but is not seeking them?

2. What can qualitative research uniquely contribute to the knowledge base of social work?

3. What gender differences would you expect to find in older people faced with widowhood?

Chapter 43
Racism Oral History

• • • • • • • • • • • • •

by Grantlin Schafer, BSW

Side A of the tape had run out, and it felt as if Mr. Malone had just started talking. He was on a roll and I hated to have to tell him to pause so I could flip the tape. As a Pop Warner and Pee Wee football coach for 36 years in this small city in this southern state not far from the Mason-Dixon line, Mr. Malone had interacted with almost every male—black, white, and Hispanic—in town. He had witnessed positive relationships, as well as incidents stifled by the ignorance of racism. Hearing all of this firsthand, plus the many other tales of a true storyteller, made me reflect on how grateful I was to be present for this learning experience. As Mr. Malone caught his breath and I started recording on Side B, I thought back to how this project started.

Little did I know that Lani Silver would change my entire perspective on social work. A renowned social activist from San Francisco, Ms. Silver spoke about remembering the Holocaust and learning from that horrible event in a way that I never thought I could do: from listening in person to the very words of survivors. She spoke about the Bay Area Holocaust Oral History project she created and directed for 16 years. She passionately voiced how she trained film director Steven Spielberg and many others to interview thousands upon thousands of survivors all over the world. I was intrigued, but not hooked, until she mentioned her current project: the James Byrd Jr. Racism Oral History Project, interviewing people about how racism has affected their lives in the hope of compiling an archive for people to learn by listening.

Racism has always been a topic I have been passionate about researching and working to eliminate. In a way, I think this passion is in my genes. Both of my parents were part of the first wave of teachers to integrate a prominent school system in the Deep South in the early 1970s, and they experienced the depth of racism first hand. Their combined total of well over 60 years of experience in public education has taught them many lessons that they, fortunately, passed on to me.

The first lesson that helped me in my oral history interviews was exposure. I attended public school and had classes, lunch, recess, and constant interaction with white, black, Indian American, and Asian American kids. I attended school in neighborhoods where I was the racial minority. The message from Dr. King, to judge others not by the color of their skin, but by the content of their character, was easily instilled in me, because the environment and my interest constantly worked together to manifest this lesson daily. It was not so much color blindness, but rather the willingness to learn from others how they are different from me, embrace those differences, and then quickly learn how more similar we are than different.

Oral history settings define the word exposure. The social work principle of "starting where the client is" is first and foremost, particularly in my situation, because I was in the interviewee's home. New sights, sounds, and smells abound and the challenge becomes staying focused and sincere. Many of the older interviewees were so excited to have a newcomer in their home that the social work skill of "directing" clients proved useful. Sure, I wanted to take the grand tour of the house and to hear about every family member's baptism, but I was on a mission, and much of what they wanted to talk about could be encompassed in the interview on tape. On the other hand, a couple of interviewees required more time to get used to me, if they even warmed up very much at all. A few times, I had to explain my authenticity in my own words, as if they wanted to see for themselves if I was really who our mutual connection claimed I was. I learned it was best to just be myself and speak from my heart.

The James Byrd Jr. Racism Oral History Project enabled me to combine my passion for researching racism with an effort to constructively use my anger at the injustice of racial hate crimes to record personal accounts of the destructive nature of racism. At first, I simply wished to volunteer, but then I decided to integrate this into my social work education. I thought about the interviewing skills class that I had taken and how this would be the perfect opportunity to practice these skills. I thought of the social work skill of networking with people in the community to meet interviewees. I thought of the exposure I would have to a research project: producing permission forms, contacting interviewees, following up with interviewees, transcribing tapes, and contributing my work for educational benefit—the racism oral history archive.

The whole project would not have been possible without a connection I had to the small and close knit African American community in this city. The administrative assistant at the campus office where I worked was the first person I thought of as my ticket in. She knew me well and was intrigued by my idea to interview her neighbors, friends, and relatives about how racism had affected their lives. She thought about who she knew that would be interested and came up with a list of community "elders," who would certainly have something to say. After she contacted them and verified that this young white student who wanted to talk to them about racism was genuine, I was presented with a contact list.

I cannot stress how important mutual connections to a community are with oral histories. I found that especially with the older population, I needed someone to blaze a path for me. This population can be reluctant to talk about deeply personal feelings, such as how racism has affected their lives, much less to have these thoughts recorded on tape by a white college kid forty plus years younger. The connection served as an icebreaker, a sort of invitation to talk about racism. Complementing the personal connection, it is vital to have a mission statement, a compelling purpose. The title of the James Byrd Jr. Racism Oral History Project was about all I needed to say in some instances. But I learned that one cannot rely on a title, especially if it stems from a recent hate crime, which some may not have been aware occurred. This is where the phrase "to learn about how racism has affected your life to add to an oral history archive so younger generations can learn from your story" became vital. Having a catalyst that gives importance and meaning beyond just our conversation is important. People are more willing to agree to give an oral history when there is an educational component, and people can learn from their story. This idea seemed to resonate well with the "elders" of the African American community where I conducted my oral histories.

After you acknowledge the mutual connection and read your mission statement, the reality of the oral history process is not always easy. To start with, the initial questions can be challenging. What should my opening line be? Should I start with something vague, and then narrow it down? Should I write down a script? These were all the questions that went through my mind on the eve of my first interview.

Before I knew it, I was knocking on Mr. Malone's door. I had never been to the predominantly African American part of the city before. My intellectual curiosity had taken me to a part of town, only a few miles away from the university, where in the days of slavery, the largest plantation in the city once stood. Down the street was the first and only African American school, named after a freed slave, formerly of that very plantation. I learned all about this in my interviews. I learned about the slow acceptance of desegregation, and the three racism-shielding elements of the African American community: education, family, and religion. I learned about police brutality and racism. I learned about a small town outside of the city that actually desegregated its schools seven years before this larger city. Some "elders" had lived in other locations in the Deep South and compared that experience to their current residence. I was even able to hear from a professor at the university about her experience of being an African American academic in the city. Some spoke of how most of the racial incidents involved members of their generation and my parents' generation, and others said they do not see much change in my generation. I heard accounts of blatant racial slurs, deeply-rooted institutional racism, and the city redevelopment project, which tore down key landmarks in the African American community all in the name of "urban renewal." Mr. Malone, though, wanted to talk mostly about football.

It was fascinating to hear Mr. Malone tell his story of encountering racism through his storied history of youth football in the city. He covered it all, from the all-black high school scrapping together a football program because they had no money and the all-white high school refused to even give them their used equipment, to people doubting whether a black man could be a successful coach. Racism had affected Mr. Malone's life since he first picked up a football as a kid, to coaching all races of kids, to providing the university team with some of its finest black players. This game had produced some of the first interracial interaction, but also had consistently allowed racism to rear its ugly head throughout the years.

I learned something about interviewing after each conversation. From the beginning, I was reluctant to say the word "racism," and instead preferred to start off by asking interviewees to tell me about growing up. They would talk about how racism was a factor in their childhood, but I knew that I had to ask specifically about racism. I knew that I had to learn to ask the tough questions—the questions that clients know they want to talk about but need the social worker to have the courage to break the silence and get to the point. I learned the importance of open-ended questions and then pursuing the tough questions that often arise, while guiding the client to keep focused on the topic: how racism has affected his or her life.

Mr. Malone spoke of his son's frequent interactions with the police before his untimely death. I wanted Mr. Malone to expand on the connection he made between racism and his son's troubles. This was the most emotionally charged part of any oral history I conducted. I asked some clarifying questions so Mr. Malone could fully explain and the people at the archive could hear how his son's life was affected by racial profiling and targeting by the nearly all-white police force.

I had to not be afraid to "go there." If the social worker is afraid of "going there," how can the client feel comfortable fully self-disclosing? These interviews empowered me to learn how to "go there" with the client, complete with the safety net of self-determination, surrounded by a good rapport and environment that allows the client to comfortably say, "No, I don't want to talk about that."

The broader implication for social work practice garnished from this experience is the importance of knowing your client. Use oral histories in your everyday practice with elders, youth, or children. Take time to listen to where they are coming from, and be present for them to relay the "person in environment" principle. You don't need a tape recorder to show interest in your clients beyond their presenting problems. I learned through the James Byrd Jr. Racism Oral History Project that I did not need to be on PBS to create my own documentary about the impact of racism on United States citizens. The power of oral histories, knowledge learned about racism, and the challenge bestowed upon me by my interviewees for my generation to eradicate racist ignorance will continue to be a fundamental part of my professional and personal life.

Think About It

1. How has racism affected the lives of others besides African Americans? Latinos, Asian Americans, Native Americans?

2. How has racism affected the lives of Anglo Americans? Do you think Anglo Americans' experience of how racism has affected their lives should be a part of the James Byrd Jr. Racism Oral History archive?

3. What could your own community learn by starting this project through your local library?

Chapter 44
Centenarians in India: Secrets to Long Life

● ●

by Murali D. Nair, MS, MSW, DSW

Imagine yourself sitting on a matted floor as a school-aged child, conversing with a person more than a hundred years old. You are about 13,000 miles from the United States, where the three oceans meet and are surrounded by spice mountains, plush forest, and a maze of backwaters. You are in the southwestern part of India—Kerala, also known as "God's own country." I have visited this area every summer for the past 10 years, and I would like to share my observations of some of the centenarians in the area and their "secrets of long life." As a social worker, I am keenly intrigued with the relationship between their longevity and their lifestyles.

Every summer, I offer a summer study abroad course called "India Experience" to social work students and professionals. We travel to Kerala, India *(http://www.csuohio.edu/india_experience)*. This area is known as the "Spice Capital of the World," "Venice of Asia," and "God's own country." *National Geographic* named Kerala as one of the "fifty places to visit in a lifetime." According to anthropologists, Kerala is one of the few places in the world where the matriarchal family system still exists. A recent United Nations study identified this as the only place in the world with an almost perfect literacy rate. The infant mortality rate is lower than in some of the cities in the United States, and there is a vibrant alternative health system. One thing that fascinates me about India is the aging population. Respect for the aged is deeply rooted in this culture. The use of honorific language and courteous manners is widely observed in these cultures when addressing the elders.

Today, as I prepare for my next trip to Kerala, I want to tell you about these people—to honor their ways so that we can learn from them. Rather than telling you about a day in *my* life, I want to tell you about factors in *their* day-to-day lives that I believe have contributed to their longevity.

Some of the recent research on centenarians includes the Okinawa Centenarian Study, New England Centenarian Study, Georgia Centenarian Study, Swedish Centenarian Study, and Human Longevity and Aging Research of the National Institute on Aging. These studies seem to focus more on genes and the impact of modern medical innovations as the main factors in the longevity of centenarians.

Over the years, I have been interacting with centenarians from different strata of the community, to obtain qualitative data on the secret of long life. My interest is more on the impact of lifestyles on longevity than on genetics. As I ventured out to interview this population in India, I became more and more convinced that the breakthrough in modern medicine alone is not the primary factor to the secret of long life.

My case studies on centenarians focus mainly on variables such as the social, culture, familial, spiritual, dietary habits, socialization patterns, feelings of worthiness, physical, and mental exercises. Several of these factors are transferable to our society in the United States in working with elders.

Even the poorest interview subjects have valuable traits within their lifestyles, which allow them to live healthy lives. In eastern cultures such as India, respecting elders and their "practice wisdom" is very much a factor in the day-to-day activities of the people. These elders may or may not be related to a person. Societal respect to this population group is a way of life. In these types of traditional cultures, elders stay with their extended family members. Relatives and the neighbors make sure that the elders' needs are taken care of in a proper manner. Children look up to the elders and learn oral histories and practice wisdoms that are generally passed on from one generation to another.

The longest continuously living civilization in the world today exists in India. There are thousands of years of oral history communicated from one generation to another through the close interaction of young and old. Many lessons on ethics, morality, and clean living are transmitted in the form of poems. Animals, birds, trees, and nature are common elements of these ancient stories, which live on through the youth.

While I was interviewing these centenarians, I was careful not to be preoccupied with "time." As in any culture, my subjects liked to tell incident after incident they had encountered in their lives. Some were positive and others were negative. As I listened to their stories, they reflected a similar growth or maturation process.

There are several common factors I was able to identify, irrespective of these centenarians' socioeconomic status, that are common factors of their long life. I did not see a pattern of siblings and parents living a long life among these centenarians.

Let me share with you some of these factors.

Positive attitude: Leading a stress-free lifestyle is very much a part of their day-to-day activities. Every single one of my subjects exhibited an aura of optimism in our conversation. This is very much visible in both their verbal and non-verbal communication with people around them. A smiling face is always visible, and it is more or less expected that others around them also project the same expression of outward happiness. They are happy with their lives and are hopeful about the future. Even if others observe negative events in the centenarian's life, such as the death of a family member, illness, or financial difficulties, to a close person, the centenarians have a tendency to bounce back from those situations very quickly. Long-term mourning is not visible among these individuals. They tend to develop positive outlooks in negative situations. Moreover, they try to instill this quality among the people they associate with on a daily basis. If they come across people who are pessimistic in their outlook, first they try to steer them to a positive way of thinking; if they are not successful, they tend to avoid them in a nonspecific pattern of exclusion from their close categories of contacts. Staying young has a lot to do with lifestyle and independence. They do not want to be dependent on others. Each morning, they awake with a new set of goals to accomplish.

Physical and mental exercise: Poor and rich alike, from the time they get up in the morning until they are ready to sleep, these centenarians are constantly involved in some form of physical or mental activity. They keep themselves physically and mentally active at all times. There is nothing called "boring" in their daily routine. You never observe them sitting in one place for an extended period of time. Walking around is very much a part of their lifestyle. They project positive energy to others, as well. They are always doing something, such as cleaning the place around them, walking, gardening, cooking, or sight seeing. To an outsider, their activities may not always appear productive. They are never lonely or stay alone for extended periods of time. However, they do seek their own space. They have a true sense of life. To stay alert mentally, they are involved in activities such as reading, writing, and memorization. For example, several of them are constantly learning new things—sometimes simple things such as memorizing telephone numbers, birth dates, special event dates, or Sanskrit poems. Two of the centenarians could recite multiplication tables from one to 59. One centenarian even recited the Gettysburg Address to my American social work students.

Eating habits: Most of the subjects are vegetarians. They consume freshly picked vegetables and fruits. Sprouted items are common in their diet. They can easily identify vegetables and fruits with healing qualities. They seldom eat refrigerated items. Every day, they eat at the same time, regularly, and in little quantities (no one is able to tempt them with larger portions, even if it is their favorite). They do not involve themselves in lengthy conversation while eating. Eating slowly and concentrating is very much a part of their routine. For instance, they say "each time you put food in the mouth you need to chew it 32 times—one for each tooth." They consume large quantities of surprisingly warm water, boiled with the herbal seed "cumin" (but not while they eat). Several types of spices and herbs are part of their diet. Even if they need to travel to other places, they insist on eating at their regular times. They make it a point not to sleep or lie down at least two hours after they eat.

Traditional healing practices: These centenarians are very proud to identify their traditional healing practices as one of the main secrets of longevity. Naturopathy, yoga, herbs, and spices are identified as some of these healing practices. For example, most of these elders awake in the morning at least one hour before sunrise and do "sun gazing." Early morning walking, meditation, yoga (including breathing exercises), and cold water bathing are part of their daily rituals.

Feeling of worthiness: Doing good things for others is paramount to this group of people. Instead of expecting anything in return, they are always eager to assist others—relatives, friends, or even strangers. Giving advice and narrating their positive lifestyles to others are part of their daily routine. It is part of the traditions to respect the elders. Even if others are not seeking anything, young and old alike receive advice from these elders on all types of things, such as: interpersonal relationships, dietary habits, financial security, and spirituality. Neighbors invite the eldest in their midst to birthdays, marriages, the birth of new babies, and other happy occasions. Blessings from these elders are accepted with great pride. People bow in front of these elders by keeping their hands together and touching the feet of the elders as a blessing. Their "practice wisdoms" are highly honored. Some of the other characteristic features include: they laugh at all times, they are very friendly, they behave like children, they develop good support networks, and extended family members and friends visit them often. There are many well wishers surrounding these centenarians. These elders have an answer for all your questions. They insist it comes with their "practice wisdom."

Socialization pattern: Feeling comfortable and friendly with others, including strangers, is a landmark of these centenarians. They feel comfortable socializing with people from different age groups. They try to keep up to date on what is happening locally, nationally, and internationally. They are always willing to learn new things. For example, on her 106th birthday, a centenarian registered to learn computers at a local school. Interacting with children and teenagers, by telling them oral histories and participating in outdoor activities, is an integral part of their lifestyles. They never feel shy and are always seen as extroverted in their interaction with others. They are willing to express their feelings very freely to others. Physical or mental limitations of these elders do not make them "slow down."

Spirituality: "Believe in something beyond what you know" is very common among this group. Every day when they wake up, before their meal, before involvement in any auspicious occasions, and before going to sleep, they take a few minutes of their time to pray. They believe in some form of "divinity" that is not known to human beings. Equating their secrets of long life to someone "divine" is commonly expressed. They are willing to share the concept of spirituality with others.

Implications for Social Workers Interested in Working With the Aging Population

Recent U.S. Census data (2002) indicates that there are now more than 58,000 centenarians living in the United States, with a projected increase to 1,095,000 by the year 2050. Social workers may encounter the aging population during their careers. Learning from them will be a challenge. Factors for long life expectancy include features beyond genetic disposition and advancement in medicine. Social workers can play a major role in the field of gerontology by concentrating on the lifestyle patterns of seniors and learning from traditions. Cultural understanding of elders is an important factor for social workers in working with the aging population.

As I look back at all we have learned from these centenarians, I look forward to taking a new group of social work students to Kerala this summer.

Think About It

1. Think about the oldest people you know. How do their lifestyles compare with those described in this chapter?
2. How can learning about the lifestyles of centenarians help you as a social worker working with the aging population in the future?

Dr. Murali Nair would like to thank his colleague Todd Pesek, M.D., Director, Center for Healing Across Cultures, Cleveland State University, for his valuable suggestions.

Appendix A—Organizations and Web Resources of Interest to Social Workers in Gerontology

This is a partial listing of professional associations, organizations, and Web resources that may be useful in exploring gerontological social work. Use it as a starting point in your search for more information on the topics introduced in this book.

Administration on Aging
Washington, DC 20201
202-619-0724
http://www.aoa.gov/

Aging, Alcohol, and Addictions
http://www.fmhi.usf.edu/amh/
schonfeld/GSA-Alcohol.htm

Alzheimer Society of Canada
20 Eglinton Avenue W., Suite 1200
Toronto, ON M4R 1K8
416-488-8772
http://www.alzheimer.ca

Alzheimer's Association
225 N. Michigan Avenue, Floor 17
Chicago, IL 60601
800-272-3900
http://www.alz.org

American Art Therapy Association
5999 Stevenson Avenue
Alexandria, VA 22304
888-290-0878
703-212-2238
http://www.arttherapy.org

American Association of Retired Persons
601 E Street, NW
Washington, DC 20049
888-OUR-AARP (1-888-687-2277)
http://www.aarp.org

American Network of Home Health Care Social Workers
1187 Wilmette Avenue, #139
Wilmette, IL 60091
847-853-9204

American Society on Aging
833 Market Street, Suite 511
San Francisco, CA 94103-1824
415-974-9600
http://www.asaging.org

Association for the Advancement of Social Work with Groups (AASWG)—An International Professional Organization
2303 Winfield Street
Rahway, NJ 07065-3620
732-669-7852
http://www.aaswg.org

As You Age: A Guide to Aging, Medicines, and Alcohol
http://asyouage.samhsa.gov/

Association for Death Education and Counseling
60 Revere Drive, Suite 500
Northbrook, IL 60062
847-509-0403
http://www.adec.org

Association for Gerontology in Higher Education
1030 15th Street, NW, Suite 240
Washington, DC 20005
202-289-9806
http://www.aghe.org

Association of Oncology Social Work
100 North 20th Street, 4th Floor
Philadelphia, PA 19103
215-599-6093
http://www.aosw.org

Association of VA Social Workers
http://www.vasocialworkers.org

Careers in Aging
http://www.careersinaging.com/careersinaging/

Center for Excellence in Aging Services
518-442-3360
http://www.albany.edu/aging/links.htm

Council of Nephrology Social Workers
National Kidney Foundation
30 E. 33rd Street
New York, NY 10016
800-622-9010
http://www.kidney.org/professionals/cnsw/index.cfm

Council on Social Work Education
1725 Duke Street, Suite 500
Alexandria, VA 22314-3457
703-683-8080
http://www.cswe.org

CSWE Gero-Ed Center
Council on Social Work Education
1725 Duke Street, Suite 500
Alexandria, VA 22314-3457
http://depts.washington.edu/geroctr/

Geriatric Mental Health Foundation
7910 Woodmont Ave, Suite 1050
Bethesda, MD 20814
301-654-7850
http://www.gmhfonline.org/gmhf/

Geriatric Social Work Education Consortium
c/o Partners in Care Foundation
101 South First Street, Suite 1000
Burbank, CA 91502
818-526-1780
http://www.geriatricsocialwork.org/

Geriatric Social Work Initiative
http://www.gswi.org/

The Gerontological Society of America
1030 15th St. NW, Suite 250
Washington, DC 20005
202-842-1275
http://www.geron.org

Huffington Center on Aging—Centenarians
Baylor College of Medicine
One Baylor Plaza, M320
Houston, Texas 77030
713-798-5804
http://www.hcoa.org/centenarians/centenarians.htm

Institute for the Advancement of Social Work Research
750 First Street, NE, Suite 700
Washington, DC 20002
202-336-8385
http://www.iaswresearch.org

International Association of Gerontology and Geriatrics
Rua Hilário de Gouveia 66 / 1102
Copacabana
Rio de Janeiro, RJ 22040-020
Brazil
Phone/fax: 55-21-22351510
http://www.iagg.com.br/webforms/index.aspx

International Federation of Social Workers
P.O. Box 6875
Schwarztorstrasse 22
CH-3001 Berne, Switzerland
41-31-382-6015
http://www.ifsw.org

Lesbian and Gay Aging Issues Network (LGAIN)
American Society on Aging
833 Market Street
Suite 511
San Francisco, CA 94103
415-974-9600
http://www.asaging.org/networks/
index.cfm?cg=LGAIN

Meals on Wheels Association of America
203 S. Union Street
Alexandria, VA 22314
703-548-5558
http://www.mowaa.org/

Medicare
Centers for Medicare & Medicaid Services
7500 Security Boulevard
Baltimore MD 21244-1850
1-800-MEDICARE
http://www.medicare.gov/

Medicare & You 2007 Guide
http://www.medicare.gov/
publications/pubs/pdf/10050.pdf

Merck Manual of Geriatrics, Chapter on Geriatric Social Work
http://www.merck.com/mrkshared/
mmg/sec1/ch9/ch9a.jsp

National Alliance for the Mentally Ill
Colonial Place Three
2107 Wilson Blvd., Suite 300
Arlington, VA 22201
703-524-7600
http://www.nami.org

National Association of Alcoholism and Drug Abuse Counselors
901 N. Washington St., Suite 600
Alexandria, VA 22314
800-548-0497
http://www.naadac.org

National Association of Area Agencies on Aging
1730 Rhode Island Avenue, NW
Suite 1200
Washington, DC 20036
202-872-0888
http://www.n4a.org/

National Association for Home Care and Hospice
228 7th Street, SE
Washington, DC 20003
202-547-7424
http://www.nahc.org

National Association of Professional Geriatric Care Managers, Inc.
1604 No. Country Club Road
Tucson, AZ 85716-3102
520-881-8008
http://www.caremanager.org

National Association of Social Workers
750 First Street, NE, Suite 700
Washington, DC 20002-4241
800-638-8799
http://www.socialworkers.org

National Center on Elder Abuse
1201 15th Street, NW, Suite 350
Washington, DC 20005
202-898-2586
http://www.elderabusecenter.
org/default.cfm

National Coalition for the Homeless
2201 P Street, NW
Washington, DC 20037
202-462-4822
http://www.nationalhomeless.org

National Council on the Aging
1901 L Street, NW, 4th Floor
Washington, D.C. 20036
202-479-1200
http://www.ncoa.org

National Institute on Alcohol Abuse and Alcoholism
5635 Fishers Lane, MSC 9304
Bethesda, MD 20892-9304
301-443-3860
http://www.niaaa.nih.gov

National Institute on Drug Abuse
6001 Executive Boulevard, Room 5213
Bethesda, MD 20892-9561
301-443-1124
http://www.drugabuse.gov

National Hospice and Palliative Care Organization
1700 Diagonal Road, Suite 625
Alexandria, VA 22314
703-837-1500
http://www.nho.org

National Long Term Care Ombudsman Resource Center
1828 L Street, NW, Suite 801
Washington, DC 20036
202-332-2275
http://www.ltcombudsman.org/

National Network for Social Work Managers
1040 W. Harrison Street, 4th Floor
M/C 309
Chicago, IL 60607
312-413-2302
http://www.socialworkmanager.org

National Parkinson Foundation
1501 N.W. 9th Avenue/Bob Hope Road
Miami, Florida 33136-1494
305-243-6666
http://www.parkinson.org

National Prison Hospice Association
P.O. Box 4623
Boulder, CO 80306-4623
303-447-8051
http://www.npha.org

NIH Senior Health
http://nihseniorhealth.gov/

North American Association of Christians in Social Work
P.O. Box 121
Botsford, CT 06404-0121
888-426-4712
http://www.nacsw.org

Oral History Association
http://omega.dickinson.edu/organizations/oha/

SeniorResource.com
4521 Campus Dr. #131
Irvine, CA 92612
http://www.seniorresource.com/

Senior Service America
8403 Colesville Road, Suite 1200
Silver Spring, MD 20910
301-578-8900
http://www.seniorserviceamerica.org/

Social Work Leadership Institute
The New York Academy of Medicine
1216 Fifth Avenue
New York, NY 10029
212-822-7200
http://socialwork.nyam.org/

Society for Social Work Leadership in Health Care
100 North 20th Street, 4th Floor
Philadelphia, PA 19103
866-237-9542
http://www.sswlhc.org

Touch Research Institute
http://www6.miami.edu/touch-research/

United States Department of Health and Human Services—Home Health Agency Center
Centers for Medicare & Medicaid Services
7500 Security Boulevard
Baltimore, MD 21244
http://www.cms.hhs.gov/center/hha.asp

United States Department of Veterans Affairs—VA Careers—Social Work
VA Placement Service
1555 Poydras Street, Suite 1971
New Orleans, LA 70112
800-949-0002
http://www.vacareers.va.gov/sw.cfm

United States Department of Veterans Affairs—VA Social Work
http://www1.va.gov/socialwork/

Appendix B—Additional Reading and Resources

Chapter 1: The Blessings of Meals on Wheels

Committee of Nutrition Services of Medicare. (2000). *The role of nutrition in maintaining health in the nation's elderly: Evaluating coverage of nutrition services for the Medicare population.* National Academy Press.

Chapter 2: Adult Protective Services

Administration on Aging (2006). *Elder rights and resources.* Washington, DC: Administration on Aging. Available at http://www.aoa.gov/eldfam/ Elder_Rights/Elder_Abuse/Elder_Abuse.asp

Clarke, E. J., Preston, M., Raskin. J., & Bengtson, V.L. (1999). Types of conflicts and tensions between older parents and adult children. *The Gerontologist, 39* (3), 261-270.

National Center on Elder Abuse. (2006). *The availability and utility of inter-disciplinary data on elder abuse: A white paper for the National Center on Elder Abuse.* Washington, DC: American Bar Association Commission on Law and Aging. Available at http: //www.elderabusecenter.org/

Quinn, M. J., & Tomika, S. K. (1997). *Elder abuse and neglect: Causes, diagnoses and intervention strategies (2nd ed.).* New York: Springer.

Chapter 3: Working With Immigrants in a Community Senior Center

Patti, R. J. (2000). *The landscape of social welfare management.* In Patti, R. J. (2000). (Ed.) *The handbook of social welfare management* (pp. 3-26). Thousand Oaks, CA: Sage Publications.

Chapter 4: When the White Cane Comes in Handy: Helping Older Adults Navigate the Health Care System

Veronica B. Smith Multi-Service Senior Center. Available at http://www. cityofboston.gov/elderly/center.asp

Chapter 5: Geriatric Community Care Management

Estes, C. L., & Swan, J. H. (Eds.). (1993). *The long term care crisis: Elders trapped in the no-care zone.* Newberry Park, CA: Sage Publications.

FastStats A to Z: Home health care. (2006). National Center for Health Statistics. Available at http://www.cdc.gov/nchs/fastats/homehealthcare.htm

Formanek, R., & Gurian, A. (Eds.). (1987). *Women and depression: A lifespan perspective.* New York: Springer Publishing Company.

Keigher, S., Fortune, A. E., & Witkin, S. L. (Eds.). (2000). *Aging and social work: The changing landscapes.* Washington, DC: NASW Press.

Kubler-Ross, E. (1969). *On death and dying.* New York: Macmillan Publishing Company.

Quinn, J. (1993). *Successful case management in long-term care.* New York: Springer Publishing Company.

Safford, F., & Krell, G. I. (Eds.). (1997). *Gerontology for health professionals: A practice guide.* Washington, DC: NASW Press.

Towle, C. (1987). *Common human needs.* Silver Spring, MD: NASW Press.

Chapter 6: Community Senior Services

Austin, C., Des Camp, E., Flux, D., McClelland. R., & Sieppert, J. (2005). Community development with older adults in their neighbourhoods: The elder friendly communities program. *Families in Society: The Journal of Contemporary Social Sciences, 86* (3), 401-409.

Centre for Home Care Policy and Research. (2003). *Lessons for communities in supporting the health, well-being, and independence of older people.* Indiana: Visiting Nurse Service of New York. Available at http://www.indiana.edu/-evergreen/institute.html

Chapter 7: Best Practices in a Community Setting

Aging in place initiative. Retrieved April 12, 2007, from United Hospital Fund Web site: http://www.uhfnyc.org/pubs-stories3220/pubs-stories_list.htm?attrib_id=4778#pubs

Change theory and psychological assessments help move pain patients toward self-management. (1999). Retrieved April 12, 2007, from http://www.pearsonassessments.com/resources/painprofile.htm

Depression in older adults. Retrieved April 12, 2007, from NAMI Web site: http://www.nami.org/Template.cfm?Section=By_Illness&template=/ContentManagement/ContentDisplay.cfm&ContentID=7515

Chapter 8: A Day in the Life of a NORC

Hamilton-Madison House. (2002). *Hamilton-Madison House/Knickbocker Village Senior Services needs assessment.* Available from: Hamilton-Madison House, 50 Madison Street, NYC 10038.

Hooyman, N. R., & Kiyak, H. A. (2005). *Social gerontology: A multidisciplinary perspective.* (7th ed.). Boston: Allyn and Bacon.

Masotti, P., Fick, R., Johnson-Masotti, A., & Macleod, S. (2006). Healthy naturally occurring retirement communities: A low-cost approach to facilitating healthy aging. *American Journal of Public Health. 96* (7), 1164-1170.

McInnis-Dittrich, K. (2005). *Social work with elders: A biopsychosocial approach to assessment and intervention. (2nd ed.).* Boston: Allyn and Bacon.

Pine, P., & Pine, V. (2002). *Naturally occurring retirement community-supportive service program: An example of devolution.* In F. Caro & R. Morris (Eds.), *Devolution and Aging Policy* (pp. 181-193). Binghamton, NY: Haworth Press.

Chapter 9: Gas Masks, Self-Affirmation, and War in Israel

Barach, P, Rivkind, A., & Israeli, A. (1998). Emergency medical services: Emergency preparedness and response in Israel during the gulf war. *Annals of Emergency Medicine, 32* (2), 224-234.

Cahn, D. (1991, Spring). Personal response systems in Israel. *International Journal of Technology and Aging, 4* (1), 75.

Dasberg, H. (2001). Narrative group therapy with aging child survivors of the Holocaust. *The Israel Journal of Psychiatry and Related Sciences, 38* (1), 27-36.

Robinson, S., Hemmendinger, J., Netanel, R., & Rapaport, M. (1994). Retraumatization of Holocaust survivors during the gulf war and scud missile attacks on Israel. *British Journal of Medical Psychology, 67* (4), 353.

Stahl, A. (1993). Changing attitudes toward the old in oriental families in Israel. *The International Journal of Aging & Human Development, 37* (4), 261-270.

Chapter 10: Firsts: Mrs. Blue Visits the ER

Crum, R. M., Anthony, J. C., Bassett, S. S., & Folstein, M. (1993). Population-based normals for the mini-mental state examination by age and educational level. *JAMA, 269* (18), 2386-2390.

Dohrenwend, A., Kusz, H., Eckleberry, J., & Stucky, K. (2003, Feb.). Evaluating cognitive impairment in a primary care setting. *Clinical Geriatrics, 11* (2), 21-29. (Available online at: http://www.clinicalgeriatrics.com/cg/attachments/1054651395-Dohrenwend.pdf.)

Folstein, M. F., Folstein, S. E., & McHugh, P. R. (1975). Mini-mental state: A practical method for grading cognitive state of patients for the clinicians. *Journal of Psychiatric Research, 12,* 189-198.

Chapter 11: Social Work in Outpatient Rehabilitation

Health and Social Work. (All volumes.) Washington, DC: NASW Press.

Chapter 12: Hospital Social Work: A Fast-Paced Environment

Gehlert, S., & Browne, T. A. (2006). *Handbook of health social work.* Hoboken, NJ: Wiley.

Chapter 13: Welcome to Geriatrics! Life as a VA Social Worker

Manske, J. E. (2006). Social work in the Department of Veterans Affairs: Lessons learned. *Health and Social Work, 31* (3), 233-238.

Chapter 14: Do Unto Others: Life Lessons Learned as a Medical Social Worker

Bachman, R., Lachs, M., & Meloy, M. (2004). Reducing injury through self-protection by elderly victims of violence: The interaction effects of gender of victim and the victim/offender relationship. *Journal of Elder Abuse and Neglect, 16* (4), 1-24.

Bell, B., Oyebode, J., Oliver, C. (2004). The physical abuse of older adults: The impact of the carer's gender, level of abuse indicators, and training on decision-making. *Journal of Elder Abuse and Neglect, 16* (3), 19-44.

Brandl, B. & Horan, D. (2002). Domestic violence in later life: An overview for health care providers. *Women and Health, 35* (2/3), 41-54.

Green, R. R. (2000). *Social work with the aged and their families.* (2nd ed.). New York: Aldine De Gruyter.

Harris, S. (1996). For better or for worse: Spouse abuse grown old. *Journal of Elder Abuse and Neglect, 8* (1), 1-33.

Hines, D. A., & Malley-Morrison, K. (2004). *Family violence in the United States: Defining, understanding and combating abuse.* New York: Sage.

Levesque, R. (2002). *Culture and family violence: Fostering change through human rights law.* Washington, DC: American Psychological Association.

Malley-Morrison, K. (2004). *International perspectives on family violence and abuse: A cognitive ecological approach.* Mahwah, NJ: Lawrence Erlbaum.

Malley-Morrison, K., & Hines, D. A. (2004). *Family violence in a cultural perspective: Defining, understanding and combating abuse.* New York: Sage.

Chapter 15: A Typical Day in Home Health

Lee, J. (2001). *The empowerment approach to social work practice.* (2nd ed.). New York: Columbia University Press

Safford, F., & Krell, G. (1997). *Gerontology for health professionals*. (2nd ed.). Washington, DC: NASW Press

Chapter 16: A Day in the Life of a Hospice Social Worker

Callanan, M., & Kelley, P. (1992). *Final gifts*. New York: Bantam Books.

Larson, D. G. (1993). *The helper's journey*. Champagne, IL: Research Press.

MacDonald, D. (1991). Hospice social work: A search for identity. *Health and Social Work, 16* (4), 274-280.

Meyer, C. (1993). *Surviving death: A practical guide to caring for the dying and bereaved*. Mystic, CT: Twenty-Third Publications.

Pietsch, J. H., & Blanchette, P. L. (2000). *Cultural issues in end-of-life decision making*. Thousand Oaks, CA: Sage Publications.

Reese, D. J. (2001). Successful interprofessional collaboration on the hospice team. *Health and Social Work, 26* (3), 167-176.

Smith, D. C. (1997). *Caregiving: Hospice-proven techniques for healing body and soul*. New York: Macmillan.

Stein, G. L. (2004). Improving our care at life's end: Making a difference. *Health and Social Work, 29* (1), 77-79.

Wolfelt, A. (1983). *Helping children cope with grief*. Muncie, IN: Accelerated Development.

Worden, J. W. (1991). *Grief counseling and grief therapy: A handbook for the mental health practitioner*. New York: Springer.

Chapter 17: The Need for Hospice Social Workers in Skilled Nursing Facilities

Byock, I. (1997). *Dying well: Peace and possibilities at the end of life*. New York: Riverhead.

Doka, K. J. (Ed.). (2002). *Living with grief: Loss in later life*. Washington, DC: Hospice Foundation of America.

Doka, K. J. (Ed.). (2005). *Living with grief: Ethical dilemmas at the end of life*. Washington, D.C. Hospice Foundation of America.

Schneider, R. L., Kropf, N. P., and Kisor, A. J. (Ed.). (2000). *Gerontological social work: Knowledge, service settings, and special populations*. (2nd ed.). Belmont, CA. Wadsworth.

Chapter 18: Social Work in a Nursing Home

Beaulieu, E. M. (2002). *A guide for nursing home social workers.* New York: Springer Publishing Company.

Chapter 19: The Mount

Bradley, D. B. (1999/2000, Winter). A reason to rise each morning: The meaning of volunteering in the lives of older adults. *Generations, 23* (4), 45-50.

Fingerman, K. L. (2001). A distant closeness: Intimacy between parents and their children in later life. *Generations, 25* (2), 26-33.

Power, M., & Maluccio, A. N. (1998/1999, Winter). Intergenerational approaches to helping families at risk. *Generations, 22* (4), 37-43.

Chapter 20: Life as a Nursing Home Administrator

Daniels, D., & Price, V. (2000). *The essential enneagram: The definitive personality test and self-discovery guide.* San Francisco: HarperSanFranciso.

Fannin, J. (2006). *SCORE for life: The secret formula to thinking like a champion.* New York: HarperCollins.

Gladwell, M. (2002). *The tipping point: How little things can make a big difference.* Boston: Back Bay Books.

Moody, H. R. (2006). *Aging: Concepts and controversies.* (5th ed.). Thousand Oaks, CA: Pine Forge Press.

Smith, S. A., & Mazin, R. A. (2004). *HR answer book: An indispensable guide for managers and human resource professionals.* New York: AMACOM.

Whiteman, V. L. (2001). *Social security: What every human services professional should know.* Needham Heights, MA: Allyn and Bacon.

Chapter 21: Investigative Social Work: The Nursing Home Surveyor

Centers for Medicare and Medicaid (CMS). (2006). *Nursing home data compendium 2005 edition.* Washington, DC: US Department of Health and Human Services. Retrieved 11/29/2006 from http://www.cms.hhs.gov/CertificationandComplianc/12_NHs.asp

Decker, F. H. (2005). *Nursing homes 1977-1999: What has changed, what has not?* Hyattsville, MD: National Center for Health Statistics. Retrieved 11/29/2006 from http://www.cdc.gov/nchs/data/nnhsd/NursingHomes1977_99.pdf

Government Accounting Office (GAO). (2003). *Nursing home quality: Prevalence of serious problems, while declining, reinforces importance of enhanced oversight.* Retrieved June 5, 2006, from http://www.gao.gov/new.items/d03561.pdf

Omnibus budget reconciliation act. (1987). Pub. L. No. 00-203 § 1819 [42 USC § 1395i-3].

Shankroff, J., Miller, P., Feuerber, M., & Mortimore, E. (2000). Nursing home initiative. *Health Care Financing Review, 22* (1), 113-115.

Spector, W. D., & Takada, H. A. (1991). Characteristics of nursing homes that affect resident outcomes. *Journal of Aging and Health, 3,* 427-454.

Streim, J. E., & Katz, I. R. (1994). Federal regulations and the care of patients with dementia in the nursing home. *Alzheimer's and Related Dementias, 78* (4), 895-909.

Chapter 22: A Day in the Life of an Ombudsman

National Area Agency on Aging. (2006). *Area agency on aging: Link to services for older adults and their caregivers.* Retrieved November 26, 2006, from http://www.n4a.org/aboutaaas.cfm

Chapter 23: Long Term Care Ombudsman: Another Perspective

Burger, S., Fraser, V., Hunt, S., Frank, B., & the National Coalition for Nursing Home Reform. (2001). *Nursing homes: Getting good care there.* Atascadero, CA: Impact.

Cockerham, W. (1997). *This aging society.* (2nd ed.). Upper Saddle River, NJ: Prentice Hall.

Gelfand, D. (1999). *The aging network: Programs and services.* (5th ed.). New York: Springer.

Greene, R. (2000). *Social work with the aged and their families.* (2nd ed.). New York: Aldine De Gruyter.

Schneider, R., Kropf, N., & Kisor, A. (Eds.). (2000). *Gerontological social work: Knowledge, service settings and special populations.* (2nd ed.). Belmont, CA: Brooks/Cole.

Chapter 24: Working With Geriatric Inpatients in Acute Mental Health

Falcone, D., Bolda, E., & Leak, S. C. (1991). Waiting for placement: An exploratory analysis of determinants of delayed discharges of elderly hospital patients. *Health Services Research, 26* (3), 339-374. Summary available at: http://www.pubmedcentral.nih.gov/articlerender.fcgi?tool=pmcentrez&artid=1069829

Jackson E., & Warner, J. (2002). How much do doctors know about consent and capacity? *Journal of the Royal Society of Medicine, 95* (12), 601-603. Full text available at: http://www.pubmedcentral.nih.gov/articlerender. fcgi?tool=pmcentrez&artid=1279286

Lieff, S., Maindonald, K., & Shulman, K. (1984). Issues in determining financial competence in the elderly. *Canadian Medical Association Journal, 130* (10), 1293-1296. Summary available at: http://www.pubmedcentral.nih. gov/articlerender.fcgi?tool=pmcentrez&artid=1483520

Pasker, P, Thomas, J. P., & Ashley, J. S. (1976). The elderly mentally ill: Whose responsibility? *British Medical Journal, 2* (6028), 164-166. Summary available at: http://www.pubmedcentral.nih.gov/articlerender.fcgi?tool=p mcentrez&artid=1687465

Shapiro, E., Tate, R. B., & Tabisz, E. (1992). Waiting times for nursing-home placement: The impact of patients' choices. *Canadian Medical Association Journal, 146* (8), 1343-1348. Summary available at: http://www.pubmedcentral. nih.gov/articlerender.fcgi?tool=pmcentrez&artid=1488570

Chapter 25: Stella's Orchestra: Social Work in Rural Geriatric Mental Health

Bytheway, B. (1995). *Ageism.* Buckingham: Open University Press.

Coleman, P. G., & O'Hanlon, A. (2004). *Ageing and development: Theories and research.* Oxford: Oxford University Press.

Gubrium, J., & Holstein, J. (Eds.) (2003). *Ways of aging.* Oxford: Blackwell.

Kitwood, T. (1997). *Dementia reconsidered: The person comes first.* Buckingham: Open University Press.

Zarit, S. H., & Zarit, J. M. (1998). *Mental health disorders in older adults: Fundamentals of assessment and treatment.* New York: Guilford Press.

Chapter 26: Social Work at the Alzheimer's Association

Taylor, R. (2006). *Alzheimer's from the inside out.* Baltimore, MD: Health Professions Press.

Chapter 27: Parkinson's Disease and Social Work Practice

Erickson, C. L., & Muramatsu, N. (2004). Parkinson's disease and depression: Current knowledge and social work practice. *Journal of Gerontological Social Work, 42* (3/4), 3-18.

Fox, M. J. (2002). *Lucky man: A memoir.* New York: Random House.

Meenaghan, T. M., Gibbons, W. E., & McNutt, J. G. (2005). *Generalist practice in larger settings: Knowledge and skill concepts.* (2nd ed.). Chicago: Lyceum.

Nausieda, P., & Bock, G. (2000). *Parkinson's disease: What you and your family should know.* Miami, FL: The National Parkinson Foundation.

Chapter 28: A Social Work Perspective on Geriatric Addictions

Ambrogne, J. A. (2002). Reduced -risk drinking as a treatment goal: what clinicians need to know. *Journal of Substance Abuse Treatment, 22,* 45-53.

American Psychiatric Association. (2000). *Diagnostic and statistical manual of mental disorders.* (4th ed., text rev.). Washington, DC: Author.

Arndt, S., Gunter, T. D., & Acion, L. (2005). Older admissions to substance abuse treatment in 2001. *American Journal of Geriatric Psychiatry, 13* (5), 385-392.

Barrick, C., & Connors, G, J. (2003). Relapse prevention and maintaining abstinence in older adults with alcohol-use disorders. *Drugs and Aging. 19* (8) 583-594.

Blow, F. C. (2004). *TIP 26: Substance abuse among older adults.* Available at http://www.ncbi.nlm.nih.gov/books/bv.fcgi?rid=hstat5.chapter.48302

Blow, F. C., & Barry, K. L. (2002). Use and misuse of alcohol among older women. *Alcohol Research and Health, 26* (4), 308-315.

Brocato, J., & Wagner, E. F. (2003). Harm reduction: A social work practice model and social justice agenda. *Health and Social Work, 28* (2), 117-125.

el-Guebaly, N. (2005). Are attempts at moderate drinking by patients with alcohol dependency a form of Russian Roulette? *Canadian Journal of Psychiatry, 50* (5), 266-268.

Fleming, M. F. M., Marlon P., French, M. T, Manwell, L. B, Stauffacher, E. A., & Barry, K. L. (2002). Brief physician advice for problem drinkers: Long-term efficacy and benefit-cost analysis. *Alcohol Clinical and Experimental Research, 26* (1), 36-43.

Futterman, R. L. M., & Silverman, S. (2004). Integrating harm reduction and abstinence-based substance abuse treatment in the public sector. *Substance Abuse, 25* (1), 3-7.

Gfroerer, J., Penne, M., Pemberton, M., & Folsom, R. (2003). Substance abuse treatment need among older adults in 2020: The impact of the aging baby-boom cohort. *Drug and Alcohol Dependence, 69,* 127-135.

Hanson, M., & Gutheil, I. (2004). Motivational strategies with alcohol-involved older adults: Implications for social work practice. *Social Work, 49* (3), 364-372.

Jackson, K. (2004). Harm reduction: Meeting clients where they are. *Social Work Today, 4* (6), 34.

Kadden, R. M. (2001). Behavioral and cognitive-behavioral treatment for alcohol: Research opportunities. *Addictive Behaviors, 26,* 489-507.

MacFarland, N., & Rockwood, A. (2004). 21st century approach to geriatric addictions. *NASW NYS Update, 29,* 12 & 22.

MacMaster, S. A. (2004). Harm reduction: A new perspective on substance abuse services. *Social Work, 49* (3), 356-363.

Marlatt, G. A., & Witkiewitz, K. (2002). Harm reduction approaches to alcohol use: Health promotion, prevention, and treatment. *Addictive Behaviors, 27,* 867-886.

Mason, S. E., & Sanders, G. R. (2004). Social work student attitudes on working with older clients. *Journal of Gerontological Social Work, 42* (3/4), 61-75.

Menninger, J. A. (2002). Assessment and treatment of alcoholism and substance-related disorders in the elderly. *Bulletin of the Menninger Clinic, 66* (2), 166-183.

Oslin, D. W. (2004). Late-life alcoholism. *American Journal of Geriatric Psychiatry, 12* (6), 571-583.

Oslin, D. W., Pettinati, H., & Volpicelli, J. R. (2002). Alcoholism treatment adherence: Older age predicts better adherence and drinking outcomes. *American Journal of Geriatric Psychiatry, 10* (6), 740-747.

Oslin, D. W., Slaymaker, V. J., Blow, F. C., Owen, P. L., & Colleran, C. (2005). Treatment outcomes for alcohol dependence among middle-aged and older adults. *Addictive Behaviors, 30,* 1431-1436.

Satre, D. D., Mertens, J. R., & Weisner. C.. (2004). Gender differences in older adult treatment outcomes for alcoholic dependence. *Journal of Studies On Alcohol, 65* (5), 638-642.

Smith, M. J. W. (2005, June). Harm reduction: Starting where the client is. *NASW NYS Update, 29,* 7 & 21.

Tatarsky, A. (2003). Harm reduction psychotherapy: Extending the reach of traditional substance use treatment. *Journal of Substance Abuse Treatment, 25,* 249-256.

Chapter 29: Working With Homeless Older Adults

Baumohl, J. (Ed.). (1996). *Homelessness in America.* Phoenix: AZ: Oryx Press.

Blau, J. (1992). *The visible poor: Homelessness in the United States.* New York: Oxford University Press.

Coates, J. R. (1990). *A street is not a home: Solving America's homeless dilemma.* Buffalo, NY: Prometheus Books.

Cohen, C. I. (1999). Aging and homelessness. *The Gerontologist, 29* (1), 5-14.

Crane, M. (1994). Elderly homeless people: Elusive subjects and slippery concepts. *Ageing and Society, 14* (4), 631-640.

Doolin, J. (1985). America's untouchables: The elderly homeless. *Perspective on Aging,* 8-11.

Keigher, S. M., & Greenblatt, S. (1992). Housing emergencies and the etiology of homelessness among the urban elderly. *The Gerontologist, 32* (4), 457-465.

Ladner, S. (1992). *The elderly homeless.* In M. J. Robertson & M. Greenblatt. (Eds.), *Homelessness: A national perspective* (pp. 221-228). New York: Plenum Press.

Pynoos, J., & Liebig, P. S. (Eds.). (1995). *Housing frail elders: International policies, perspectives, and prospects.* Baltimore, MD: The Johns Hopkins University Press.

Tully, C. T., & Jacobson, S. (1994). The homeless elderly: America's forgotten populations. *Journal of Gerontological Social Work, 22* (3/4), 61-81.

Weiss, L. M. (1992). *There's no place like... no place: Confronting the problems of the aging homeless and marginally housed.* Washington, DC: American Association of Retired Persons.

Chapter 30: Tapping Into the Creative Parts: Art Therapy With Older Adults

Butler, R. N. (1963). The life review: An interpretation of reminiscence in the aged. *Psychiatry, 26,* 65-76.

Magniant, R. C. (2004). *Art therapy with older adults.* Springfield, IL: Charles C. Thomas Publishing.

Shulman, L. (2005). *The skills of helping individuals, families, groups and communities (5th ed.).* Itasca, IL: F. E. Peacock.

Spaniol, S. (1997). Art therapy with older adults: Challenging myths, building competencies. *Art Therapy, 14* (3), 158-160.

Chapter 31: Integrative Touch and the 15-Minute StressOut

15-Minute StressOut Program & Forum. Retrieved from http://jerryvest. pages.web.com/

Elder abuse. Retrieved from http://courts.co.calhoun.mi.us/book004.htm

Ichazo, O. (2006). *Master level exercise: Psychocalisthenics.* Kent, CT: Oscar Ichazo Foundation.

McInnis-Dittrich, K. (2005). *Social work with elders: A biopsychosocial approach to assessment and intervention.* (2nd ed.). Boston: Pearson.

Montagu, A. (1981). *Growing young.* New York: McGraw-Hill.

Montagu, A. (1986). *Touching: The human significance of the skin.* New York: Harper & Row.

Nelson, D. (1993). *Compassionate touch: Hands on caregiving for the elderly, the ill and the dying.* Barrytown, NY: Station Hill Press.

Stoller, E. P., & Gibson, R. C. (2000). *Worlds of difference: Inequality in the aging experience.* (3rd ed.). Thousand Oaks, CA: Pine Forge Press.

Vest, G., Ronnau, J., Lopez, B., & Gonzales, G. (1997). Alternative health practices in ethnically diverse rural areas: A collaborative research project. *Health and Social Work, 22,* 95-100.

Chapter 32: A Win-Win Partnership: Intergenerational Social Work

Adkins, V. K. (1999). Grandparents as a national asset: A brief note. *Activities, Adaptation and Aging, 24* (1), 13-18.

Cote, N., Mosher-Ashley, P., & Kiernan, H. (2003). Linking long-term care residents with elementary students via pen pal program. *Activities, Adaptation and Aging, 27* (1), 1-10.

Marken, D. M. (2006). One step ahead: Preparing the senior center for 2030. *Activities, Adaptation and Aging, 29* (4), 13-18.

Chapter 33: Social Work in a Law Firm

Aiken, J., & Wizner, S. (2003). Promoting justice through interdisciplinary teaching. Practice and scholarship law as social work. *Washington University Journal of Law and Policy, 11* (63).

Albert, R. (2000). *Law and social work practice (2nd ed.)*. New York: Springer Series on Social Work.

Forgey, M. A., Moynihan, A., & Litman, N. (1999, September/October). Law and social work team practice: Communicating about the basics. *Interdisciplinary Report on At-Risk Children and Families, 2* (65).

Chapter 34: Geriatric Care Management in Private Practice

Berkman, B. (Ed.). (2006). *Handbook of social work in health and aging.* New York: Oxford University Press.

McInnis-Dittrich, K. (2005). *Social work with elders: A biopsychosocial approach to assessment and intervention. (2nd ed.)*. Boston, MA: Pearson Education, Inc.

National Association of Professional Geriatric Care Managers. *Geriatric care management journal.* All issues.

Chapter 35: Caregiver Psychoeducational Support Groups: Gerontological Social Work in Business and Industry

Akabas, S. (1995). Occupational social work. In R. L. Edwards (Ed.). *Encyclopedia of Social Work (19th ed.)*, pp. 1779-1786. Washington, DC: NASW Press.

Bengston, V. L., & Lowenstein, A. (2003). *Global aging and challenges in families.* New York: DeGruyter.

Germain, C., & Gitterman, A. (1980). *The life model of social work practice.* New York: Columbia University Press.

Hooyman, N. R., & Kiyak, H. A. (2005). *Social gerontology: A multidisciplinary perspective.* (7th ed.). Boston: Pearson Education.

Koenig, T. L. (2004). From the woman's viewpoint: Ethical dilemmas confronted by women as informal caregivers of frail elders. *Families in Society, 5,* (2), 236-242.

Moody, H. R. (2006). *Aging: Concepts and controversies.* (5th ed.). Thousand Oaks, CA: Sage Publications.

Pace, P. R. (2006, July). Styles of aiding workers evolve for EAPs: Employee assistance programs handle an array of issues. *NASW News. 51* (7), 4.

Swanberg, J. E., Kanatzar, T., Mendiondo, M., & McCoskey, M. (2006) Caring for our elders: A conundrum for working people. *Families in Society, 87* (3), 417-426.

Zastrow, C. (2004). *Work-related problems and social work in the workplace.* In *Introduction to Social Work and Social Welfare.* (8th ed., pp. 379-404). Belmont, CA: Brooks/Cole Thomson.

Chapter 36: Community Organizing in State Government

Estes, C. L. (2001). *Social policy and aging: A critical perspective.* Thousand Oaks, CA: Sage Publications Inc.

Chapter 37: Gray and Gay: Lesbian, Gay, Bisexual, and Transgender Aging

Cahill, S., South, K., & Spade, J. (2000). *Outing age: Public policy issues affecting gay, lesbian, bisexual and transgender elders.* Washington, DC: National Gay and Lesbian Task Force Policy Institute.

Harwood, G. (1997). *The oldest gay couple in America: A 70-year journey through same sex America.* Secaucus, NH: Carol Publishing.

Kimmel, D., Rose, T., & David, S. (Eds.). (2006). *Lesbian, gay, bisexual and transgender aging: Research and clinical perspectives.* New York: Columbia University Press.

Chapter 38: Field Placement in Geriatric Case Management

Herdt, G., & DeVries, B. (2004). *Gay and lesbian aging: Research and future directions.* New York: Springer.

McInnis-Dittrich, K. (2004). *Social work with elders: A biopsychosocial approach to assessment and intervention (2nd ed.).* Boston: Allyn and Bacon.

Quam, J. K. (1997). *Social services for senior gay men and lesbians.* New York: Haworth Press.

Chapter 39: A Graduate Student's Experience in the Hartford Practicum Partnership Program

Tompkins, C. J., & Rosen, A. L. (Eds.). (2007). *Fostering social work gerontology competence: A collection of papers from the first national gerontological social work conference.* Binghamton, NY: Haworth Press.

Chapter 40: Learning the Ropes as a BSW Intern

Butler, S. S., & Kaye, L. W. (2003). *Gerontological social work in small towns and rural communities.* Binghamton, NY: Haworth Press.

Kaye, L. W. (2005). *Perspectives on productive aging. Social work with the new aged.* Baltimore: NASW Press.

Keigher, S. M., Fortune, A. E., & Witkin, S. L. (2000). *Aging and social work. The changing landscapes.* Benton Harbor, MI: Batson Printing.

Markson, E. W. (2003). *Social gerontology today. An introduction.* Los Angeles: Roxbury Publishing.

McInnis-Dittrich, K. (2005). *Social work with elders. A biopsychosocial approach to assessment and intervention (2nd ed.).* Boston: Allyn and Bacon.

Naleppa, M. J., & Reid, W. J. (2003). *Gerontological social work. A task-centered approach.* New York: Columbia University Press.

Ronch, J. L., & Goldfield, J. A. (2003). *Mental wellness in aging. Strengths-based approaches.* Baltimore: Health Professions Press.

Schneider, R. L., Kropf, N. P., & Kisor, A. J. (2000). *Gerontological social work. Knowledge, service settings, and special populations (2nd ed.).* Belmont, CA: Wadsworth.

Westerfelt, A., & Dietz, T. J. (2005). *Planning and conducting agency-based research. (3rd ed.).* Boston: Allyn and Bacon.

Chapter 41: Teaching Aging by Concept and Example

Albom, M. (1997). *Tuesdays with Morrie.* New York: Doubleday.

Quadagno, J. (2004). *Aging and the life course.* (3rd ed.). New York: McGraw Hill Publishing.

Vaillant, G. E. (2002). *Aging well.* Boston: Little, Brown and Company.

Worthington, C. E., Dryden, T. J., & Chauner, D. M. (Eds.). (2006). *Healthy aging: Inspirational letters from Americans.* Unionville, PA: Educational Television Network, Inc.

Chapter 42: One Day in the Life of a Qualitative Researcher

Corbin, J., & Strauss, A. (1990). Grounded theory research: Procedures, canons, and evaluative criteria. *Qualitative Sociology, 13* (1), 3-21.

Gubrium, J. F. (1992). Qualitative research comes of age in gerontology. *The Gerontologist, 32* (5), 581-582.

Moore, A. J., & Stratton, D. C. (2002). *Resilient widowers: Older men speak for themselves.* New York: Springer Publishing.

Moore, A. J., & Stratton, D. C. (2004). *The current woman in an older widower's life.* In K. Davidson & G. Tennell (Eds.) *Intimacy in later life.* London: Transaction Publishers.

Chapter 43: Racism Oral History

Gates, H. L., & McKay, N. Y. (Eds.). (2004). *Norton anthology of African American literature (2nd Ed.)*. Norton and Company.

Griffin, J. H. (1961). *Black like me*. Signet.

Toomer, J. (1923). *Cane*. New York: Boni & Liveright.

Chapter 44: Centenarians in India: Secrets to Long Life

Anderson-Ranberg, M., & Shroll, J . (2001). Healthy centenarians do not exist, but autonomous centenarians do: A population-based study of morbidity among Danish centenarians. *Journal of American Geriatric Society, 49,* 900-908.

Archer, S. (2002). Centenarians in Barbados: The importance of religiosity in adaptation and coping. *The Gerontologist, 42 (*1), 49-50.

Barzilai, N. (2003). Discovering the secrets of successful longevity. *The Journals of Gerontology, 58A* (3), 225.

Brickey, M. (2001). The extended life: Four strategies for healthy longevity. *Futurist, 35,* (5), 52-56.

Buettner, D. (2005, November). The secrets of long life. *National Geographic,* 2-26.

Chopra, D. (1993). *Ageless body and timeless mind.* New York: Crown Publishers Inc.

Ellis, N. (2002). *If I live to be 100: Lessons from centenarians.* New York: Crown Publishers.

Mills, T. (2003). Listening from the sidelines: The telling and retelling of stories by centenarians. *Generations, 27* (3), 16-20.

Murray, M. (1963). *My first hundred years.* London: Williams Kimber.

Perls, T., Silver, M., & Lauerman, J. (1999). *Living to 100: Lessons in living to your maximum potential at any age.* New York: Basic Books.

Perls, T., & Terry, D. (2003). Understanding the determinants of exceptional longevity. *Annals of Internal Medicine, 139* (5), 445-449.

Selim, A. J., Fincke, B. G., Berlowitz, D. R., Miller, D. M., Zian, S. X., Lee, A., Cong, Z., Rogers, W. H., Selim, B. J., Ren, X. S., Spiro, A. III, & Kazis, L. E. (2005). Comprehensive health status assessment of centenarians: Results from the 1999 large health survey of veteran enrollees. *Journal of Gerontology: Medical Sciences, 60A,* 515-519.

Stathakos, D., Pratsinis, H., Zachos, I., Vlahaki, I., Gianakopoulou, A., Zianni, D., & Kletsas, D. (2005). Greek centenarians: Assessment of functional health status and life-style characteristics. *Experimental Gerontology, 40,* 512-518.

Suzuki, M., Wilcox, B., & Wilcox, C. (2004). Successful aging: Secrets of Okinawa longevity. *Geriatrics and Gerontology International, 4,* 180-181.

Tafaro, L., Cicconetti, P., Piccirillo, G., Ettorre, E., Marigliano, V., & Cacciafesta, M. (2005). Is it possible to predict survival in centenarians? A neural network study. *Gerontology, 51,* 199-205.

Wu, Z., & Schimmele, C. (2006). Psychological disposition and self-reported health among the 'oldest-old' in China. *Aging and Society, 26.*135-151.

Web Sites on Centenarians

Georgia Centenarian Study
http://www.geron.uga.edu/research/centenarianstudy.php

Human Longevity and Aging Research
http://www.nia.nih.gov/AboutNIA/BudgetRequests/HLAgingResearch.htm

International Centenarian Study
http://www.geron.uga.edu/research/intlcentenarianstudy.php

Living to 100: What's the Secret?
http://wifle.org/pdf/Living_to_100.pdf

New England Centenarian Study
http://www.bumc.bu.edu/Dept/Home.aspx?DepartmentID=361

New England Centenarian Study
http://www.med.harvard.edu/programs/necs/centenarians.htm

Swedish Centenarian Study
http://www.ncbi.nlm.nih.gov/entrez/query.fcgi?cmd=Retrieve&db=PubMed&list_uids=9438877&dopt=Abstract

Appendix C—Glossary of Terms

- **AAA (Area Agency on Aging):** Established under the Older Americans Act of 1973, AAAs respond to the needs of Americans aged 60 and over in every local community.

- **ADL (Activities of Daily Living):** Activities that people perform daily for self care, such as bathing, dressing, eating, and toileting.

- **Alzheimer's Disease:** An irreversible form of dementia that involves impairments in cognitive, social, and motor function.

- **APS (Adult Protective Services):** Agency that employs workers who strive to protect vulnerable older adults from abuse and/or neglectful situations.

- **Assisted Living:** A private-pay living arrangement in which people with special needs live in a facility that provides help with activities of daily living, such as bathing, dressing, and taking medication.

- **CARF (Commission on Accreditation of Rehabilitation Facilities):** A non-government accreditation agency that evaluates rehabilitation facilities to make sure that the facilities are providing the best care and rehabilitation possible.

- **Delirium:** A condition of severe confusion and rapid changes in brain function. It is usually caused by a treatable physical or mental illness. (See http://www.nlm.nih.gov/medlineplus/ency/article/000740.htm.)

- **Dementia:** The broad category of cognitive disorders characterized by memory loss and other mental functions.

- **Depression:** Depression may be described as feeling sad, blue, unhappy, miserable, or down in the dumps. True clinical depression is a mood disorder in which feelings of sadness, loss, anger, or frustration interfere with everyday life for an extended time. (See http://www.nlm.nih.gov/medlineplus/ency/article/003213.htm.)

- **DSM (Diagnostic and Statistical Manual of Mental Disorders):** A diagnostic tool used by mental health professionals to aid in the diagnosis of mental health issues.

- **Elderly Waiver:** A program financed by Medicaid to keep an older adult in his or her home environment. It provides in-home services to people who are age 65 and over, have significant health care needs, and meet certain income requirements.

- **Geriatrics:** The branch of medicine that deals with the diagnosis and treatment of diseases and problems specific to older adults.

- **Gerontology:** The scientific study of the biological, psychological, and sociological aspects associated with old age and aging.

- **Health Care Power of Attorney:** A form that when completed will designate a person of choice as the one who will be solely responsible for making health care decisions, in case the older adult is unable to make these decisions anymore.

- **HIPAA (Health Insurance Portability and Accountability Act):** This act, which was passed in 1996, provides rights and protections for participants and beneficiaries in group health plans. It also addresses the safety and privacy of health-related information.

- **IADL (Instrumental Activities of Daily Living):** Activities that are related to independent living and include grocery shopping, preparing meals, managing money, ability to do housework, and using the telephone.

- **ICF (Intermediate Care Facility):** This is a facility that provides 24-hour nursing care to individuals who require a lower level of care than those in a Skilled Nursing Facility (SNF). ICFs serve patients who have a disability, are elderly, or have a non-acute illness. *(See SNF.)*

- **LifeLine:** A medical alert company that provides immediate in-home service in case an older adult or caregiver has a medical emergency.

- **LIHEAP (Low Income Home Energy Assistance Program):** A program developed to help pay for heat or cooling for low income older adults. It was authorized by Congress in 1981 and began in 1982.

- **MDS (Minimum Data Set):** A clinical assessment that is completed for all residents in a skilled nursing facility who are using Medicare and/or Medicaid forms of payment.

- **Medicaid:** Health insurance, funded by the states and federal government, for the poor of all ages. Also known as Medical Assistance.

- **Medicare:** Health insurance program for citizens age 65 or older and those who have been declared disabled. It is provided by the federal government.

- **MMSE (Folstein Mini Mental Status Exam):** Created in 1975, this 30-minute test assesses a person's capacity to make decisions on his or her own, evaluates one's competency, and screens for any cognitive impairment.

- **NORC (Naturally Occurring Retirement Community):** A community or neighborhood where senior citizens age together, as neighbors.

- **Parkinson's Disease:** Disorder that affects nerve cells in the part of the brain controlling muscle movement. People with Parkinson's disease often experience trembling, muscle rigidity, difficulty walking, problems with balance, and slowed movements. (See http://www.mayoclinic.com/health/parkinsons-disease/DS00295.)

- **PPP (Practicum Partnership Program):** An initiative funded through the John A. Hartford Foundation beginning in 1999. It is focused on strengthening field education in gerontology in selected MSW programs throughout the U.S.

- **SAMS (Social Assistance Management System):** An information database for all consumer data and service delivery. This database is used in some state (such as Pennsylvania) Area Agencies on Aging to manage client data and the services that have been provided to these clients.

- **SNF (Skilled Nursing Facility):** This is a facility that provides 24-hour nursing care to individuals who need full-time care. These facilities can also provide rehabilitation. These include free-standing nursing facilities, as well as distinct units within hospitals.

- **SSI (Supplementary Security Income):** Federal program that provides a supplement to income designed to aid those who are older, blind, and/or disabled. One must have little or no income to receive this benefit.

ALSO PUBLISHED BY WHITE HAT COMMUNICATIONS:

BOOKS

Days in the Lives of Social Workers
edited by Linda May Grobman

The Field Placement Survival Guide
edited by Linda May Grobman

*Improving Quality and Performance
in Your Non-Profit Organization*
by Gary M. Grobman

*An Introduction to the Nonprofit Sector:
A Practical Approach for the Twenty-First Century*
by Gary M. Grobman

More Days in the Lives of Social Workers
edited by Linda May Grobman

The Nonprofit Handbook
by Gary M. Grobman

*Fundraising Online: Using the Internet to
Raise Serious Money for Your Nonprofit Organization*
by Gary M. Grobman and Gary B. Grant

*The Social Work Graduate School
Applicant's Handbook*
by Jesús Reyes

MAGAZINE

The New Social Worker
(available free online at www.socialworker.com)

VISIT OUR WEB SITES

www.socialworker.com
www.socialworkjobbank.com
www.whitehatcommunications.com

"Days in the Lives of Social Workers" Books

DAYS IN THE LIVES OF SOCIAL WORKERS
54 Professionals Tell "Real-Life" Stories from Social Work Practice (3rd Edition)
edited by Linda May Grobman

Did you ever wish you could tag along with a professional in your chosen field, just for a day, observing his or her every move? In this third edition of our "best seller," you can read about social workers in 54 different settings, including mental health, schools, prisons, adventure-based therapy, private practice, HIV/AIDS, public health, hospice, nursing homes, international social work, public policy, and more.

410 pages • 5 1/2 x 8 1/2 • ISBN 1-929109-15-6 • 2005 • $19.95 plus shipping

---

MORE DAYS IN THE LIVES OF SOCIAL WORKERS
35 "Real-Life" Stories of Advocacy, Outreach, and Other Intriguing Roles in Social Work Practice
edited by Linda May Grobman

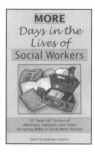

This book, like its popular predecessor DAYS IN THE LIVES OF SOCIAL WORKERS, illustrates through first-person narratives that there are no "typical" days in social work. In this volume, there is more of a focus on macro roles than in the first. This book illustrates ways in which social workers combine macro, mezzo, and micro level work in their everyday practice. You will read about working on a national level, program development and management, advocacy and organizing, policy from the inside, training and consultation, research and funding, higher education, specialized roles in the court system, faith and spirituality, domestic violence, therapy and case management, and employment and hunger.

252 pages • 5 1/2 x 8 1/2 • ISBN 1-929109-16-4 • 2005 • $16.95 plus shipping

Order from White Hat Communications, P.O. Box 5390, Dept. DG, Harrisburg, PA 17110-0390 with order form in the back of this book.

See http://www.daysinthelivesofsocialworkers.com for tables of contents and additional details about these books.

THE SOCIAL WORK GRADUATE SCHOOL APPLICANT'S HANDBOOK
Second Edition

Are you thinking about getting a master's degree in social work?

Find out from a former admissions director how you can improve your graduate school application. In *The Social Work Graduate School Applicant's Handbook,* you will learn about the admissions process from an insider's perspective. Discover what will help (and hurt) your chances of being accepted to the school of your choice, and find tips on deciding which school is right for you.

Read this book and find out:
- What factors to consider when determining your interest in a school of social work
- What admissions committees look for in an applicant
- Whether your GPA and test scores matter
- How to gain social work related experience to help your application
- Who to ask for letters of reference (and who not to ask)
- What to include in your personal essay
- Which schools are accredited by the Council on Social Work Education, and why this is important
- Where to find out about social work licensing in your state.

The author, Jesús Reyes, AM, ACSW, is Acting Chief Probation Officer of the Circuit Court of Cook County, IL, Adult Probation Department, as well as Director of the Circuit Court's Social Service Department. As former assistant dean for enrollment at one of the top ranked schools of social work in the U.S., and as a private consultant to MSW applicants, he has advised thousands across the country on their school applications and personal statements and on ways to improve their chances of getting into the school of their choice.

Price: $19.95 plus $7.00/shipping (to U.S. addresses) for first book, $1.00 shipping each additional book, $12/shipping per book to addresses outside the U.S.
306 pages 5 1/2 x 8 1/2 ISBN: 1-929109-08-3

Order the current edition of this book from:
WHITE HAT COMMUNICATIONS
P.O. Box 5390, Dept. DG, Harrisburg, PA 17110-0390

Questions? Call 717-238-3787.
Credit card orders: call 717-238-3787 or fax 717-238-2090
or order online at http://www.socialworker.com
or use order form in the back of this book.

THE FIELD PLACEMENT
SURVIVAL GUIDE
What You Need to Know to Get the Most
From Your Social Work Practicum
edited by Linda May Grobman

Field placement is one of the most exciting and exhilarating parts of a formal social work education. It is also one of the most challenging. This book brings together in one volume over 30 field placement-related writings from THE NEW SOCIAL WORKER magazine. A goldmine of practical information that will help social work students take advantage of all the field placement experience has to offer.

253 pages • 5 1/2 x 8 1/2 • ISBN 1-929109-10-5 • 2002 • $21.95 plus shipping

Order from White Hat Communications, P.O. Box 5390, Dept. DG, Harrisburg, PA 17110-0390 with order form in the back of this book.

The Journal of Social Work Values and Ethics

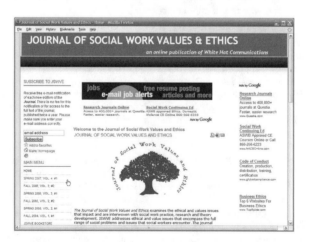

Read the latest research and writing on social work ethics and values. The *Journal* is available **free of charge** in full text at:

http://www.socialworker.com/jswve

2 GREAT WEB SITES—1 GREAT PROFESSION!

THE NEW SOCIAL WORKER Magazine

www.socialworker.com

- **Download** the latest and back issues of *THE NEW SOCIAL WORKER* magazine in PDF format, published quarterly (FREE)

- **Read articles** from *THE NEW SOCIAL WORKER* magazine, and sign up for free notification of each new issue

- Get **continuing education credits** for reading

- Subscribe to the **FREE e-mail newsletter,** *The Social Work E-News*

- Participate in **stimulating discussions**

- Find **social work events** listed on our online calendar ...and lots more!

Real jobs for social work professionals!

SocialWorkJobBank.com

- **Search** current job listings
- Read **articles** in our online career center
- **Apply** online easily & quickly
- Sign up for e-mail **job alerts**
- **Post** a confidential résumé

Hiring faculty or staff?
- Post job announcements
- Receive applications online
- Quick, easy, affordable

Recent job postings have included:

- direct practice in child welfare, mental health, aging, medical, homeless, and other settings
- supervisory positions
- academic faculty positions
- advocacy positions
  ...and many others!

Job seeker services are free.

ORDER FORM

I would like to order the following:

Qty.	Item	Price
_____	Days in the Lives of Gerontological SW @ $19.95	_____
_____	Days in the Lives of Social Workers @ $19.95	_____
_____	More Days in the Lives of Social Workers @ $16.95	_____
_____	Field Placement Survival Guide @ $21.95	_____
_____	Social Work Grad. School App. Hdbk. @ $19.95	_____

Please send my order to:

Name _____

Organization _____

Address_____

City_____ State____ Zip _____

Telephone_____

Please send me more information about ❑social work and ❑nonprofit management publications available from White Hat Communications.

Sales tax: Please add 6% sales tax for books shipped to Pennsylvania addresses.

Shipping/handling:
❑Books sent to U.S. addresses: $7.00 first book/$1 each add'l book.
❑Books sent to Canada: $9.00 per book.
❑Books sent to addresses outside the U.S. and Canada: $12.00 per book.

Payment:
Check or money order enclosed for $_____
U.S. funds only.

Please charge my: ❑MC ❑Visa ❑AMEX ❑Discover
Card #: _____
Expiration Date _____ 3- or 4-digit # on card _____
Name on card: _____
Billing address (if different from above): _____
_____
Signature: _____

Mail this form with payment to:

WHITE HAT COMMUNICATIONS, P.O. Box 5390, Dept. DG
Harrisburg, PA 17110-0390

Questions? Call 717-238-3787.
Credit card orders: call 717-238-3787 or fax 717-238-2090
or order online at http://www.socialworker.com